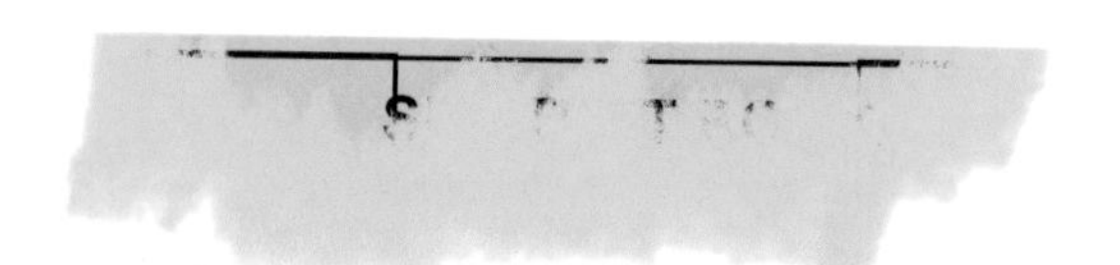

Published in 2016 by WJEC, 245 Western Avenue, Cardiff CF5 2YX

Author: Chris Stockton

ISBN 978-1-86085-691-4

Printed by Xpedient Print Services

A resource to support the teaching and learning of A level Year 1 and AS Business. The materials provide an introduction to the main concepts of the theory of the subject and should be used in conjunction with other resources and sound classroom teaching.

This book covers the content in the WJEC Eduqas A level Year 1 and AS Business specification.

Chapters 1 – 10: Business opportunities

Chapters 11 – 41: Business functions

The book is also available in the format of digital resources, including PDF format and Word format (to allow centres to edit and customise their teaching notes), free of charge via the WJEC Eduqas resource website http://resources.wjec.co.uk.

Interactive resources linked to the business content are also available on the resources website free of charge; these activities are signposted in this book in the relevant place.

Table of contents

Chapter 1
Enterprise and business planning

Business activities have a major impact on our lives – both as consumers and employees. Business is in every sector of the economy:

In the **primary sector**, providing the food we need, farming, supplying the power we use through mining or extracting oil from the North Sea

In the **secondary sector private** enterprises provide us with a massive amount of consumer goods; manufacturing cars, processing food, making clothes, designing and producing consumer electronics – in fact all the goods that surround us in the shops we visit, that help satisfy our every want

In the **tertiary (service) sector** private companies provide gyms, offering financial advice, operating fleets of buses and trucks, prepare marketing campaigns and so much more

- In the UK there are almost 5 million separate businesses, employing a total of 24 million people.
- Of these businesses, over 3.3 million are sole proprietors.
- There are around 500 000 businesses that are partnerships.
- There are also 1.2 million registered limited companies.
- SMEs (small and medium-sized enterprises) employ around 14.4 million people and have a combined turnover of £1,600 billion.

Why do people start their own business?

- **To gain a profit** – the motive for profit is generally thought of as the prime reason why people start businesses. For an entrepreneur who is starting a small business for the first time, it is rarely just about money – even so, earning a decent income in the form of profit will be a major focus.

- **To turn a hobby or a pastime into a business** – many new entrepreneurs are able to turn a hobby or a pastime into a business. For example, every surf school in the country is likely to be owned by a surfer and fantasy games shop is likely to be set up by a player. Being fully involved in your hobby and creating an income from it is probably as satisfying a business experience as the small business person is likely to find. Often these entrepreneurs do not try to fully maximise profits, instead they balance work, customer satisfaction, and their own freedom to live a lifestyle that they are content with. This is known as 'satisficing' – decision making that aims for a satisfactory result, and not using all energies trying to maximise income.

- **To use redundancy money** – some new business people are forced into setting up a business because of redundancy. Losing a job, with little chance of finding another one in the near future, is often reason enough to start a business. Most people who have been made redundant will receive a redundancy payment and this can be used as capital to start a business.

- **To be their own boss** – often people just want to be their own boss, in control of their own destiny, not being an underappreciated 'cog' in a huge corporate machine. These sort of potential entrepreneurs are often searching for an idea that they can turn into a successful business.

The following article is from the Company Bug website (dated 18 December 2013), which refers to figures from the enterprise website Startup Britain:

Record number of new businesses started in 2013

New business formation data shows that 2013 has been a record-breaking year for start-ups, with over 520 000 new businesses expected to have been formed by the end of the year.

The Startup Britain figures, which are verified and subsequently audited by Companies House, are certainly impressive.

By mid-December 2013, 499 000 businesses had already been formed, so the 500 000 barrier is certain to be broken for the first time by December 31st.

The statistics also show a significant rise in start-up numbers compared to previous years; 440 000 were formed in 2011 and 484 224 last year.

Emma Jones, who co-founded the site, commented; "We've been looking at these figures for three years since the campaign began and it's clear the UK's start-up community is fit and healthy – and shows no sign of abating."

Small businesses have often been referred to as the 'life blood' of the UK economy, especially by politicians. For good reasons too.

According to the Department of BIS [*Business, Innovation and Skills*] data, 99.2% of all UK businesses are defined as 'small' (i.e. they have between 0 and 49 employees).

Interestingly, this 99.2% of businesses is responsible for 47% of all private sector employment in the UK, and around one third of all turnover created by private enterprise.

Surprisingly, the number of people deciding to start up businesses on their own has increased each year since 2000, despite the recession. The Government estimates that the total number of business entities increased from 3.5m to 4.9m between 2000 and 2013.

We can see from the article above that studying business is not just about looking at big businesses like BP, Apple, Sony and hundreds of others who are worldwide (multi-national) enterprises, with billions of £s in assets and profits. It is just as much the study of what makes a successful small business. The article tells us about the importance of small businesses to the economy. A huge number of separate enterprises are helping to innovate and drive economic growth – creating opportunities for employment and satisfying consumers' needs and wants.

Needs and wants are not fixed: they can change quickly as fashions and lifestyles change and also over the longer term as incomes increase and population changes. This means that markets are always changing. The business world does not stay still – new opportunities are constantly arising. An entrepreneur with an idea, commitment, funds and a little luck can succeed even in the most competitive of markets.

Needs and wants

Needs – economists say that needs are what people require to survive – for example, food, warmth, shelter and clothing. We could also include education, healthcare and security – being safe.

Wants – what we desire, what we would like to have. For example, nicer clothes, not just basic functional items, a new phone every year, a massive flat screen TV, a detached house with pool, holidays in the Maldives etc.

What is an entrepreneur?

An entrepreneur is someone who starts and runs a business. Perhaps he or she makes a product and then sells that product, or perhaps they provide a service. They quite possibly employ people and, of course, try to make a profit.

Many countries and governments place great value on entrepreneurs and how they create wealth in an economy. Many entrepreneurs are innovators. They bring new ideas to the market and drive the development of new technologies. James Dyson, of Dyson vacuum cleaner fame is a classic example of an entrepreneur, bringing a range of new products to the market.

The following article is a brief history of the development of the Dyson vacuum cleaner from the Idea Finder website:

Dyson vacuum cleaner

James Dyson was vacuuming his house when he realized his top-of-the-line machine was losing suction and getting clogged. An industrial designer by training, Dyson went to work re-engineering vacuum cleaner technology to fix this problem. But that wasn't his only challenge. Fifteen years and more than 5000 prototypes later, he launched Dyson Limited to produce his design when no other manufacturer would take it on.

Invention:	Dyson vacuum cleaner
Function:	Cyclone technology uses 150 000 g's of centrifugal force in the cyclones to filter dust and remove dirt from the airflow efficiently. Because there is nothing to obstruct the airflow, the Dyson doesn't clog and doesn't lose suction.
Patent:	4 377 880 issued 1983 for vacuum cleaning appliances 5 090 976 issued 1992 for Dual cyclonic vacuum cleaner
Inventor:	James Dyson
Birth:	1947 in Norfolk, Great Britain
Nationality:	British
Milestones:	

1974	Strikes out on his own to develop the Ballbarrow. Designs a water-filled plastic garden roller.
1977	The Ballbarrow wins the Building Design Innovation Award.
1978	James invents the Trolleyball – a boat launcher with ball wheels.
1978	James stumbles across the idea of a bagless cleaner while renovating his country house.
1979	Spends five years developing the cleaner, and builds 5127 prototypes of the Dual Cyclone™.
1981	Files U.S. Patent application.
1982	James Dyson spends two years trawling, looking for someone to license the product.
1983	Dyson produces his first prototype vacuum cleaner, a pink machine called the G-Force.
1985	Dyson takes his product to Japan where he begins to work with a company that imports Filofax.
1986	The Japanese start to sell the G-Force.
1995	The Dyson DC01 becomes the best-selling vacuum cleaner in the UK.
1995	The Dyson Dual Cyclone™ DC02 is launched, and becomes the second highest seller.
1996	Launches DC02 Absolute, the first with both HEPA filtration and a bacteria-killing screen.
1997	James Dyson's autobiography 'Against the Odds' is published.
2001	New Root^{8}Cyclone technology is the most powerful upright vacuum cleaner on the market.
2002	Dyson brings Western Europe's top-selling vacuums to the United States.
2005	The Dyson DC15 (The Ball™) replaces conventional wheels with a ball.

The Story:

You know the feeling when some everyday product lets you down. You wish someone could solve the problem. James Dyson does that. He is a man who likes to make things work better. With his research team he has developed products that have achieved sales of over $10 billion worldwide.

In 1978, while vacuuming his home, James Dyson realized his bag vacuum cleaner was constantly losing suction power. He noticed how dust quickly clogged the pores of the bag and blocked the airflow, so that suction dropped rapidly. He set to work to solve this problem. Five years and 5127 prototypes later, the world's first cyclonic bagless vacuum cleaner arrived.

James Dyson offered his invention to major manufacturers. One by one they turned him down, apparently not interested in new technology. They seemed determined to continue selling bags, worth $500 million every year. Later, Hoover's vice president for Europe, Mike Rutter, said on U.K. national TV, "I do regret that Hoover as a company did not take the product technology off Dyson; it would have lain on the shelf and not been used."

What are the key characteristics of an entrepreneur?

- **Being a risk taker** – entrepreneurs are not always about new products or new ideas. They are often just doing things better than they were done before. However, they are all risk takers – they risk capital and their own time to try to create profits. They may remortgage the house, borrow from friends and family, or give up well-paid jobs to try to make a success out of their business idea.

- **Taking the initiative and being proactive** – successful entrepreneurs are able to take the initiative when required. They do not panic and allow events to overwhelm them – they are proactive and able to change as needed.

- **Being an effective organiser** – an ability to organise effectively is central to running a business effectively. The entrepreneur may need to undertake a wide range of activities; from hiring labour and buying inputs, such as raw materials, to producing the finished product for sale.

- **Having creativity and being innovative** – creativity in business means the ability to come up with innovative concepts and ideas, or developing a better way of doing things. Two American college students working in their college dorm in 2003 had the view that there had to be a more efficient way of gathering data for internet search engines – we now have Google, one of the biggest brands in the world!

- **Being hard working** – successful entrepreneurs are, generally, hard working. It is estimated that entrepreneurs in the UK work for around an average of 52 hours a week, plus another 40 hours thinking or worrying about their business venture. Compare this to the average working week of 38 hours for an employed person.

- **Being determined and having perserverance** – entrepreneurs also need to be determined, as new businesses have low success rates. Entrepreneurs must also have considerable perseverance, and be willing to keep trying if initial ideas fail.

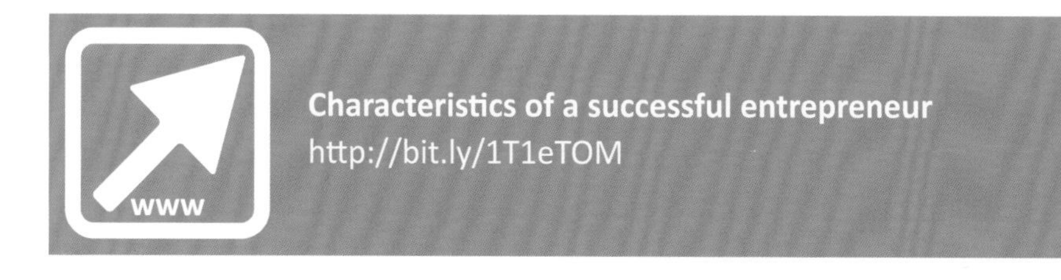

Discussion themes
The website startups.co.uk has a section on young entrepreneurs (link below). http://startups.co.uk/being-a-young-entrepreneur/ Choose two or three of the young business people described and list factors that are consistent in the reasons for their success.
Read the article 'Dylan Jones-Evans on why the backbone to the small firm sector is a 'family affair''. Then use notes and information in the article to answer the following question: Big business benefits an economy much more than the activities of small businesses. Discuss. WalesOnline Business http://www.walesonline.co.uk/business/business-opinion/dylan-jones-evans-backbone-small-firm-7101903
'Big businesses make the headlines, so why bother about the growth of small businesses.' Do you think that this statement undervalues the importance of SMEs to the UK economy?
Discuss the following statement: 'All successful entrepreneurs are risk takers.'
To what extent do you agree with the following statement: 'Business success is down to having a good idea.'

Identifying business opportunities

Potential business opportunities occur when a **market need** exists. This market need is preferably one that has not yet been targeted or not yet been targeted effectively. Therefore, a new entrepreneur wanting to start and run a successful business will need to find a product or service that isn't already available, or one that can be improved on. A starting point might be to find out what is missing in the local area.

Another way of investigating opportunities might be to ask the question: 'What can be offered to other businesses that would help them increase their sales, improve their service, or reduce their costs?' A business can service other businesses. These other businesses have customers who are different businesses. They may supply office equipment, cleaning, marketing services, transport, IT services, financial services etc.

Sometimes identifying a potential business opportunity can occur through word of mouth. Are people complaining about lack of access to a product, or describing a need, or criticising a business? All of these could present an opportunity.

Many new businesses are based on accessing customers through new market places – products or services can be bought here. Moving away from bricks and mortar reduces costs and allows prices to be cut. Obviously the internet is the best example of this – Amazon and Ebay are prime examples of new businesses which are based on price, buying opportunities and convenience. However, it is not only big businesses who can succeed through this method. The example of Foulgers Dairy shows how a small firm targeting a specific market (raw milk) can take advantage of new ways of accessing customers nationwide.

Often new businesses are founded on the idea of how innovative methods could help meet a need. For example, is there a kind of website or app that would improve what is already available or make it a more efficient process? Comparison websites have changed the way people buy insurance, book holidays and hotels, choose electrical goods etc. MoneySavingExpert, which covers the whole range of financial services and shopping, was founded by a sole trader – Martin Lewis. The site is focussed on allowing consumers to access the best deals on everything from buying cars to the weekly shop. Martin Lewis founded MoneySavingExpert.com in 2003 for £100. It's now the UK's biggest money site, with over 14 million monthly users.

Finally, business opportunities can come from an entirely new product developed by the entrepreneur/inventor. Fortunes used to be made by inventors working with limited resources, but times have changed, with most new consumer products now coming from mega corporations. However, exceptions still occur. Worldwide success and the rapid growth of small businesses (or even one-man bands) have come through using marketing platforms such as the ITunes Store and the Android Market to promote and sell apps.

We have seen then that there are a number of ways of identifying where the potential lies when establishing a business. But whatever the business and however the opportunity has arisen, the next stage for the budding entrepreneur is to prepare a business plan.

Developing a business plan

The business plan makes clear the objectives of the business and how the business intends to achieve these objectives. A business plan is often likened to a map. This road map analogy is important – business plans are not to be written and forgotten, they are ongoing. The objectives that are set – whether financial, sales, marketing or production – are there for future guidance and not to be ignored. Start-up businesses that develop and follow a business plan are more likely to survive than those who do not.

The overview or executive summary

When preparing a business plan the entrepreneur should first of all clearly describe the business idea. This overview of the business will briefly describe the business opportunity that is to be exploited. It should summarise the strategies that will be employed and how finance will be obtained. This overview is very important in setting out the overall aims and objectives of the business. There is no set pattern for a business plan but there are key elements that need to be included – the plan needs to be flexible and able to adapt to changing market circumstances.

The marketing plan

This is an important part of any business plan and it should be based on both field and desk research. The market **research** carried out needs to establish if possible the size of the market, the needs of the customers and the level of competition. Once market research findings have been examined then the marketing plan (strategy) can be prepared. If market research has identified weaknesses with the initial idea, this may be the time to adapt the product to more closely meet the needs of the customer or clearly differentiate it from the competition.

The operations plan

This will include details of where the business will be located, production methods and any equipment needed. In addition, information on the costs of production and where the business will buy supplies may also be included.

The human resources plan

The number of employees and the skills, experience and qualifications they require will be outlined. Any management team will also be identified.

The financial plan

A variety of forecasting will be necessary:

- a sales forecast indicating potential revenues;
- a cash flow forecast for the first 12 months;
- a profit and loss and balance forecast for the end of the first year;
- a break even analysis.

In addition, information should be provided on where the finance for starting and running the business will come from. This will indicate the available start-up capital as well as any potential borrowing.

What are the potential benefits of a business plan?

When complete the business plan presents the business owners with a clear set of instructions on how to run the business. A comprehensive business plan will allow business owners to check progress against objectives, monitor cash flow and take action when objectives are not being achieved. Business owners can clearly see when things are going wrong.

A business plan is also needed for potential investors or when seeking finance from banks. Without a business plan it is highly unlikely that capital could be attracted from people or institutions outside of the business.

What are the potential drawbacks of a business plan?

Even with all these positive factors for having a business plan, there are downsides. Market research costs time and money, resources which might be better spent elsewhere in the business. For many start-up businesses this will be the hardest part of preparing a business plan. How do you predict what your income will be? Market research should provide an idea, but how reliable is the data? The estimate of sales revenue, money flowing into the business, should be based on accurate market research, but the truth is that most new businesses will at best be making an educated guess on how much money will be generated. The need for this guesswork is a potential weakness of any business plan.

An inaccurate business plan with unachievable objectives can give entrepreneurs false hope, leading to failed investments. Some experienced entrepreneurs have enough market and business knowledge to move from year to year without reference to marketing plans, or financial forecasts, and they do happily survive. However, for such businesses growth is unlikely without forward planning. Identifying and adapting to change in the market may then result in crisis management.

Discussion themes
Business Wales Guide to Business Plans http://business.wales.gov.uk/starting-business/starting-business-0/preparing-business-plan
Business plan templates and advice www.gov.uk/write-business-plan
Why is it important to consider 'the audience' when preparing a business plan?
What financial aspects of the business should always be contained in a business plan?
Discuss the following statement: 'Most business plans are not worth the time spent in preparation.'
To be effective business plans need to be flexible. Explain why.

Chapter 2
Market structure, types and segmentation

There are a variety of differing market structures which are separated by the levels of competition that exist within each market and the market conditions in which the businesses operate.

Competition increases as the number of businesses in the market increases:

Perfect competition

Characteristics

- There are a **large number of businesses** competing and no one business is large enough to influence the activities of others.
- There are no market leaders and no price leaders, so each business must accept the going price on the marketplace – they are **price takers**.
- The goods sold are **homogenous** – there is no difference between the goods sold by one business or any other business. This means that there is no branding, no product differentiation, no way of telling goods apart.
- Businesses have **equal access to technology**, meaning that they have equal levels of productivity and each business will benefit in the same way from any economies of scale that are available.
- Consumers in a perfectly competitive market have **full market information**, they know what is being sold and the price the goods are sold at. They can access a wide number of suppliers to the market.
- Businesses are free to leave or enter the market at any time: there are **no barriers to entry or exit**.

These unrealistic conditions mean that perfect competition is merely a model.

In reality there is always some sort of branding or differentiation – whether it is the quality of products, price of products or the location of where products are sold. It has some use as the starting point to analyse the behaviour of other market structures in the real world.

Monopoly

Characteristics:

- **A single producer within a market** – one business has 100% of the marketplace. This is known as a pure monopoly.
- They are likely to **erect barriers** to prevent others from entering their market.
- Monopolists are called **price makers** as they have a significant influence on price. Nonetheless, they cannot simply charge what they want as the law of supply and demand still operates.

Pure monopolies were not uncommon in the UK 30 years ago. The average household only had the option of one gas supplier, one home telephone supplier, and one electricity supplier etc. With the introduction of competition into these markets through deregulation and privatisation, these monopolies have in the main disappeared. Until recently the Royal Mail had a monopoly over the delivery of letters in the UK, but even this is now opening up to competition.

Pure monopolies with 100% of the market are now very rare.

The UK and EU competition authorities regard any business with over 25% of the market as having potential monopoly power, and will investigate situations where it believes this power is being abused.

Monopolies can, however, offer advantages to consumers. Being big or very big they can benefit from massive economies of scale, reducing prices and making goods affordable. Also the profits earned can be used for investment into improving products, improving production techniques and developing new products.

Oligopoly – oligopolistic competition

Characteristics:

- There are many businesses but **only a few dominate** the market.
- Each business tends to have differentiated products with a **strong brand identity**.
- **Brand loyalty** is encouraged by the use of heavy advertising and promotion.
- Prices can be stable for long periods, although **short price wars** do occur.
- **Some barriers to entry** do exist: for example, high start-up costs in relation to manufacturing.

Many of our largest industries, whether manufacturing, retailing or service industries, are oligopolistic in nature. In retailing, the grocery market is dominated by Tesco, Sainsbury's, Morrisons and Asda. In clothing retailing, each age group have just three or four major chain stores that dominate their marketplace.

When businesses in an oligopolistic market act together (collude), a cartel is formed. Cartels try to keep prices high, whilst the businesses involved share the market between themselves. This type of collusion has occurred in a wide range of industries: for example, the airline industry and the sports clothing industry. This formal collusion is illegal.

However, oligopolies are not without advantages to consumers. Large size leads to economies of scale, high profits means money for innovation and investment, and oligopolies targeting a wide range of market segments provide variety and choice. A very good example of the advantages of the oligopolistic market structure can be found in communications. By communications we mean mobile phones, landlines, the internet and television. A small number of very large businesses have put huge amounts of investment into these industries over the last 30 years, meaning that service and customer choice has improved dramatically.

Monopolistic competition

Characteristics:

- A large number of relatively small businesses in competition with each other.
- There are few barriers to entry.
- Products are similar, but differentiated from each other.
- Brand identity is relatively weak.
- Businesses are not price takers; however, they only have a limited degree of control over the prices they charge.

You are likely to be aware of local business in specific markets that are quite similar to each other – for example, hairdressers or take-away restaurants. Within every monopolistic market sector each business tries to offer something different and possess an element of uniqueness, but all are essentially competing for the same customers. Differentiation may take a number of forms in this market structure. For example, businesses could use physical product differentiation. This is where businesses use size, design, colour, shape, performance and features to make their products different from competitor businesses. For example, pizza outlets produce their products with stuffed crusts, thin and thick bases and in all shapes and sizes. They may also attempt differentiation through methods of purchase and distribution such as online purchases and free delivery. Often attached to delivery is a promotional promise such as 'if we are late you get it for free'.

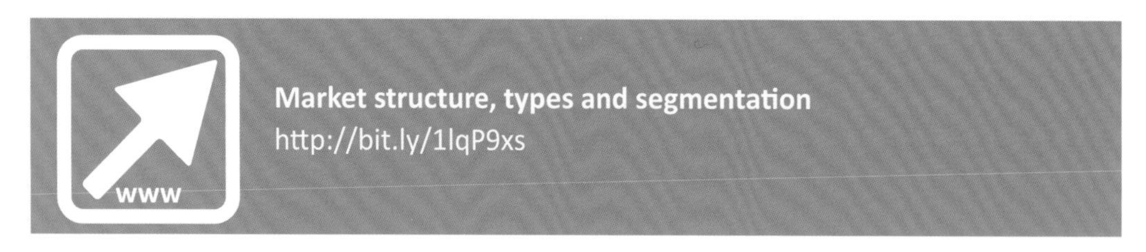

Businesses and markets

Different businesses can operate in very different markets – some are local, others global. Some businesses are focussed on consumer markets (B2C), others sell to other businesses (B2B). For many businesses there will be large seasonal variations in their sales; others may find much more constant sales throughout the year. Although mass market businesses may seem to dominate the retail world there is still plenty of space for niche market businesses. Each business will still use the marketing mix, but how they adapt their strategy depends largely upon the target market. In most markets there is one dominant (mass) segment and several smaller (niche) segments.

Mass marketing

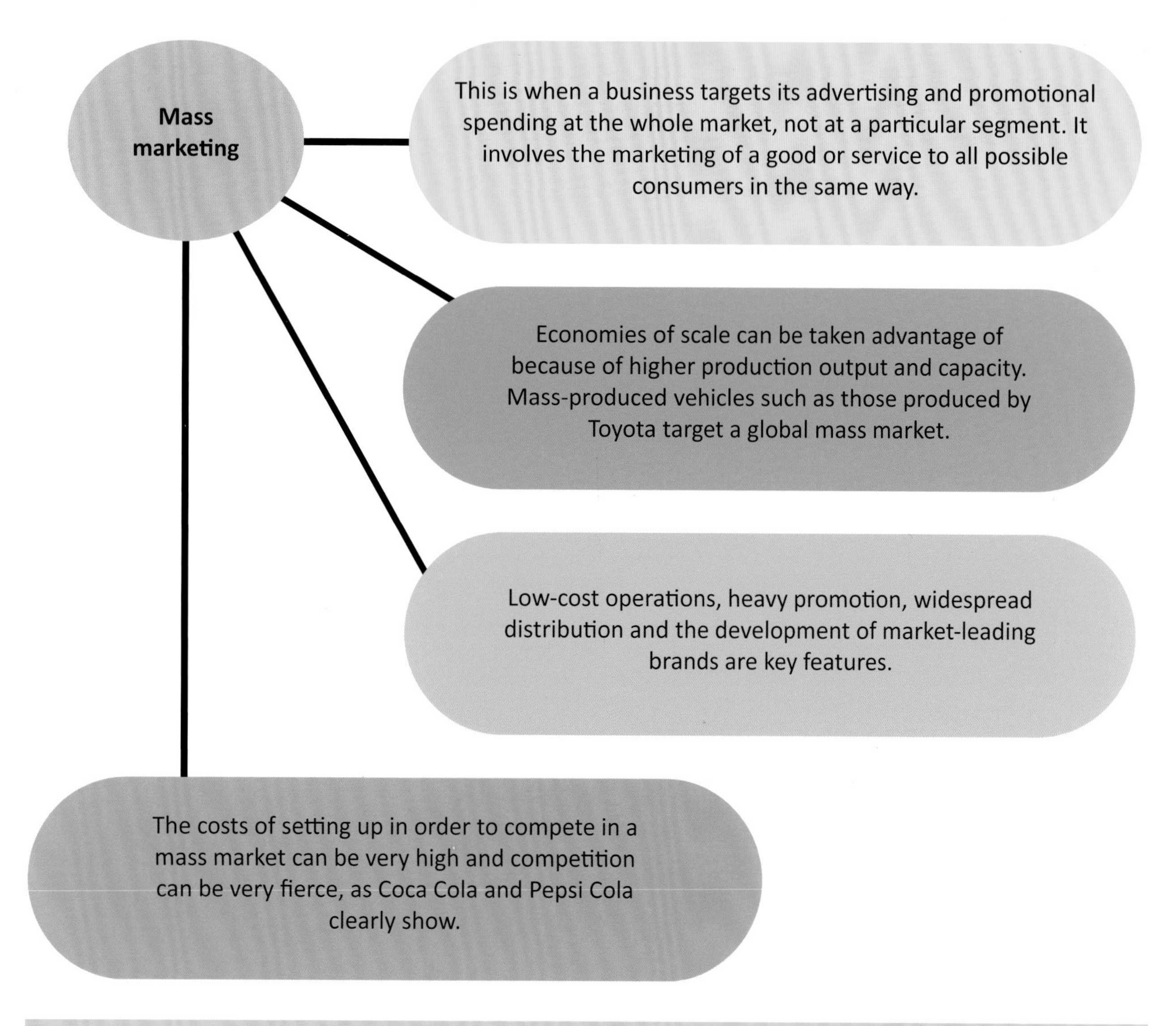

Niche marketing

Niche marketing is where a business targets a smaller segment of a larger market, where customers have specific needs and wants.

- One or more **specific segments** of the market are targeted with niche marketing.
- A **higher price** can often be charged – customers are prepared to pay for expertise and tend to be loyal.
- There must be a **full understanding** of the desires and needs of the niche. This understanding can be gained through market research, but is often initially based on more of a 'gut feeling' and an understanding that comes through personal experience.
- Niche marketing businesses are able to **concentrate on their strengths**, developing products from what the business is good at. As niche businesses can gain expert knowledge of the targeted part of the market, their products or services directly meet the needs of customers, giving the niche marketing business a real advantage over potential competitors.
- **Lower start-up costs** help niche market businesses in their early stages. The business may have the market to themselves (at least for a while), because competition may ignore the niche, either because of lack of awareness or because it is too small for large businesses to focus on.
- However, market niches **can disappear** as a result of changes in economic conditions, fashion or taste.
- Alternatively, **mass market businesses can target the niche** if it grows in value or size and existing small businesses may find this competition impossible to deal with.

Market segmentation

A market segment is any sub-group of a larger market. Mass market businesses divide their target markets into segments (sub-groups) that have common features, or are made up of individuals that make purchasing decisions based on common factors. When this is done businesses produce and market products aimed at each of these segments.

Types of segmentation

Demographic	Age, social class, gender, income.	Example: Banks offer different accounts to different age groups.
Psychographic	Allows targeting of groups on personality and emotionally based behaviour – attitudes, opinions and lifestyles.	Example: Differentiating cars by emphasising different features – safety and capacity for the family car.
Geographic	Regions of the country – rural, urban, suburban. Global marketing often requires different products for different countries.	Example: Global brands such as McDonalds and Coca Cola require different ingredients in different countries.

What rules must apply to market segmentation?

- Firstly, segments must be **recognisable**. They must be different enough from other segments to make producing for that segment worthwhile. For example, housing is built for different groups of people: flats for single people, two bedroom houses and starter homes for young couples, three or four bedroom houses for families, bungalows for retired people.
- Also segments must have **critical mass**. This means that they must be big enough or produce enough sales value to make the production of products or services targeted at the segment worthwhile. The market for two-seater sports cars has grown rapidly in recent years making the segment attractive: not only to niche market businesses such as Lotus, but also to mass market businesses like Toyota, Honda and Nissan.
- Segments have to be **targetable**. Having their own identity means that they can be promoted to, and have marketing directed towards them. On daytime TV, there are many adverts for retirement plans, or funeral expenses plans, often sold in a reassuring but concerned manner. They are targeted at a segment which is aware of the potential problems of costly funeral expenses, or leaving a loved one without financial support.

Once segments have been identified, then businesses can use a **segment-orientated marketing approach**. This approach offers a number of advantages for both businesses and customers. Targeted marketing allows the business to stress those product features that are most relevant for each particular segment (e.g. price vs. quality vs. brand identity). This targeting will occur even if the product being sold to different segments is almost identical.

Finally, customers change their preferences and patterns of behaviour over time (the customer life cycle). **Sustainable customer relationships** in all phases of the customer life cycle can come from segmenting markets. Businesses that serve different segments along a customer's life cycle can lead their customers from stage to stage by always offering them a special solution for their particular needs. For example, most car manufacturers offer a product range that caters for the needs of all phases of a customer life cycle: a first car for students/young workers, a fun car for young professionals, a family car for young families, SUV for growing families etc. Skincare cosmetics brands often offer a branded series of products for babies, teens, young adults, mums, and more mature skin.

Global markets

Global marketing is all about selling goods or services to overseas markets. With global marketing different marketing strategies are implemented, based on the region or country the company is marketing to. This may mean different packaging, pricing and promotional strategies.

When businesses are considering moving into overseas markets there are several possible advantages.

- **Higher earnings** – firstly there are likely to be higher earnings, especially if margins in overseas markets may exceed those found at home.
- **Spread risks** – by moving into new markets risks are now spread. Decline in one market may be smoothed out by increased demand in an overseas market.
- **Saturation of the home market** – often businesses are encouraged to make their first moves into a global market because of saturation of the home market – the business may have the finance to expand, but be unable to do so because of competition.
- **Economies of scale** – this move into global markets is likely to lead to increased economies of scale.
- **Survival** – some businesses need to be global to survive, for example automobile businesses. The biggest of these companies (Ford, GM, Toyota, and VW) will not have the sales volumes in domestic markets to fully support their operations. The trick for these businesses is to design products that will, with perhaps a few adjustments, meet the needs of a number of consumers in a number of individual markets.

Trade markets (B2B)

Trade marketing is the marketing role that focuses on selling and supplying to distributors, retailers, wholesalers, and other supply chain businesses instead of the consumer. So for the producer the objective of trade marketing is to increase demand for products/services supplied within the supply chain. Through effective trade marketing there is an increased likelihood that the product will end up in front of the final consumer. Trade marketing is not an alternative to brand and consumer marketing, but rather acts as a support to traditional consumer-focussed marketing strategies and helps ensure effective establishment of place in the marketing mix. Trade marketing will include price discounts, promotional support, special offers (two for one), point of sale display provision and even competitions.

Seasonal markets

Many markets have large seasonable variations. Classic examples are ice cream (during the pre-summer period), fireworks and diet plans (in January). Seasonal marketing will have a huge influence on the activities of businesses involved in these industries as each will have a critical sales period, which can make or break a business. Few businesses are totally immune to seasonality of sales. Lines of stock are adapted and changed – the big supermarkets have titled seasonal aisles. All of these seasonal changes have to be thought about and planned several months in advance to ensure that all aspects of the marketing mix are in place when required.

Market types
http://bit.ly/1RR4kyK

Discussion themes
List three features of each market structure described above.
Explain why price stickiness may occur in an oligopoly.
What is a cartel, and what advantages do cartels bring to members?
Give three reasons why perfect competition is unlikely to exist in any consumer market.
Explain how market structure can influence marketing strategies used by businesses.
Explain why both mass and niche market businesses attempt to identify market segments.
Why is success in trade markets important to achieving success in consumer markets?
Read the article and explain four reasons for adapting the niche marketing approach. Entrepreneur.com
Explain how niche marketing businesses can survive and thrive in the long run. LinkedIn Article https://www.linkedin.com/

Chapter 3
Demand and supply

Demand is the amount of a product that consumers are willing and able to purchase at any given price. It is assumed that this is **effective demand**, i.e. it is backed by money and an ability to buy.

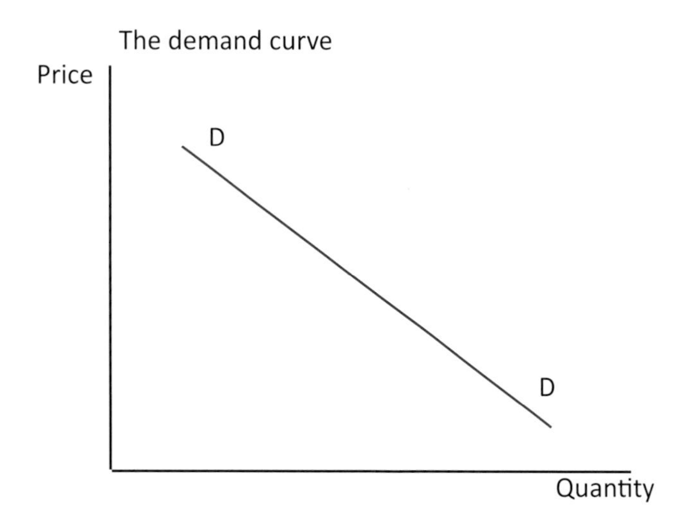

The law of demand states that the higher the price, the lower the quantity demanded; and the lower the price, the higher the quantity demanded. Naturally, consumers are willing and able to buy less as the price rises. This results in a downward sloping demand curve.

Movements along the demand curve are therefore caused by changes in price.

Supply is the amount of a product which suppliers will offer to the market at a given price.

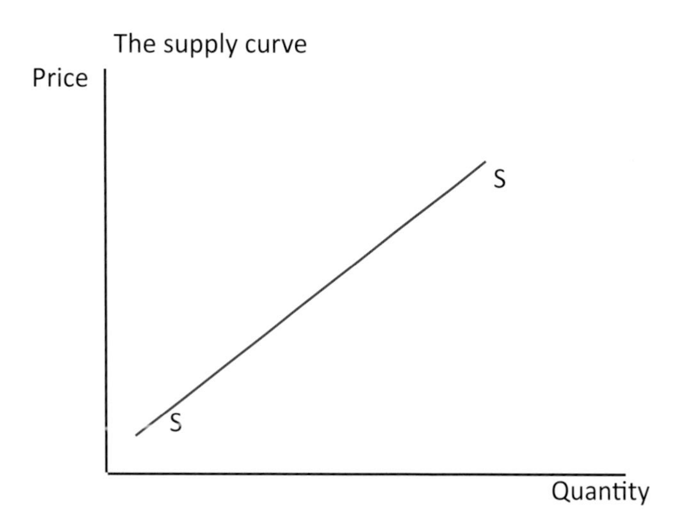

As the price of an item goes up, suppliers will attempt to maximize their profits by increasing the quantity offered for sale. This means that the lower the price, the lower the quantity supplied; and the higher the price, the higher the quantity supplied. At low price levels only the most efficient suppliers can make a profit so supply is limited. As price increases, the profit motive attracts new resources to supply and the higher price allows less efficient producers to make a profit. So as price increases, supply increases.

Movements along the supply curve are therefore caused by changes in price.

Equilibrium

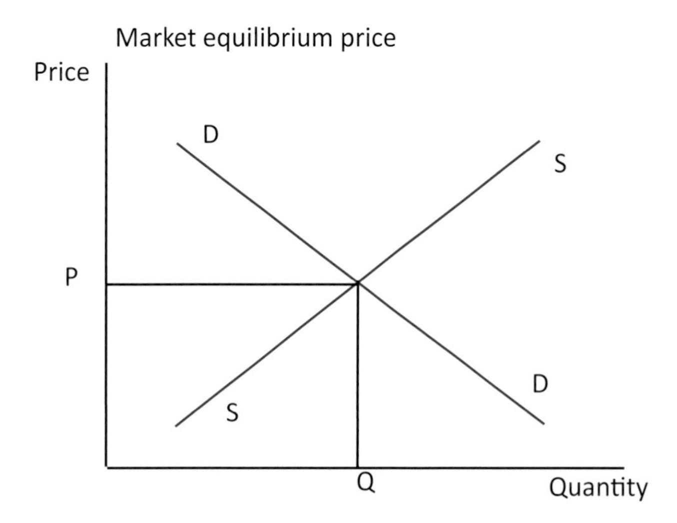

Where the demand curve and the supply curve intersect, we have a point where the quantity that consumers are willing to purchase matches the quantity that suppliers are willing to supply at a given price. This point is known as the **market equilibrium**. From the market equilibrium we can derive market price and market quantity. This market equilibrium is not fixed; it is likely to change over time due to changes in the patterns of demand and supply.

Label the diagram (demand and supply)
http://bit.ly/1QkYiVe

Shifts in demand and supply

As well as price there are a number of other factors which affect the demand and supply for a product. Whereas a change in price will cause a movement up or down the demand and supply curves, other factors might cause the curves to **shift**. This means that more or less of a product will be demanded or supplied at any given price.

Shifts in the demand curve

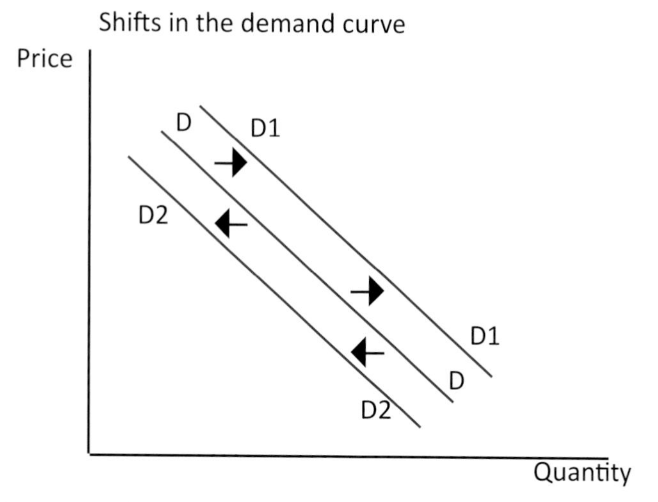

The demand curve can shift outward (to the right) or inward (to the left). If the demand curve shifts out, this means that more is demanded at each price level. This **increase in demand** is shown by the shift to a new demand curve, D1 in the diagram. An inward shift to a new curve at D2 indicates a **decrease in demand** – this indicates that less is demanded at each price level.

Factors that affect demand

- Firstly, an increase in consumers' **incomes** is likely to shift a demand curve to the right for most normal and luxury goods. With more disposable income people buy more of the things they want. So as incomes increase, the demand for cars, holidays, consumer electronics etc. also increases. A fall in incomes will cause the demand curve to shift inwards and to the left – demand decreases.
- **A change in tastes and fashion** can also shift the demand curve. If goods become more fashionable the demand curve shifts to the right, increasing demand at all price levels. If goods go out of fashion, the demand curve shifts to the left.
- Other factors which shift the demand curve include a **change in the price of other goods**: *Complimentary goods* are those used alongside another good. For example, if demand for holidays increases, demand for luggage or perhaps suntan lotion will also increase. A change in the price of *substitute goods* will also shift the demand curve. A substitute is a good used instead of another good. For example, if train fares increase some people will switch to private transport and travel by car. This may lead to an increase in the demand for petrol, shifting the demand curve for petrol to the right. If the price of airline tickets were to increase, then it is likely that demand for holidays at home in the UK would increase.
- A successful **advertising** campaign can cause the demand curve for a product to shift to the right. However, bad publicity will have the opposite effect and cause a shift to the left.
- **Changes in population** will also affect demand. The UK has an ageing population with those of retirement age forming a larger proportion of the population. This has resulted in an increase in demand for retirement homes, stair lifts and numerous other products that are used by the elderly.
- **Government legislation** may also have an impact on the demand for certain products. When legislation was passed making child seats compulsory in vehicles there was a significant increase in demand at any given price.

The effect on equilibrium price of a change in demand

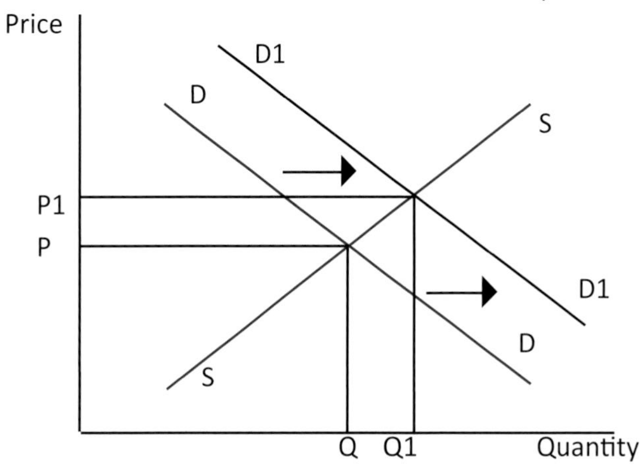

The diagram shows a shift outwards of the demand curve (caused by perhaps increasing incomes or the increasing price of the substitute good). Initially at market equilibrium we have price P and quantity Q. A new equilibrium is created where D1 cuts the original supply curve. Price rises to P1 and quantity demanded and supplied expands to Q1 .

Shift in the demand curve – fall in price

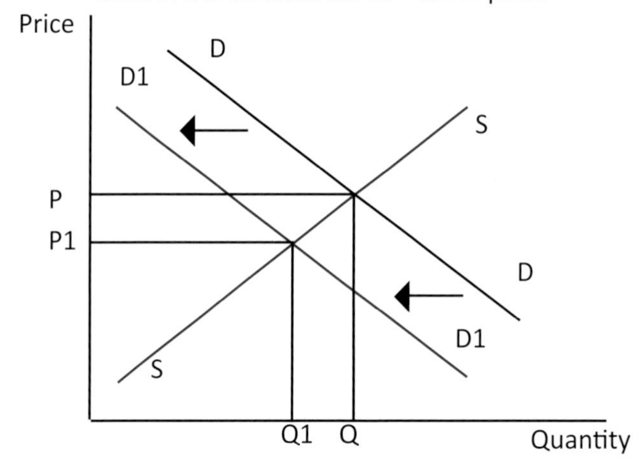

In this diagram we see a shift to the left of the demand curve (perhaps caused by a fall in price of a substitute). Again we start with equilibrium with price P and quantity Q. After the shift in demand curve we have a new equilibrium with price P1 and quantity Q1. The impact of the shift in of the demand curve has been to reduce price and to cause a contraction in the quantity demanded and supplied.

Shifts in the supply curve

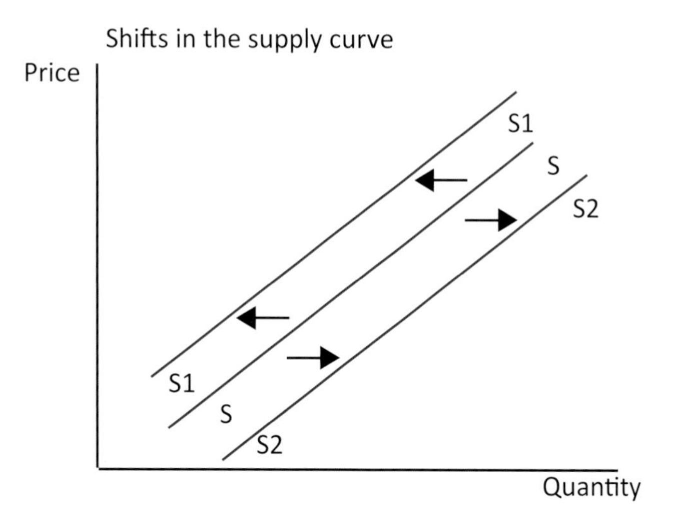

Like demand, supply can also change – independent of any change in price. Supply at each price level can increase (shift outwards to S2) or the amount supplied at each price level can decrease (shift inwards to S1).

Factors that affect supply

- One of the most important factors that changes supply, independent of any change in price, is a **change in costs**. If producers' costs fall resulting from a factor such as a fall in the price of raw materials or cost of labour, this will increase supply, shifting the supply curve outwards and to the right. Now at each price level more is supplied. Rising costs will have the opposite effect and shift the supply curve inwards and to the left.
- **Weather** can have a significant impact on the supply of agricultural products. Increased output is likely to result from a good harvest – this again shifts the supply curve outwards and to the right. Bad weather, of course, has the opposite effect.
- **Introduction of new technology**, especially in production techniques, also increases supply: this increase in productivity shifts the supply curve outwards and to the right.
- **Legislation** can also have a significant impact on the supply of some products. Increasingly businesses find their costs are increasing because they have to comply with new anti-pollution legislation introduced by the government. This shifts the supply curve inwards and to the left. When the government imposes a tax on a good or service, this too will cause the supply curve to shift to the left.

The effect on equilibrium price of a change in supply

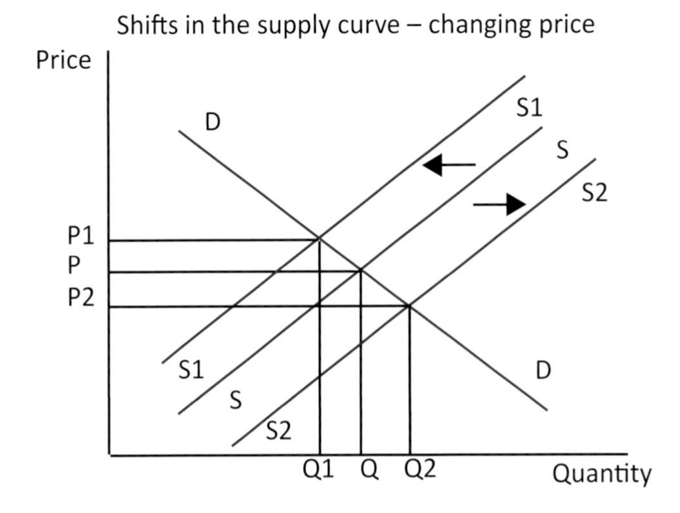

The diagram shows a shift outwards to the right of the supply curve (S2) (perhaps caused by falling costs). Initially at market equilibrium we have price P and quantity Q. The shift outwards results in a fall in price to P2 and an increased quantity demanded and supplied at Q2. The diagram also shows a shift of the supply curve (S1) (perhaps caused by a bad harvest). Initially at market equilibrium we have price P and quantity Q. The shift in the supply curve to the left results in an increase in price to P1, and fall in quantity demanded and supplied to Q1.

The concept of elasticity

Price elasticity of demand measures the responsiveness of demand to a change in price.

Understanding price elasticity of demand is very important to business managers who need to know the impact of changes in price on likely levels of demand. They need to know how **sensitive** the demand for their good or service is to a change in price.

Price elastic/Price sensitive

In markets approaching perfect competition, elasticity of demand is likely to be highly **elastic** – this means that a change in price will cause a more than proportional change in the quantity demanded. Price goes up, demand falls dramatically. When price falls, the reverse happens. Given the conditions of near perfect competition, where goods are largely undifferentiated, this impact of the change in price on demand levels is quite predictable. Why should people buy a higher priced good when a virtually identical good is immediately available at a lower price?

Price inelastic/Price insensitive

If a good has **inelastic** price elasticity of demand then a change in price causes a less than proportional change in the quantity demanded. So if price goes up, demand falls just a little. If price goes down demand increases just a little. Inelastic price elasticity of demand is likely to occur when the levels of competition are low, when there are a few substitutes, the goods are necessities or perhaps addictive. In these circumstances the business involved has much more control over the price than companies in highly competitive markets. Of course for many retailers and producers price elasticity of demand is likely to be somewhere between highly elastic/sensitive and highly inelastic/insensitive. But knowing and understanding price elasticity of demand is important in decision-making, especially with regards to the marketing of goods.

The objective of most businesses would be to make the price elasticity of demand of their goods or services more inelastic. This means that they have more control over their price, they are price makers and not price takers. If price elasticity of demand is inelastic and increasing price causes a less than proportional fall in the quantity demanded, this means **revenue would increase**. This is a much more preferable situation to a situation where price elasticity of demand is elastic and there is an increase in price which leads to a more than proportional fall in the quantity demanded, resulting in a fall in revenue.

Businesses can make demand for their goods more price inelastic if they do the following:

- **encourage consumer loyalty;**
- **reduce or restrict competition in the market;**
- **increase brand value.**

Income elasticity of demand

Income elasticity is the responsiveness of demand to changes in income.

Business managers like to look at the relationship between changing (increasing or falling) incomes and changing demand levels for different types of goods or services. Generally real incomes increase over time ('real' means allowing for the impact of inflation), leading to increased wealth and rising demand for most, but not all, goods and services. As people get richer they consume more, driving up demand for many goods and services.

When we link this pattern of changing demand to changing income we can measure the income elasticity of demand for each type of good or service.

- Income elasticity of demand can be elastic: a change in income causes a more than proportional change in the quantity demanded. For example, a 5% increase in incomes leads to a 10% increase in demand for pizzas.
- Income elasticity of demand can be inelastic: a change in income causes a less than proportional change in the quantity demanded. For example, incomes fall by 4% but demand for toothpaste falls by just 2%.
- Income elasticity of demand can also be negative when a rise in incomes causes a fall in demand. For example, incomes increase by 6%, and this causes a 5% fall in demand for supermarkets' own brand lemonade.

Normal, luxury and inferior goods

When real incomes of customers increase, the demand for **normal goods** responds as we might expect. As people become better off they buy more of this type of product. The majority of everyday items fall into this category – for example, cars, furniture, washing machines etc.

Luxury goods also fall into the category of normal goods but tend to be more sensitive to changes in real income. If incomes increase, demand for gym membership booms; if incomes fall many people quickly cancel their gym memberships in an attempt to save money.

Inferior goods are those goods that have negative income elasticity of demand – demand rises when real incomes fall. Supermarket own-label products are a good example of inferior goods. During a recession, consumers may turn to such products in order to economise. However, as incomes rise, they do not buy more of the own-label products but may switch to buy higher priced branded products instead.

Elasticity of demand
http://bit.ly/1P2GmOf

Discussion themes
Discuss the following statement: 'Businesses can do little to alter the price elasticity of demand for their goods.'
Explain the differing circumstances where a) a fall in price increases revenue; b) an increase in price increases revenue.
Explain how demand for different types of goods (normal, inferior and luxury) responds to changes in income.
Read the article http://www.dailymail.co.uk/news/article-2608359/Choc-horror-It-Easter-world-running-chocolate-demand-China-outstripping-cocoa-bean-production-forcing-prices-up.html Draw a diagram (with explanation) to show how the impact of Chinese chocolate demand has impacted on price. What is likely to happen in the long run to chocolate prices if the actions of Mondelez International are successful?

Chapter 4
Market research

Businesses regard having an understanding of the market place as a major priority. This is because of the following factors:

- the expense of launching new products;
- the importance of maintaining market share;
- the importance of preserving the profile and brand value of existing products.

After all, businesses like Proctor and Gamble (whose portfolio includes Gillette, Fairy, Ariel, and pet food IAMS, etc.) spend over £5 billion a year on worldwide marketing. Therefore, when it comes to designing new products or moving into new markets, businesses do not particularly like taking a leap in the dark. They need to understand their markets, in order to design products and marketing campaigns that meet the needs of customers. Market research undoubtedly reduces risk.

The objectives of market research

Market research is the process of collecting information and data about a business's customers, the market place and the activities of competitors within that marketplace.

The intention is to gather evidence that can enable marketing and production decisions to be made in a more scientific way than would otherwise be possible.

Businesses will attempt to do the following:

- **Discover the needs of customers** – who are these customers and how many are there likely to be? What motivates them to purchase the product? How much are they willing to spend?
- **Understand the structure of the market** – market research needs to tell the business managers if the market is subdivided or segmented or if the market is separated by geographical differences, socioeconomic differences or other differences.
- **Discover whether or not market demand is increasing**, in order that future sales predictions can be made (this is called the 'extrapolation of trends'). What might be the sales and profit potential of the product or service and its likely future success?
- **Establish at what stage is the product in its life cycle** – is it near maturity or in decline? From this information the business can then consider if it is worth investing in the product – for example, should extension strategies be used?
- **Test consumer response to new products or services**. Once consumer reactions have been discovered, product adaptation and development can be undertaken to meet consumer needs.
- **Assess the effectiveness of previous promotion campaigns**. Have the intended aims been achieved? Questions asked will reveal if the target market knows of the product, its uses, brand values and purpose?
- **Monitor competition and understand the activities of existing, new and potential competitors**. What are their strengths and weaknesses in relation to their products/services, finances, pricing, distribution and packaging?

Types of market research

Primary research

Also known as *field research*, primary research gathers first-hand information. This means that the data gathered is new (primary data), and should be directly relevant to the needs of the business. Primary research is carried out when there is a need to collect information which is specific to the business and its products or services.

Methods of primary (field) research:

- **Questionnaires** – these are designed to gain specific information, based on a series of questions. Questionnaires are often carried out face-to-face, but information is increasingly gathered through postal surveys and online.
- **Focus groups** – these meet regularly to have chaired discussions on themes set by a market researcher. Political parties often use these so that they can understand the issues that are of greatest concern to different groups within a population.
- **Consumer panels** – these are similar to focus groups, but are more product orientated, and are made up of consumers of products. The objective here is to gain opinions on different aspects of a product, such as taste, packaging and shape. For ongoing long-term research, consumers can be asked to keep diaries of their shopping and consumption behaviour. Market researchers will then examine the diary and ask follow-up questions.
- **Test marketing** – this is often used after a product has moved through development stages and is nearly ready for launch. This is a trial release of the product in a restricted area, designed to gather customer responses. Once responses have been gathered, changes based on these responses may be made to the product before the final launch. Test marketing is one of the best ways of finding out if potential customers like the product, and is often used by the film industry. Cinema audiences can be shown the same film before general release, but with different endings, and responses to the alternative endings will be judged.

Secondary research

Secondary research involves the use of previously collected information. So with secondary (or desk) research, the information used has not been gathered specifically for the business, but is instead adapted for its use. Secondary research data is often more easily available and accessible at a lower cost than primary research.

Methods of secondary (desk) research:

- **Official publications** – traditional methods of desk research have involved using official publications. The most popular for desk research are census reports and social trends surveys; this information is available online.
- **Industry magazines** – many industries produce their own 'industry magazine', which provides a wealth of information on specific retail and product areas. One of the best known examples is *The Grocer*, a 'must-read' for all food retail marketing professionals.
- **Yellow Pages** – this business telephone listing gives basic details of businesses operating in different market sectors. For example, if you are considering setting up as a local dog grooming service, first check to see how many others do the same. *Yellow Pages* are, of course, available online, along with other equivalent listings which provide the same basic information.

- **Internal information** – the use of a business's internal information, such as sales and customer data figures has boomed as a source of useful data over the last two decades. Database profiles are used more and more, and data can be gathered by the use of loyalty cards. Using the database created, retailers are able to build up detailed profiles of their customers and their spending habits. This information is then used to create targeted marketing, improve customer service and even alter product ranges. Businesses have learned that adapting to the specific needs of existing customers and directly applying marketing to these needs is a sure-fire way of increasing customer loyalty and revenue from these customers.
- Online desk research – this offers a huge range of potential information. There is an incredible amount of data available online, on the internet, but of course sorting out what is useful from the rest can be difficult. Competent IT businesses can gather user and customer profiles, by the process of registration and customer comments on websites. For start-ups, simple Google searches often provide relevant data.

Who undertakes the research?

Field research is an expensive and time-consuming activity and because of this businesses are turning more and more to market research companies. These market research companies are continually gathering data from questionnaires, census reports, trade information sheets, sales figures etc. From the information gathered they develop a comprehensive database on the spending patterns of consumers, market activity, etc. This data can be interpreted in a way that meets the research needs of the customer's business. This use of data that was previously collected by market research companies is in essence desk research, but it is quite usual for findings from this sort of desk research to be refined by further field research.

What's the difference between quantitative and qualitative research?

Quantitative research

Quantitative research aims to gather information based on facts that can be tested.

By asking closed questions that allows the collection of data, quantitative research findings will lead to objective conclusions and hypotheses that can be tested. They are statistically valid. Findings must be in a mathematical form, or they can be interpreted using figures.

For example – What is the average income of our customers? What is their weekly spending on food? How often do they take foreign holidays? The requirements of this type of market research can be stated in very specific and set terms.

With the use of quantitative research, subjective judgements (based on opinion) can be eliminated; findings should be clear and unambiguous. But the questions asked are often closed in nature, not leading to fuller responses. This means that quantitative research fails to encourage continuous investigation.

Quantitative research sets a pattern of research with little potential for following up or developing findings. After carrying out quantitative research, research leaders could be left asking questions like 'why is this pattern of spending shown?'

Qualitative research

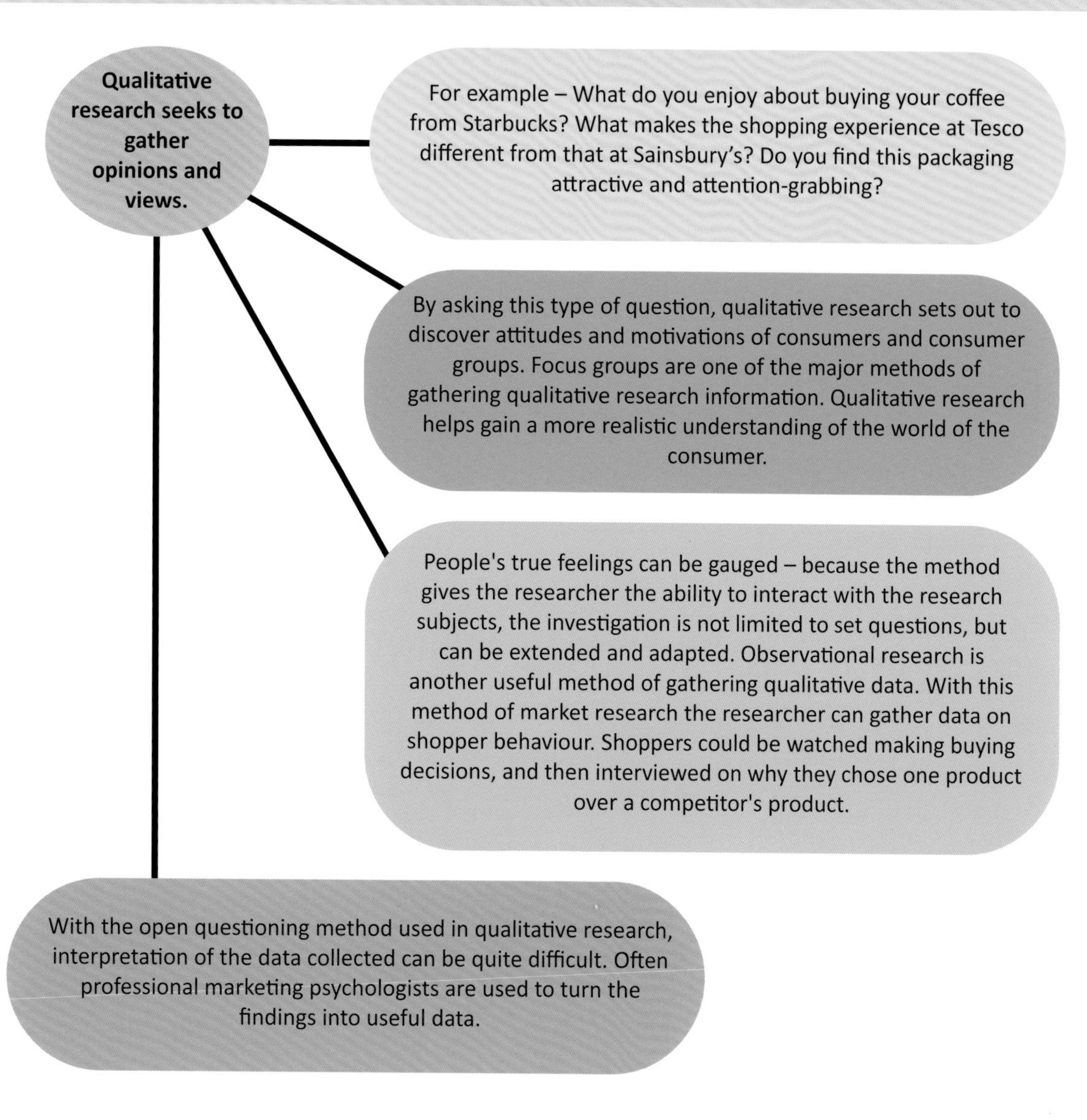

Qualitative or quantitative
http://bit.ly/1QbkzmC

The importance of sample size market research

A **sample** is a group of respondents to a market research exercise who are selected to be representative of the views of the target market as a whole. The size of the sample used is very important as it needs to be large enough to make the data statistically valid. When a business decides upon an appropriate market size for a survey it must bear in mind two issues:

- If the sample size is very large the research will take a long time and may prove to be very expensive.
- If the sample size is too small then there is a greater chance that random factors will make the results inaccurate.

This gives large businesses with big marketing budgets a significant advantage over smaller businesses – a good example of an economy of scale.

Bias is something that may cause data within a sample to be weighted towards one side. Such statistical bias occurs when a sample has an overweighting towards one subgroup – for example, too many teenagers between the ages of 16–19 within a research sample. To avoid bias and collect data that is statistically valid, sampling methods, such as random sampling and quota sampling, must be used to determine the market research sample. With questionnaires (as with all forms of research) it is important to gather data from a sample that reflects the whole population.

Random sampling – every member of the population has an equal chance of being interviewed.

- This is not easy to achieve and must not be confused with haphazard sampling.
- Random samples are drawn from local electoral registers and interviewees are contacted at home.
- The interviewer must call three times before giving up on the address – this is to overcome the fact that busy people are those least likely to be at home at certain times.
- Attempting to achieve randomness in this way creates expensive fieldwork costs so many businesses tend to adopt quota sampling instead.

Quota sampling – the population is segmented into a number of groups which share specific characteristics.

- The sample is often segmented on the basis of age or sex – known as the demographic profile.
- Therefore, if it is known that 20% of your buyers are men, interviewers would be instructed to interview one man for every four women in the sample.
- This is a relatively cheap method of sampling compared to many others.
- Results using quota sampling cannot be regarded as statistically representative of the population – they are not randomly chosen.

Discussion themes
In what ways is this method of research useful to Asda? Asda observational research https://www.youtube.com/watch?v=3f-lmYUTB70
Teacher video on marketing, introducing market research. Market research – customer needs https://www.youtube.com/watch?v=WPTz5uJJXPQ Define and give examples of primary and secondary data. Explain the reasons why secondary data may be misleading. Using examples from the video describe three methods of primary research. Using examples from the video describe three methods of secondary research.
A short film (4.50) showing test marketing in Columbus Ohio. Adventures in test marketing https://www.youtube.com/watch?v=7wx5B2p8qyg Why is Columbus chosen as a site for test marketing?
Money spent on market research would be better spent on other business functions. Discuss.
When it comes to making marketing decisions quantitative data is a better tool than qualitative data. Discuss.
Explain why an understanding of market data is an important part of future business success.

Chapter 5
Consumer protection

Why do consumers need protection?

Many businesses are managed in an ethical fashion and focus on providing excellent quality goods and services to meet customer expectations. However, this is not always the case and the drive to maximise profit overwhelms some organisations resulting in them resorting to dubious tactics in order to increase sales and revenue. There are a huge number of suppliers and retailers operating in the UK and this gives the opportunity for unscrupulous traders to set up in business. Poor quality goods, substandard services, misleading information and pressurised selling tactics are among the practices that the UK government seeks to discourage.

In order to control the way in which businesses conduct themselves and offer protection to consumers, the government has passed a number of laws and set up various organisations. These laws and organisations are together known as 'consumer protection'.

Consumer protection legislation

The latter half of the twentieth century saw a massive rise in consumerism (the number of goods bought and sold). The government recognised the need to regulate business practices and passed a number of important pieces of legislation such as the Sale of Goods Act 1979. Some of the main pieces of legislation are outlined below:

Consumer Rights Act 2015

The **Consumer Rights Act 2015** is the major piece of law covering the purchase of goods, services and digital content. Every time a consumer buys a product or a service, they make a 'contract' with the retailer. The Consumer Rights Act regulates this contract (agreement). It states that all goods must be of satisfactory quality, fit for the purpose for which they were bought and must correspond with any description given. For example, if you buy a car it must be capable of reliably transporting its passengers or if you buy a pair of wellington boots they should be waterproof. If a consumer buys a product that isn't satisfactory or doesn't match the description etc., they are entitled to return the goods to the retailer and ask for a refund. If the retailer refuses to reimburse the consumer, the consumer can then take court action, i.e. sue the retailer in court and ask for compensation or repair/ replacement of the product.

The Consumer Rights Act 2015 also states that services must be carried out for a reasonable price (unless agreed beforehand), within a reasonable time, and with reasonable care and skill. For example, if you visit a hair salon to dye your hair, the hairdresser would not be providing a service with reasonable care and skill if they dyed your hair the wrong colour.

Consumer Credit Acts 1974 and 2006

These laws, together with the **Consumer Credit Regulations 2010,** control the way that businesses lending money operate. These laws require the creditor (lender) to give certain key information to the debtor (borrower) before the contract is made including the interest rate, how much the repayments will be and the cancellation rights of the debtor. Credit companies have to publish a figure known as the Annual Percentage Rate (APR). This percentage not only reflects the rate of interest charged but also how it is calculated and added and any arrangement fees. The APR enables consumers to compare credit deals. The laws also give the debtor a 'cooling off period' after signing a credit contract during which they can change their mind. (In many cases this is 14 days). All organisations involved in credit must obtain a licence from the appropriate government authority – it is a criminal offence to operate without one.

Consumer Protection from Unfair Trading Regulations 2008

This is a very broad piece of legislation that makes it a criminal offence for businesses to engage in unfair business practices. This means that businesses can be prosecuted and fined for engaging in these practices, such as making untrue statements about a product or service, using aggressive sales techniques such as harassment or misleading consumers about the price of a product or service. For example, if a car dealer tells you that a vehicle has 50,000 miles on the clock but knows the true figure to be 70,000, they are omitting a key fact which would affect your decision to purchase the car.

Manufacturers and retailers have to take a great deal of care about information presented on the packaging of their goods, or within advertisements and any other form of promotional material.

The Consumer Contracts (Information, Cancellation and Additional Charges) Regulations 2013

These help protect consumers who buy over the phone or online. These are distance sales, which mean that there was no face to face contact at the time of purchase. If businesses break these regulations then the consumer is not bound by the purchase contract. These regulations provide the consumer with a cancellation period of 14 days: the 'cooling off' period during which consumers are entitled to change their minds and cancel the contract and receive a full refund, regardless of whether the product is defective.

These regulations also apply to goods or services purchased at your home, or 'off-premises'. For example, if a sales person visits you at your home and you agree to buy a new mobile phone, you have the right to change your mind and cancel the agreement, within 14 days. Also consumers are not bound by charges they have not expressly agreed to – such as hidden delivery or card payment costs.

The role of the ombudsman

Ombudsman services are available for various industries and offer complaints procedures for dissatisfied customers. Ombudsman services are set up by the government and are free for consumers to use. Examples of ombudsman services include the Health Service Ombudsman, the Legal Services Ombudsman and the Energy Ombudsman. Consumers can usually complain to the relevant ombudsman once they have tried to resolve any dispute with the relevant business and also followed up any other complaints procedures. The ombudsman services are the last port of call before full legal action in court is taken. When consumers take a complaint to an ombudsman, the ombudsman will look at all written information provided by the consumer and the business and make a decision accordingly. The decision is final and can only be overturned by a court.

Trading Standards departments

All local authorities have a Trading Standards department. The department is responsible for checking that local businesses are complying with the various trading laws e.g. Consumer Protection from Unfair Trading Regulations 2008. Trading Standards officers visit businesses and carry out spot checks. They investigate whether goods are correctly described, priced clearly and sold in the correct quantities. (For example, if a restaurant has 'locally sourced Welsh beef' on their menu, the officers will establish whether this is a true statement). They will also ensure that no counterfeit goods are being sold. Trading Standards officers can prosecute businesses if necessary and this process can result in fines and, in extreme cases, imprisonment.

The Competition and Markets Authority (CMA)

The Competition and Markets Authority (CMA) was set up by the government in 2014 and replaces the former Office of Fair Trading and Competition Commission. Its mission statement is 'to make markets work well for consumers' and, in order to pursue this aim, the CMA carries out investigations into various markets such as the groceries market and the energy market. The purpose of these investigations is to ensure that the businesses operating in these markets are not engaging in any 'anticompetitive business practices' that restrict competition within the market. These practices would include activities such as 'price agreements' where businesses agree not to compete on price or 'boycott activities' where suppliers refuse to supply to retailers if they stock the goods of a competitor. The CMA investigates markets and can elicit 'undertakings' (promises) from businesses to change their business practice if they uncover anticompetitive activities. If a business fails to honour these undertakings, it can result in more stringent measures such as fines.
The CMA also investigates proposed mergers if the merger would result in a company with such a large market share that it may restrict competition.

The CMA works closely with the government's Department for Business, Innovation and Skills (BIS) and local Trading Standards departments.

Competition policy is focussed on controlling the power of big business. If businesses in a monopoly or near monopoly are able to hold a dominant market position, then they are likely to have control over price or the amount produced within the market. Governments (UK and EU) will therefore put in place laws and regulators to limit the potential abuse of market power and thereby protect consumers.

One role of the CMA (see text box) is to examine situations where companies act together, forming an illegal cartel to limit the competition within an industry. Businesses, if they have a choice, will not compete on price and they may take the view that by creating a dominant market position by working with other large businesses, they can limit price competition. Because of the potential of cartels and collusion between businesses, legislation allows for guilty parties to be fined up to 10% of turnover for each year of illegal activity.

Role of the CMA

- investigating mergers which could restrict competition
- conducting market studies and investigations in markets where there may be competition and consumer problems
- investigating where there may be breaches of UK or EU prohibitions against anticompetitive agreements and abuses of dominant positions
- bringing criminal proceedings against individuals who commit the cartel offence
- enforcing consumer protection legislation to tackle practices and market conditions that make it difficult for consumers to exercise choice
- co-operating with sector regulators and encouraging them to use their competition powers

Consumer advice

Consumers can access advice about consumer problems via a number of websites. For example, *www.citizensadvice.org.uk*, *www.consumer-rights.org.uk* and Consumerline *www.nidirect.gov.uk/* consumerline.

Ethical issues related to consumer protection

Ethics relate to what is morally right and wrong and businesses have to make ethical decisions. How they treat their customers is part of the wider field of 'business ethics'. Other ethical issues include how businesses deal with their suppliers (Do they pay a fair price? What are the working conditions like in their overseas factories?) and their workers.

Many of the practices that consumer protection laws seek to ban are unethical. Giving false information about a product (e.g. claiming eggs to be free range when they are not or stating that a garment is 100% silk when it isn't), putting pressure on a consumer to purchase something or supplying poor-quality goods that break easily are all examples of unethical behaviour on the part of businesses.

Business ethics is a complicated field and, because ethics relate to opinions, there is sometimes disagreement over whether a particular practice is unethical or not. Marketing in particular can cause disputes in this area. For example, some stores display sweets at the checkout. This is regarded as unethical by some because it encourages 'pester power' (children repeatedly asking parents to buy the sweets for them). As sweets are unhealthy food, this practice can be seen as unethical. However, others argue that people have a choice whether they purchase them or not and it is up to parents to educate their children about healthy foods.

Some businesses have tried to reinvent themselves because their marketing has been labelled unethical. McDonalds 'supersize' was once a marketing winner, but with increased worries about people's weight problems, the campaign was dropped. McDonalds now focus a large part of their advertising and product development on healthier meals.

Consumer protection
http://bit.ly/1QbAQYy

Discussion themes
Visit the website of the Competition and Marketing Authority and look for two examples of recent investigations. What were the findings and recommendations?
Use online consumer advice sites such as www.citizensadvice.org.uk, www.consumer-rights.org.uk and Consumerline www.nidirect.gov.uk/consumerline to research consumer protection laws. Turn the advice around and design a brief guidance document advising SMEs on what they must do to avoid breaching the various pieces of legislation.
Should ethics be part of a business's marketing approach?
Discuss the following statement: 'With so much choice available, consumers are capable of looking after themselves.'

Chapter 6
Business structure

The public sector

The public sector is made up of organisations that **are owned and run by the government**. This part of the economy is huge, and includes some of the largest employers in the UK. The government spends over £450 billion a year running public sector organisations and providing public sector services. The largest public sector organisation, the NHS, is the biggest civilian employer in Europe, costing nearly £120 billion a year to run.

Why do we need a public sector?

Some goods and services which we need in our everyday lives would simply not be provided by the private sector who are looking to make profits. These necessities include street lighting, defence (army, navy, air force) and the police. The problem with these goods is that we can all benefit from them without paying for them. So if someone paid for, and installed street lighting, anyone walking down that road would benefit. If you are benefiting without paying, why pay? These goods which will only be provided by the government are called **public goods**.

Public goods (and services) have two features:

- non-excludability;
- non-rivalry.

Non-excludable: this means that individuals cannot be prevented from enjoying the benefits of the provision of public goods or services. We all gain from having violent criminals kept behind bars, as the threat to our family's well-being is reduced. No individual is excluded from this benefit. The same non-excludability would apply to having public goods such as street lighting – if street lights are provided by a local authority all will benefit from this provision as nobody can be excluded from the benefits.

Non-rivalry: this means that one person gaining from consumption of a good or service does not prevent others from also gaining from the good or service. If an individual eats an ice cream for example, then less ice cream is available for others to consume. Rivalry exists here. However, if an individual benefits from gaining justice in the Law Courts, this does not prevent any other individual from also being able to benefit from such a public service. They are not rivals for this service.

Not all goods provided by the public sector are public goods. There is another group of goods and services that is supplied by both the private and public sectors, but if left to just the private sector the quantity supplied of these goods and services is likely to be much less than the level of provision which is most efficient for the economy.

The two best examples of these **merit goods** are education and health care. There are of course private schools and private hospitals but most patients are treated by the NHS, and most children go to state schools. The government spends a great deal of money trying to ensure that we have an effective Health Service and schools and colleges that supply a well-educated and trained workforce. We would **underconsume** merit goods if it were left to the market. Some consumers could not afford the goods; others would fail to see the full benefit of consuming these goods.

These merit goods are said to have **positive externalities**. This means that the consumption of these goods will have positive effects not only on the individual that consumes them, but also on society in general. By attending school, individuals become better educated and skilled. Some individuals may use their knowledge and skills to set up businesses which employ people who themselves will pay tax and contribute to society. So there are positive externalities to education. Also if individuals succeed in school they are less likely to commit crime or require the safety net of the benefits system.

It is because of these positive externalities and likely underconsumption if left to the market, that the government provides merit goods (mainly) free at the point of delivery. Instead of paying to consume these goods or services directly, we pay for them through general taxation.

The public sector is focussed much more on needs than wants. There are public-owned leisure facilities, theatres, museums and so on that look to attract paying customers, but the core role of the public sector is to create a **fair and just society** and, if possible, an efficient economy.

The private sector

This is the part of the UK economy that is operated by businesses owned by shareholders or private individuals.

Although making profits, and giving a return to owners (increasing shareholder value), will always be the number one and two priorities of businesses in the long run, in the short term there can be other important objectives to pursue.

Public or private sector
http://bit.ly/20bCfDm

Objectives of private businesses

Objective	Description
To make a profit	To make a return on the capital (money) invested in the business. Profit maximisation is a key expression when considering how successful a business is.
To increase shareholder value	Measured by the dividend paid and the share price. Often the main objective for directors of limited companies. Many senior managers have bonus schemes related to increasing share prices and dividends; achieving the targets within these schemes will then become the main focus of the business.
Survival	In the shorter term this can be more important than making profits as the majority of new businesses fail within the first two years. For a small business, the initial objective is to survive the difficult start-up time of gaining customers, establishing a good local name, and building a reputation. Larger businesses may also have this objective as a priority during recessions when the market is very competitive.
Gaining market share	Businesses may spend to gain customers, reducing profits in the short run, but hopefully increasing profits in the longer term. Some may concentrate on establishing their brand name, becoming the most recognised business in their market. This costs money, so reduces profits.
Improving ethics	For example, there are businesses that will try to minimise the impact of their activities on the environment or ensure that their suppliers get a good deal. Such ethical objectives are likely to increase costs and reduce profits.

Different business structures

Sole traders

- Sole traders are the most popular form of business in the UK and are run by a single individual. A quick examination of a business directory such as Yellow Pages will show that there are thousands in every town or city.
- Sole traders are easy to set up; it is just a matter of informing the Inland Revenue that an individual is self-employed and registering for class 2 National Insurance contributions within three months of starting in business.
- Costs are low due to the simplicity of setting up and no legal formalities, so there is little administrative cost.
- Also no formal audited accounts are required, though it makes good business sense to keep a full set of business records.
- The sole trader benefits from fast decision-making and may (within employment law) hire and fire as they please.

However, there are a number of problems that arise with the sole trader structure:

- Firstly there is often **limited capital**. Sole traders often rely on their own savings and perhaps secured business loans.
- It is likely that the sole trader will have a **limited range of skills**. A sole trader may be an expert plumber, but is he or she an expert at marketing, managing staff, and controlling cash flow? With the need to be effective at all these tasks comes immense pressure.
- All the **decisions** and the future success of a business **rest with one person**.
- The sole trader has **unlimited liability**. This means that the business owner is liable for all the debts of the business, up to and including the value of all assets held.

One of the major problems of running a small business is the likelihood of falling into debt. With one in three businesses failing within two years of starting, it is probable that a good proportion of those unsuccessful entrepreneurs will not only lose the money that they initially invested, but additional money too.

Imagine a situation where a sole trader opens a shop selling fashion accessories. The shop premises are let on a two year lease; she (the entrepreneur) arranges a phone contract for the shop, leases equipment like a checkout till and shop fittings – all for the same two years. The total amount payable per month comes to £1300. Unfortunately after 9 months she has run out of cash, sales were dismal and she can't afford to continue.

She tries to walk away, handing the keys back, cancelling the phone contract and the lease deals. However, it is not that easy, she is in fact liable for ongoing costs – paying for a further 15 months charges, a total of £19 500 (15 months times £1300). Her creditors (those she owes money to), will chase her through the courts for payment, and if she has assets, the creditors can ask the courts to seize and sell these assets to pay the money owed. Assets can be anything of value – a car, computer, TV or even a house. The problem is that sole traders (and most partnerships) have unlimited liability – the owners of the business are liable for all the debts of their business, and have to pay those debts if they are able.

Sole traders
http://bit.ly/1QbmlnI

Advantages/Disadvantages of sole traders
http://bit.ly/1NipHRe

Partnerships

- Partnerships involve the **joint ownership** of a business. Normally there can be between two and 20 partners, but in certain businesses such as accountancy firms, there can be many more partners than this.
- Partnerships are **often found in professions** such as lawyers, accountants and doctors, but can be found in any type of business activity.
- The rules of partnership are laid down in a **Partnership Agreement**, or the Deed of Partnership. The Deed of Partnership lays out such rules of operations as the amounts of capital invested, the share of profits each partner is to receive, the roles and responsibilities of each partner, the voting shares of the partners, what is to happen on the death of a partner and the rules for dissolution of the partnership.
- Should a dispute arise without a partnership agreement giving methods of settling the dispute, then the dispute would be settled according to the **1890 Partnership Act**. This is best avoided, particularly where unlimited liability is involved, as the act states that each partner is equally responsible for any debts – each partner is 'jointly and severally' liable.
- There are a number of advantages of the partnership structure over that of a sole trader. These include a wider range of skills, greater availability of capital, shared decision-making, and pressure is likely to be reduced with different partners having separate key roles.

However, becoming a partner does not overcome all the disadvantages of being a sole trader:

- **Capital can still be limited**, with the same problems of raising external capital that a sole trader has.
- The partners still have **unlimited liability** of partners (sleeping partners who invest, but take no part in the day-to-day running of the business can have limited liability).
- Also partnerships are **dissolved on the death of a partner** and this can cause complications in re-establishing the partnership.
- Although there are many advantages when partners become involved in a business for the first time (such as increased capital, greater input into decision-making, a wider spread of skills), new partners can, and do, cause **strains** within a business.

Limited companies

There are two types of business structure that have limited liability:

- private limited companies (Ltd);
- public limited companies (PLC).

These businesses exist separately from their owners, who are known as **shareholders**. Employees are employed by the Ltd or PLC, and assets (buildings, machinery) are owned by the Ltd or PLC. This separate legal existence is known as **incorporation** – the business exists in the eyes of the law. Any legal action is taken against the business and not the shareholders. Shareholders are only liable to lose the amount of money they have invested in the business – hence, their liability is limited.

Although they have the same type of liability there is one major difference. Public limited companies trade their shares on the stock market. In the UK there are two main stock markets. These are:

- The Alternative Investment Market (AIM) – for smaller companies;
- The London Stock Exchange (LSE) – for larger businesses.

Shares on these stock markets are freely bought and sold: so in effect the ownership of PLCs are changing all the time. This change of ownership normally has very little impact on the running of the business. One small shareholder sells their shareholding, another small shareholder buys, and this happens thousands of times a day.

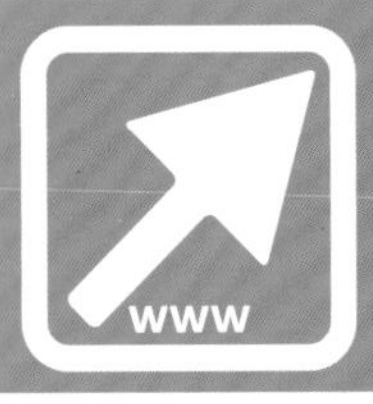

Limited companies
http://bit.ly/1StRxBU

Advantages of private limited companies include:

- limited liability;
- shares can only be sold if all the shareholders agree – control is not lost to outsiders;
- capital can be raised through increasing shareholders;
- other businesses and lenders are more likely to trade and invest;
- the business continues if one of the owners dies;
- possible tax advantages for the owners.

However, disadvantages include:

- legal procedure in setting up, increases costs;
- profits have to be shared with shareholders;
- shares cannot be sold to the public which may restrict the investment of additional capital;
- financial information is in the public domain.

Advantages of public limited companies include:

- limited liability;
- the business continues if one of the owners dies;
- capital can be raised through selling shares to the public;
- it is easier to raise finance from banks and other lenders who are more willing to lend to PLCs;
- they are likely to have economies of scale;
- increased market presence and dominance.

However, disadvantages include:

- increased costs in setting up;
- anyone can buy shares so there is an increased threat of losing control;
- increased legal requirements;
- the company accounts are in the public domain – more information has to be published than private limited companies;
- divorce of ownership and control;
- the increased size may result in inefficiencies, increased costs and distance from their customers.

Comparison of different business structures
http://bit.ly/1ZJVneM

Not-for-profit organisations

There are a growing number of business organisations that are not in business for the money – they are not out to maximise profits. Instead their focus is on social or ethical objectives. Within this group of organisations we find charities, co-operatives and social enterprises, between them providing a range of goods and services, and more often than not competing with 'for-profit businesses'. These not-for-profit organisations cannot just sell on the basis of who they are or what they stand for – if they just did this it is unlikely they would last for long. They have to provide a quality and value-for-money service, just like any other business.

Charities

Charities are established with the aim of collecting money from individuals and spending it on a cause, which is usually specified in its title. Although they are not established to make profits, they can earn surpluses. Many well-known charities such as Oxfam, Friends of the Earth and Save the Children have been around for a long time and employ many people. Oxfam was started in 1942; the RSPCA began over 100 years earlier, in 1824. Charities can often have a narrow focus (single issue) in what they are trying to achieve. For example, the Big Issue's mission statement is:

> Our mission as a UK charity for people who are homeless, is to connect vendors with the vital support and personal solutions that enable them to rebuild their lives; to find their own paths as they journey away from homelessness.

Other charities have a broader perspective (multi-issue). Greenpeace state that their mission is to:

> Defend the natural world and promote peace by investigating, exposing and confronting environmental abuse, [and] championing environmentally responsible solutions.

Charities still raise the majority of their finances through voluntary donations, but more and more charities now operate retail outlets as well. Oxfam have been doing this for a number of years and their shops contain new items often produced as a result of their development projects, as well as donated items such as books and clothes. There are hundreds of local charities who operate handfuls of shops within specific areas, all relying on donated goods. These shops have thrived as vacant premises have appeared on high streets up and down the country. Rents are cheap, and costs are low – often volunteer staff work in the shops.

Co-operatives

Business co-operatives were initially set up in the 19th century as part of a social movement by working people. They were established around workplaces or in districts of industrial towns, and were designed to prevent profiteering and exploitation by company shops and tallymen (door-to-door lenders).

> The historic background of British Co-operatives can be found on the Guardian newspaper website. To find out much more just enter the term 'co-operative history', in the Guardian website search box.

A co-operative is an organisation owned by its members. Employees of co-operatives automatically become members after a short probationary period, and shoppers at co-operative shops such as 'the Co-op', can apply to become members: acceptance is automatic. Members benefit through the payment of a dividend (their share of the co-operatives profits) in the form of money-off vouchers. Just like any business, co-operatives have managers and there is a business hierarchy, but it is much flatter than that found in a typical business – there are fewer layers to the hierarchy. Pay differentials between the most senior and most junior workers may be just 2 or 3 times (it is likely to be 30 times or more in a PLC). When major decisions need to be made, each member has an equal vote. Shoppers at the 'Co-op' have the right to vote for elected members and can actually stand in the election for representatives of the Co-operative Group.

Worker co-operatives are businesses which are owned and controlled by those who work in it. They often take the form of producer co-operatives, where people work together to produce a good or a service. As owners of the business, all employees are likely to be well motivated because they are all working towards the same goal. Some examples in the UK include various farmers' co-operatives and the Edinburgh Bicycle Co-operative, which retails bicycles.

Social enterprises

Social enterprises are a booming organisation structure. They are businesses with clear social objectives and are currently thriving in a number of industries and sectors of the economy.

- Social enterprises trade to help solve social problems, improve the communities they operate in, and improve the environment.
- Many social enterprises aim to make profits from selling goods and services in the open market; but then, instead of paying dividends, they reinvest these profits, towards achieving their social objectives.
- The chef Jamie Oliver has had great success with his '15' chain of restaurants, providing training in a range of cooking and catering skills for homeless and unskilled young people. Profits from the first restaurant go towards opening new restaurants and spreading the benefits to a larger number.
- The government is looking at the social enterprise model as a way of providing services such as child protection. Other social enterprises operate in the housing, drinks and holiday sectors, as well as many other sectors, and the number of social entrepreneurs is rapidly growing.
- Many young people, fresh out of university, are looking for a type of satisfaction from work that cannot come from employment in a large business, and the social enterprise structure offers them this motivational opportunity.

Discussion themes
Discuss the following statement: 'With a thriving and competitive private sector, the UK has no need of a public sector.'
Discuss the following statement: 'Maximising profits will always be the number one business priority.'
Explain the motivation shareholders of a private limited company may have in deciding to take their company public.
Discuss the following statement: 'Co-operatives will never be able to compete and be successful in the modern business environment.'
Discuss the following statement: 'Unlimited liability is the biggest disadvantage of operating as a sole trader.'
Explain why limited companies are more likely to be successful than unlimited businesses in obtaining external finance in order to expand.
See the article about what makes a social enterprise for an in-depth description of how social enterprises operate: http://www.socialenterprise.org.uk/advice-services/publications/social-enterprise-explained
What features of being a sole trader are shown in the video?
Teachers TV Video Watch the video on DC7 vending

Chapter 7
Stakeholders

Stakeholder groups and business

Stakeholders in a business are any individual or group which is **affected by** the business and so has an **interest in** its activities. These stakeholders are not all driven by the same objectives; in fact it is likely that different stakeholder groups will want very different things from the business concerned. Therefore it is not unusual to find different stakeholders and stakeholder groups coming into conflict over a business's activities and objectives.

- **Shareholders** are the owners of a limited company. In theory, all shareholders share the common objective of sustained long-term growth, giving both capital gain and increasing income. However, the reality is that even shareholders can come into conflict. Institutional shareholders (investment and pension funds) are often driven by the need to achieve in the short term. This means that they require high dividends and strategies to achieve short-term growth from the businesses that they have invested in. However, these strategies may be at odds with achieving long-term growth through reinvestment of profits and investing in brand value, which are what the individual, long-term investor may be looking for. Unfortunately for the small private shareholder, the institutional view is the one that more often than not wins the day.

- **Directors and managers** in large organisations focus their efforts on achieving the long-term objectives of the business. They use the resources under their control to achieve maximum benefits for the business and to gain the most from the assets that they manage. Often the success or failure of the business will be reflected in the rewards they receive. Unfortunately for some businesses, the main long-term objective of some managers is the protection of their position. This idea of self-preservation is sometimes a motivator for **middle managers** which can result in the establishment of whole layers of hierarchy whose role is to preserve their position. **Senior managers** are also sometimes accused of personal objectives ahead of those of the business by attempting to maximise their salaries and benefits, whilst cutting costs through redundancies and rationalisations.

- **Employees/workers** from middle management down receive a wage and possibly fringe benefits such as pensions. Naturally, a major concern of this category of stakeholders is job security. With many businesses seeking to incorporate technology, and reduce the size of the workforce, there will be obvious conflicts in the views of stakeholders. In the past this conflict would have often led to industrial action. However, over the last two decades it seems that the labour force has become more aware of the realities of modern employment, and are therefore less likely to take part in strikes. The labour force is more willing to accept job restructuring, and redundancy and to move jobs, relocate and retrain. However, industrial action does still take place and those employees who are members of strong trade unions are able to influence their pay and conditions to a greater extent than non-unionised workers.

- **Customers** are an increasingly important stakeholder: satisfying customers' needs profitably should lead to financial success to satisfy the other stakeholders. Customers want efficient service and a quality product, at a competitive price. These requirements should not be at odds with good business practice, but unfortunately sometimes they are. The short term nature of businesses can mean that achievement of immediate profit comes ahead of long-term customer satisfaction. Also customers like to feel needed and respected; it is all too easy to alienate your customer base. Maintaining good public relations is increasingly important – something which the banking and financial industry has come to realise in relation to the treatment of its customers.

- **Suppliers** depend on the success of businesses for their sales – and businesses depend upon suppliers in order to carry on their operations. They are mutually dependent. Suppliers want a fair price for their products whilst businesses wish to minimise costs. Following supply and demand theory, each market should achieve an equilibrium price, which should allocate rewards between supplier and buyer efficiently in a competitive market. However, unfortunately for suppliers, the power in the market often rests with the buyer, and we are seeing this market imperfection more and more. The big four supermarkets dominate the UK's farming industry, continually forcing down the prices they pay to producers, reducing farm incomes (for example, consider the recent milk price war and its impact). The situation is often worse when suppliers are based in developing countries, with the original producer receiving a tiny proportion of the product's final sale value. Fair trade goods try to make the supplier–buyer relationship more balanced.

- **Government** benefits from business success as it results in increased tax revenues, higher employment and lower benefit payments. However, the same economic success also means increased pollution, increased traffic, and loss of greenfield sites through development. In the past the priority was invariably given to growth, but increased environmental awareness has forced the government into limiting developments, encouraging development of brownfield sites, and into imposing taxes such as the Climate Change Levy and the Landfill Tax. These taxes on businesses increase business costs, reduce competitiveness, and potentially increase unemployment. As a stakeholder the government has to balance business and economic growth against external costs of business activity.

- **Local communities** need to be considered as a stakeholder. There are a number of benefits to a local community that stem from local business activity. These may include employment, increased regional wealth, improved facilities and infrastructure. Often the economic prosperity of a community may depend on one large employer in their area – the presence of which may support a range of other businesses such as shops, garages and hairdressers. Businesses may also support local charities as well as being involved with local schools and colleges. However conflicts can also occur between local communities and the businesses that operate close to them. This can involve potential pollution, environmental damage and loss of open space. Heavy transport moving 24/7 can affect the peace and quiet of a community.

Discussion themes
Discuss the following statement: 'The only important business stakeholders are customers and owners.'
Discuss the following statement: 'Meeting the needs of all stakeholders can only impact negatively on a business's bottom line.'
Explain how the interests of the owners of a business may conflict with the employees.
The Guardian Supermarkets' milk price war leaves a sour taste for dairy farmers http://www.theguardian.com/business/2014/mar/07/supermarkets-milk-price-war-dairy-farmers-tesco-cuts Explain how different stakeholders have been affected by the 'milk price war'. Could there be a long-term impact on consumers from the action of the supermarkets?

Chapter 8
Location

For many industries location is now far more complex than was previously the case. Apple, for example, has its headquarters in California, but most of its products are produced in Asia. A cloud computing company may have its head office in Dublin, but have its servers located in India, the UK and Germany. Nonetheless, even with these modern complications some basic rules still apply. Location for new and existing businesses is still largely determined by:

- access to customers;
- access to factors of production;
- minimisation of costs.

Location
http://bit.ly/23ceixZ

Key location factors

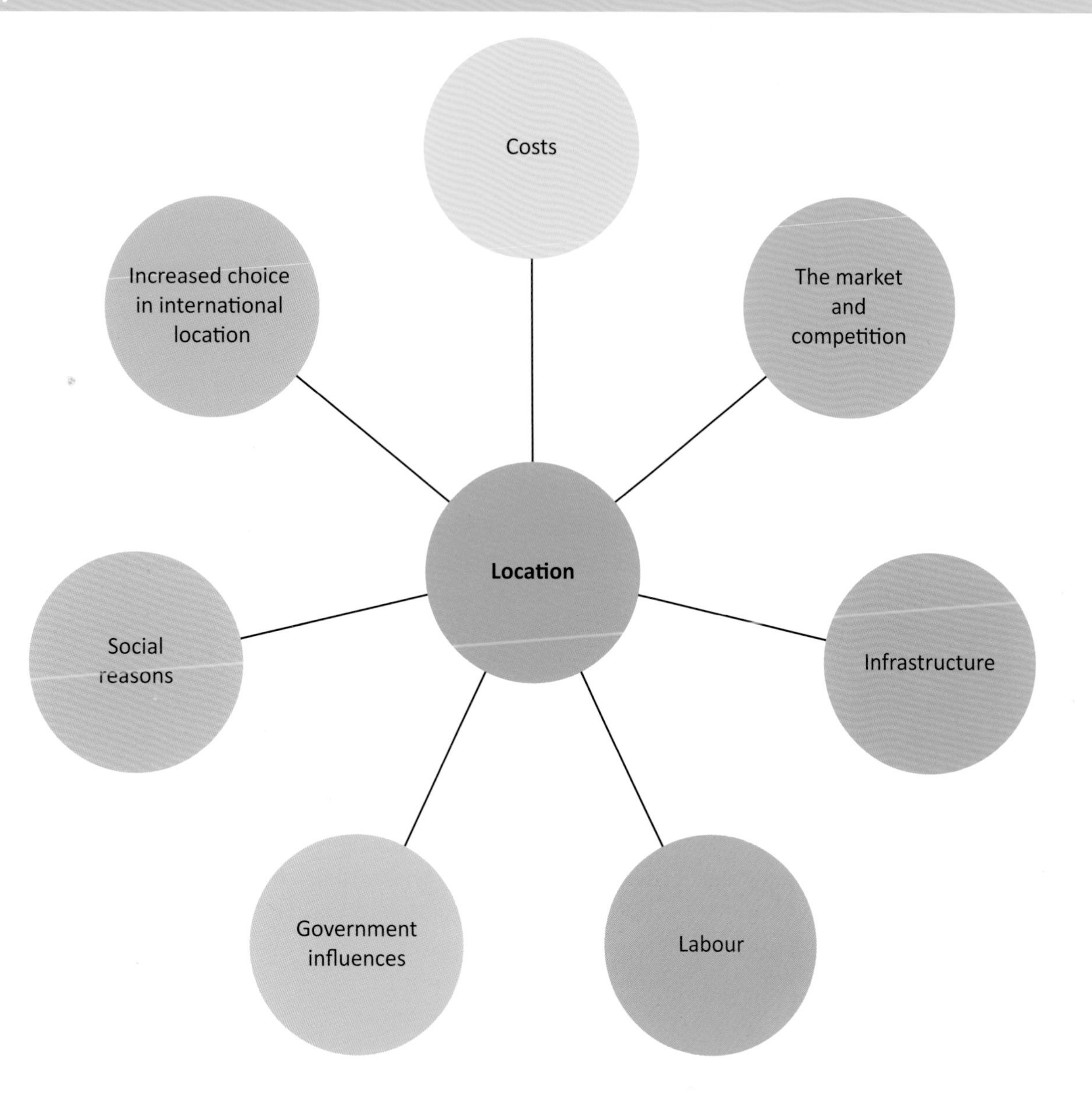

Costs

- For most new businesses the most important location factor is likely to be the cost. New businesses, especially sole traders, will have limited capital so they will need to keep their costs low. The setting up of a new business will incur a number of location costs including:
    - planning permission;
    - purchasing or rental/leasing;
    - refurbishment;
    - business rates;
    - labour costs;
    - transport costs.
- A new business may be unable to choose the ideal location for their business as they may not be able to afford the location costs. Therefore new businesses will often consider locating elsewhere, accepting that they are not selecting the optimum location. In the longer term they may have an objective to relocate when they have built up a customer base and have increased capital.
- A new business will need to consider the importance of location on its success. This will depend on its products and services and the market it will operate in.
- Because a new business may be limited in its choice of a suitable location due to costs, it will need to consider the other key location factors and determine what the most important factor is for them.

The market and competition

- The **market** is the place where buyers and sellers meet. Most commercial B2C exchanges (buying and selling in consumer markets) still take place face-to-face, so a physical location is required.
- Retail location should be driven by access to customers, but there will be a balance between customer footfall and rental/lease costs.
- Costs of location will vary according to likely sales and customer potential, but within each price band there will be both good and bad locations. Identical stores from the same chain with the same staffing levels and sales square footage can have significant variations in annual turnover.
- Retail location is not just about **footfall**, it is about type of footfall. If a new retail store is looking to locate in a shopping centre, it is a must to look carefully at the image of the anchor tenant. An anchor tenant is usually the first and the leading tenant in a shopping centre whose prestige and name recognition attracts other tenants and, it is hoped, shoppers. The **anchor** tenant sets the tone and image of the shopping centre, so the business owners need to examine the **demographics** of customers and whether their product would match the customer profile. Sometimes being near similar stores can help.
- Sometimes, being in **close proximity to competitors**, a business can benefit from their marketing efforts.
- Large businesses spend a sizeable proportion of their advertising budget on driving consumer traffic to their locations, a flow of customers that a competitor business can take advantage of. There are also competitor businesses that, by congregating in the same area, create more customer interest and higher individual sales. A good example of this situation would be antique emporiums and book shops, where a collection of shops attract customers from a wide catchment area.
- Regional markets also apply to B2B (Business to Business) relationships. Manufacturers of components in many industries need to be located close to the users of their products. This has become increasingly true with the increased use of **just-in-time systems**, where being 'on the doorstep' is now the expected norm.

Infrastructure

- The type and quality of infrastructure also affects access to markets. **Infrastructure** used to mean roads, rail and shipping. However, a more modern definition includes electronic communication systems, training agencies and financial services.
- For many modern businesses, such as those that are **e-commerce** based or the rapidly growing call centre industry, quality infrastructure has a very different meaning from that understood by road hauliers and heavy goods manufacturers.
- In the UK there is a major imbalance in development between the South East and the rest of the country. Improved infrastructure is being planned to resolve this problem (for example, HS2); but it is likely that this will be a very long-term solution.
- **Economies of concentration** or agglomeration occur when a number of businesses in the same, or related industries, locate close together. They are able to gain mutual advantages. New businesses are attracted by existing infrastructure clusters and in high-tech industries it is often worthwhile for specialist businesses and universities to undertake research, provide education, training and information, from which all businesses can benefit. We can see this occurring in London around the new Sir Francis Crick Institute.

Labour

- The factor of production **labour** can also be a deciding factor in determining location. By labour we mean cost of labour, availability of labour, and the skills of labour.
- Businesses can be attracted to certain areas by the skilled labour that may be available. For example, the aero technology workers in Coventry and Bristol, or the thriving community of software developers in Cambridge, linked to the university. Cardiff is rapidly developing a booming media industry which is attracting new international investors looking to recruit talented workers.
- The cost of labour is also a determining factor. International location has a habit of following low-cost labour to wherever it is available. Many UK manufacturing businesses have relocated to the Far East and China where labour costs are very low; although there is some evidence that this trend will be reversed as wage rates in these areas start to increase.

Government influences

- The cost of labour can be affected by the availability of **government grants**, giving incentives to move to particular regions of a country, and by **government taxation policies**.
- The availability of **low cost and suitable land** resources can also be an important factor when determining location. National governments, along with regional development agencies, often work hard to ensure that planning permission is available to allow large developments to proceed and they also offer incentives such as tax breaks and help with recruitment and training of workers.

Social reasons

- These too can also have an impact on location. Managers want to live in an environment that suits them and their families. They want leisure facilities, good schools, and low crime.
- Alternatively managers can often retain a commitment to their existing workforce, even when it makes economic and business sense to relocate a business.

Increased choice in international location

Footloose businesses are those that move from location to location, basing themselves wherever best suits their needs at a particular point in time:

- changing patterns of trade;
- improved communications;
- freer flows of capital.

All of the above mean that the largest businesses, though still influenced by the same factors that dictate national location of business, do have the alternative of locating their production facilities virtually anywhere in the world. As long as there is a stable political background and an available workforce, most countries will offer the possibility of hosting a production (or even a remote service) base.

The main influences on international location beyond politics and labour force factors are likely to be maximising **economies of scale**. If businesses are able to have a single plant supplying all their requirements for a type of product or range of components, then the business's average costs of production can fall. Therefore there are huge factories providing cakes to sell throughout Europe, or producing injection-moulded plastics for distribution throughout the world.

The falling **costs of international transport** have allowed this to occur. Back in the 1950s the final cost of selling imported goods included transport costs which made up around 25% of the selling price. Through **containerisation** and increased efficiency of systems this proportion has fallen well below 5%.

Political factors can also have an influence on location. Tariff and quota-free access to trading blocs such as the EU, or NAFTA (North American Free Trade Association) may depend on setting up a production facility within that trading bloc. Far Eastern companies such as Toyota and Honda, wanting free access to European markets, have large production units in the UK today.

Companies sometimes establish head office operations where taxation levels are lower than their home base. This can allow **transfer costing** to take place. Transfer costing is a process by which businesses are able to inflate their profits in countries where taxation levels are relatively low, and decrease their profits where taxation levels are relatively high. A number of companies, including Starbucks and Amazon, have hit the headlines recently for this sort of activity.

Comparative international wage levels also need to be considered when deciding on worldwide location. High-tech industries can often choose from willing and skilled workforces from many different global locations. One famous directory enquiry service answers enquiries in a Cardiff office during the day, and then switches between the hours of 10pm and 8am to an office in Manila.

Freedom from restrictions which would otherwise increase costs or constrain production methods can be a driver of location. Businesses can reduce their costs if they locate operations in countries where red tape is less present or employment law is less strict. For example many merchant ships use flags of convenience. This means that the ships are registered in countries that impose fewer restrictions on wages, manning levels, working hours etc. Clearly, there are ethical issues to consider here.

Locating a restaurant
http://bit.ly/1RR6EFO

Discussion themes
Explain three likely reasons why IKEA chose this location. BBC News: IKEA opening riots http://news.bbc.co.uk/1/hi/england/london/4252421.stm
Explain how Starbucks takes advantage of transfer costing. Reuters: How Starbucks avoids UK taxes http://uk.reuters.com/article/2012/10/15/us-britain-starbucks-tax-idUSBRE89E0EX20121015
Evan Davis at Exeter University Why is London so dominant in the UK? https://www.youtube.com/watch?v=scCH_M5D9PQ Evan Davies – Mind the Gap Why London Dominates Part 1 https://www.youtube.com/watch?v=DIpakXL6F6I Part 2 https://www.youtube.com/watch?v=EpUNIKB-WaU Is London's growing success good for the UK in general? Will improved infrastructure help close the economic gap between London and Manchester/Leeds/Bradford? Using examples explain what is meant by economies of concentration/agglomeration.
Discuss the following statement: 'Location is the key to business success.'
Discuss the following statement: 'Access to customers is the most important location factor.'
Explain what is meant by 'footloose'.

Chapter 9
Business finance

Businesses cannot survive without finance, whether in the form of **initial funds** to start the business, **working capital** to run the business day-to-day, or **investment capital** to help the business grow. For a new business starting out it is unlikely that external forms of finance will be available. Apart from capital provided by the entrepreneur and friends and family, *sources of finance are likely to be severely limited*. These new sole traders and micro-businesses are likely to continue to struggle to find external sources of finance until they establish an effective trading record.

The most suitable finance option for a business depends on many things:

- how much funding is needed;
- the amount of time the money is required for;
- what the finance will be used for;
- the affordability of repayments;
- whether or not personal or business assets are available as security;
- whether or not the business owner is willing to give up a share of ownership, perhaps through taking on a partner or selling shares.

Internal sources of finance

Retained profit

This is regarded as the single most important source of finance and is also the cheapest source of finance. As a business becomes more profitable, it makes sense to build up and retain some profit (reserves). This will provide a liquidity buffer and potential funds for growth. Reserves, reinvested profits, come with only one cost – the loss of profit distribution to owners. Short-term pressures to pay profits to owners (normally shareholders) can, however, restrict the availability of this form of finance.

Working capital

By reducing their trade credit period and collecting debts more efficiently, a business may receive money from customers more quickly. However, this is likely to drive customers away and may have the opposite effect on making finance available. Reducing stock holdings is another way to release finance but a sudden surge in demand could result in lost sales if the business is unable to meet delivery dates.

Sale of assets

Established businesses are able to sell off assets that are no longer required, such as buildings and machinery. Smaller businesses are unlikely to have such unwanted assets and, if growth is an objective, they are much more likely to want to acquire assets as opposed to losing them.

External sources of finance

Bank loans

Any new business will need a bank account, but it is unlikely that any bank will provide loan finance to a new start-up unless security is offered. A loan is borrowing a fixed amount, for a fixed period of time, perhaps 3–5 years. Payments made up of interest and capital are made monthly. Security, if available, will very often come in the form of property. Offering security against a loan can make it much easier to get funding and reduces interest rates charged – but increases risk to personal assets. If the business owner is not able to maintain payments, homes can be lost or business assets removed.

Overdrafts

As a business develops an effective trading record then an overdraft facility may be provided by the bank. An overdraft is the facility to withdraw more from an account than is in the bank account, resulting in a negative balance. Businesses often depend upon authorised overdrafts to provide working capital. The nature of business often means that money is paid out on costs before revenue is received. This leaves a funding deficit. An overdraft is designed to cover this funding deficit and provide working capital. Unfortunately overdrafts can be withdrawn by a bank with just 30 days' notice. This means a long-term dependency on an overdraft has dangers. The business relying upon an overdraft for day-to-day funds may find that with a withdrawal of the overdraft facility, they do not have money for paying bills, wages, suppliers etc.

Trade credit

This is an interest-free way to raise finance. Businesses buy items such as fuel and raw material and pay for them at a later date – possibly 30–90 days later. Many suppliers today, however, offer discounts for early payment so delaying payment may result in higher costs in the long run. Businesses that take a long time to pay their bills also tend to gain a bad reputation in the marketplace.

Factoring

An alternative to an overdraft is for a business to use a factoring service. Factoring is a method of turning invoices into cash. Banks and other financial organisations offer factoring services which pay a proportion of the value of an invoice (80–85%) when the invoice is issued. The balance, minus a fee, is paid to the business when the invoice is paid. This flexible form of finance keeps pace with business growth as the funding is directly linked to the turnover of the company. The factor will also undertake all credit management and collections work.

The use of this service results in savings in administration costs, which can be substantial, and faster customer payments means lower interest costs on any overdraft facility. Bad debt protection can also be built into the service. Factoring services are only offered to businesses with a good trading record and reliable customers. It is, however, an effective alternative to an overdraft, as the cost is generally lower.

Leasing and hire purchase

Leasing and hire purchase are methods of gaining the use of capital goods, whilst paying a monthly fee. With a business lease the company gains use of a productive asset, without ever owning it. Businesses often lease office equipment like computers and photocopiers. Many business vehicles are leased, and the practice even extends to ships and planes. With hire purchase a business's payment includes a hire charge and a payment towards purchase. At the end of the hire purchase period the business will own the asset.

These methods are regarded as medium-term forms of finance and the business, by avoiding paying outright for the item, gains from an increase in capacity without the use of existing capital. Any existing capital can then be used for other purposes within the business. The major disadvantages of these forms of finance is that they cost more than outright purchase and the business is obliged to pay the lease or complete the hire purchase contract. This can cause real problems if the business later struggles financially or ceases trading. A sole trader will still be liable for these contracts and the same applies to most partnerships.

Commercial mortgages

If a business owns property a commercial mortgage may be available. With a commercial mortgage the property is used as security against the loan and the loan can be as much as 60 or 70% of the value of the property. Because security is being offered to the lender, the interest rates will be lower than an unsecured loan. Payments are made monthly for the term of the mortgage. Failure to make repayments may lead to the property being repossessed by the lender. Commercial mortgages might run for 10 or 15 years so generally have predictable costs – this can be helpful with budgeting and predicting cash flow.

Sale and leaseback

Another asset-based method of raising funds for SMEs (small and medium-sized enterprises) is sale and leaseback. Sale and leaseback involves the business selling assets (buildings, machinery) to a finance company and then leasing the asset back. This method of raising finance means that the capital that is produced can be reinvested into growing the business. This means that an asset owned by the business can be turned into capital for reinvestment in the business. Sale and leaseback also carries potential tax benefits as the leasing costs are offset as an operating expense.

Share capital

A long-term method of providing funds for growth is to sell shares. This means that the business may move from being a partnership or sole trader to becoming a limited company. There are a number of advantages to being a limited company which include limited liability and reduction in risk for the owners. However, the main reason is to bring in new shareholders who invest capital for growth. This is the scenario often seen on Dragons' Den, the BBC television programme. The question business owners have to answer is how much of a business is the owner willing to give up to gain the finance they need.

Share capital is a form of permanent capital; this means it does not have to be repaid. Owners of shares have a say in how the business is run, but the amount of influence they have depends upon the percentage shareholding they own. The major disadvantage of bringing in shareholders is of course loss of control. The business owner or owners will have decisions influenced by new investors. Also the new shareholder investors may be looking for an exit strategy within a few years. This means that they are expecting the business to grow rapidly and then they expect to be able to sell their shares, taking their capital gain.

Venture capitalists

Venture capitalists are professional investors who can invest large amounts of capital into small and medium-sized businesses. Venture capitalists and venture capital companies (who exist to invest into growing businesses), will not only take a shareholding but also expect to be fully involved in running the business. They will take seats on the board and appoint managers and advisors to help generate success and growth. From the business owners' point of view, all this input of skills and capital allows the business to grow at a speed that was previously impossible. Some of the best-known internet businesses (Facebook, Google, Twitter) depended upon venture capital to fund growth. Venture capitalists are often quite happy to focus on growth for the short and medium term, with the expectation that profits will come later.

Government assistance

Although hard to come by, both local and central government may offer finance to business start-up schemes. The qualifying criteria do tend to be quite narrow and businesses setting up in regions of high unemployment tend to be favoured. The amounts available tend to be relatively small and are for a limited period of time.

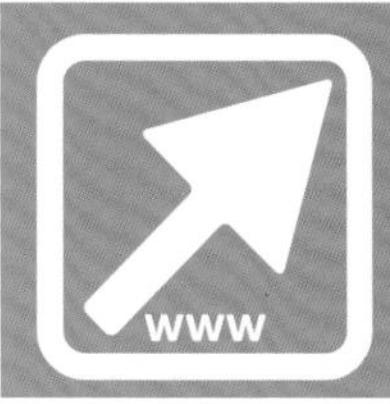

Suitable sources of finance
http://bit.ly/1ZJWURY

Discussion themes
Apart from potential access to a loan for a business start-up, what advantages are there to a young entrepreneur of participating in the Enterprise programme? The Prince's Trust Enterprise programme http://www.princes-trust.org.uk/need_help/enterprise_programme/about_the_enterprise_programme.aspx
Define the following types of finance: micro loans; technology venture investment; business loans or debt investment; equity investments. Finance Wales: What we do http://www.financewales.co.uk/what-we-do/finance-for-welsh-smes.aspx
Explain the problems that can affect businesses when overdraft facilities are withdrawn at short notice. Banks withdraw overdraft facilities http://www.telegraph.co.uk/finance/newsbysector/banksandfinance/10279439/Banks-cancel-smaller-companies-overdrafts-as-cash-crisis-continues.html
Why, at least in the short term, is liquidity often more important to business than profits?
Describe three types of short/medium-term finance.
Describe three types of long-term finance.
Explain why a venture capitalist is a suitable investor in a new business.

Chapter 10
Revenue, costs and break-even analysis

Revenue

Revenue is the money a business makes from sales. In other words, it is the value of the sales and is also referred to as turnover. The total amount of money a business receives from its sales is called total revenue.

Total revenue = quantity sold x selling price

By calculating the total revenue a business can then work out if they have made a profit or a loss.

Profit = total revenue – total costs

Of course, all businesses want to make a profit. However, if total costs are greater than total revenue then the business will make a loss.

Fixed costs

In every business some costs will remain the same whatever the level of output produced or products sold. For a shop, even if no customers visit, the rent or mortgage will have to be paid. There will still be business rates to pay, and the electricity for lighting, fridges etc. will still have to be paid. A software business will find that the value of its hardware depreciates (falls in value) even if it is not being used. An ice cream salesman in his van will have to pay insurance and road tax even if no ice creams are sold. These are all **fixed costs**. Fixed costs are costs that do not vary with output. No matter how much is made or how little is sold, fixed costs still have to be paid.

Variable costs

Variable costs behave quite differently from fixed costs. Variable costs vary in direct proportion to output – as output increases variable costs increase, as output falls variable costs fall. Using the example of a tailor's shop, variable costs would include cloth, cotton, buttons etc. None of these raw materials of the suits or dresses made would be used if no goods were produced. So when output or sales are nil, then variable costs are nil. However, as soon as output starts, then these raw materials start being used. As more and more suits and dresses are made, so more and more cloth, buttons and cotton are used. We can therefore say that at output zero, variable costs are zero; but as output increases variable costs also rise.

We assume that there is a constant relationship between output and variable costs, but in most cases this constant relationship does not hold true. Businesses who produce more often benefit from purchasing economies of scale, so as output increases variable costs per unit produced start to fall.

Not all costs can be defined as fixed or variable. Some costs, such as labour, could be fixed (a permanent member of staff working a 38 hour week) or variable (the member of staff being asked to work 5 hours overtime due to increased demand). These types of costs are called **semi-variable**.

Total costs

Total costs are found by adding together fixed costs and variable costs. At every level of output (apart from nil), a business's costs will be a combination of fixed and variable costs – the two added together make total costs. At zero output the business only has fixed costs, there are no variable costs. So at zero output, fixed costs = total costs. However, once the business starts production or starts making sales then total costs will be made up of fixed and variable costs.

Average total costs are the average cost of producing each unit of output. Because total costs consist of fixed and variable costs, as output increases then **average total costs** start to fall. This fall in average total costs will continue until a point is reached where diseconomies of scale force variable costs to rise sufficiently to push up the average total costs of production.

It is important for managers to be able to judge profitability. Decisions need to be made on continuing or discontinuing production – whether to make an investment in developing a product, whether to start training programmes or input more human resources. Without information on profitability, or lack of profitability, effective decisions cannot be made. To enable these decisions to be made businesses must have a method of allocating costs to each product, department, branch or factory. One method of implementing this cost allocation is to divide a business's costs into **direct costs and overheads**.

Direct costs are costs that arise specifically from the production of a product or the provision of a service. Examples of direct costs include:

- rent on a shop;
- materials or components;
- direct labour;
- expenses such as copyright payments on a published book, or licence fees for use of patents.

These direct costs can be totalled to give the direct costs of producing the product. However, revenue minus direct costs does not indicate profitability. The business must also apportion **overheads** or **indirect costs** to the product.

The production of any product results in a business paying costs not directly related to production or service provision. For example, a factory producing 10 different goods, to each of which managers allocate direct costs, will employ a secretary or receptionist. The overhead cost of employing the secretary or receptionist needs to be apportioned or allocated to the products to gain a picture of true profitability. For retailers, advertising is an overhead; the cost of advertising should be shared out amongst retail outlets to better judge profitability. So the true profitability of a product, factory, outlet etc. can only be judged if we take from revenue both direct costs and overheads. Overheads are therefore costs not directly related to production.

Calculating costs

Output	Fixed costs	Variable costs	Total costs	Average total costs
0	1016	0	1016	0
10	1016	600	1616	161.60
20	1016	1150	2166	108.30
30	1016	1650	2666	88.87
40	1016	2100	3116	77.90
50	1016	2450	3466	69.32
60	1016	2800	3816	63.60
70	1016	3300	4316	61.66
80	1016	3850	4866	60.83
90	1016	4450	5466	60.73
100	1016	5100	6116	61.16
110	1016	6000	7016	63.78

In the above table we see the business has fixed costs (per week) of £1016. At zero output, variable costs are zero. As output increases, variable costs start to increase, as do total costs. However, the increase is not constant, i.e. not in direct proportion to output.

To find the average total costs we simply divide total costs by output.

Break-even analysis

To gain an understanding of calculating break-even we will use the example of a young entrepreneur wishing to start up a business delivering packages of fruit and veg.

He knows that the last local shop in his area closed last year. Sensibly, he has carried out market research which indicates that there will be a good level of demand, but before he begins he needs to know how profitable the business might be. He has also fully researched the costs of starting up as a deliveryman and the costs of purchasing supplies. The costs he has researched are as follows:

- cost of delivery van purchase £6000;
- insurance and road tax £100 per month;
- petrol £10.00 per day;
- average cost of fruit and veg box £5.00;
- wages (the amount the owner draws from the business) £1150 per month;
- loan repayment to cover the cost of the van £500 per month for twelve months.

His market research indicates that the fruit and veg boxes will have an average sales price of £9.00.

The question then is how many boxes will he need to sell to cover all his costs, i.e. to break even? He decides to calculate break-even on a monthly basis.

Calculating the break-even point

The first step is to calculate his monthly costs. We separate costs into fixed costs and variable costs. **This division into fixed and variable costs is very important in break-even analysis.** So the first stage in our deliveryman's calculation of his monthly break-even sales level is the division of his costs into fixed and variable costs. The loan must be repaid each month, no matter how many boxes he sells. So this is a fixed cost. As he intends to follow the same route each day, the petrol cost will not vary with sales, therefore this is another fixed cost. He will still need his £1150 per month to live on no matter how many boxes he sells; this is therefore a fixed cost.

The fruit and veg is to be ordered from the wholesaler on a daily basis. He will order what he needs, therefore cost will vary with sales – this is a variable cost.

We can now prepare a monthly cost table:

Fixed costs	Total fixed costs £2000 per month	Loan repayment £500 per month	Petrol costs £250 per month	Insurance and road tax £100 per month	The amount the owner draws from the business £1150 per month
Variable costs	£5.00 per box				
Sales revenue	£9.00 per box				

Calculating break-even point using the contribution method

Once we have calculated costs, the next step in calculating break-even output or sales is finding out how much **contribution** each item sold produces for the business.

Every product made has a variable cost and a selling price (which must obviously be higher). The difference between the selling price per unit and the variable cost per unit is known as the **CONTRIBUTION** towards covering the business's fixed costs. There is a simple formula for calculating break-even output.

Break-even output = Fixed costs divided by the contribution per unit

In the above case the selling price is £9, the variable cost is £5 – the contribution is therefore £4 per unit sold.

Fixed costs are £2000 per month and his contribution is £4 per box. If we divide fixed costs per month by contribution we will find out how many fruit and veg boxes must be sold to break even:

£2000/£4 = 500 boxes

We can now see that to break even our deliveryman must sell 500 fruit and veg boxes per month.

- If he sells more than 500 boxes he will make a profit.
- If he sells less than 500 boxes he will make a loss.
- At break-even point the total contribution (contribution per item X number sold) equals the total fixed costs.

Calculating profit and loss

Break-even analysis also allows us to calculate the profit or loss a business will make at different levels of output. This will always be important – after all our grocery seller may wish to go into business only if his profits are likely to be at a certain level.

First of all calculate the break-even output, in the above case we know it is 500 boxes per month.

As a result of his market research he believes that he can sell 650 boxes a month. He now wants to know what his profit will be at that level of sales. To find out how much profit will be made, we again use the idea of contribution.

In this case predicted sales are 650. Break-even sales are 500.

We then take the difference between predicted sales and the break-even point and multiply this by the contribution. This will give us the profit figure.

150 x £4 contribution = £600. His profits per month on sales of 650 boxes will be £600.

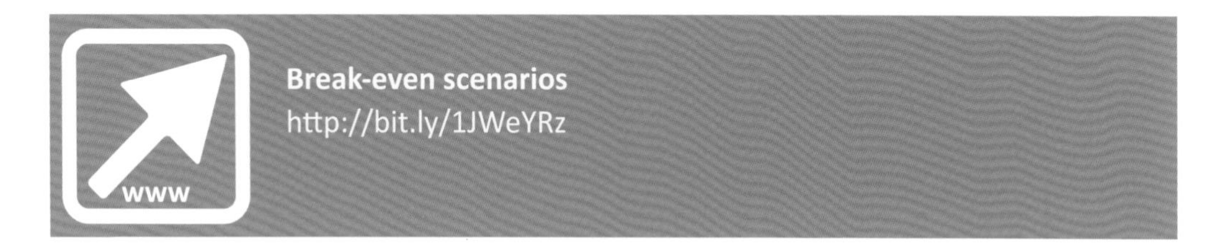

The break-even graph

For our grocery delivery business we are asked to calculate the break-even output per month. Therefore, as with the mathematical method, we must divide our costs into fixed and variable costs. Using the information above, our costs have already been broken down. We can now draw the **fixed costs line** on the break-even chart.

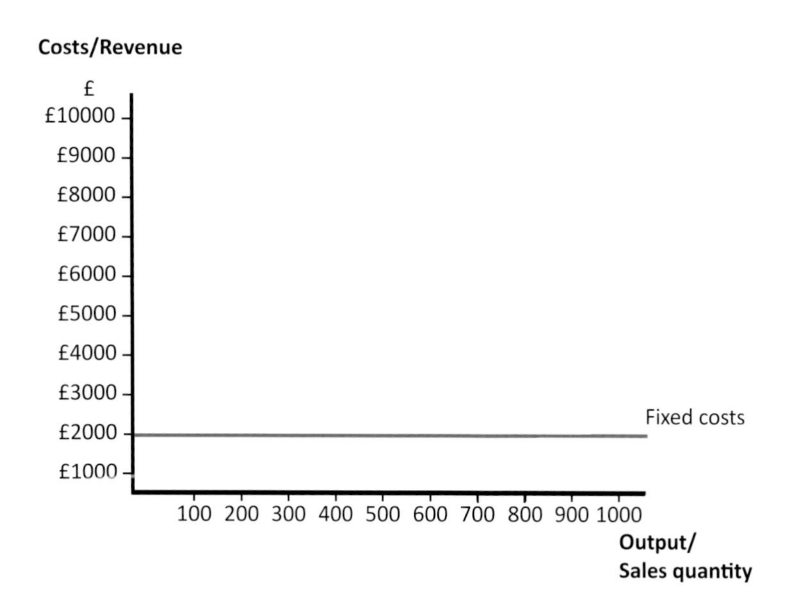

On the graph you can see that the vertical axis shows the level of costs and revenue, while the horizontal axis shows the level of output and sales. We can also see on the chart the fixed costs line which has been drawn at a level of £2000 for all levels of output. As *fixed costs remain unchanged at all levels of output*, the fixed costs line will always be horizontal.

The next step is to add **the variable costs line**. When calculating variable costs we must work out the variable cost per unit made or sold. The units in this case are the boxes of fruit and veg. To draw the variable costs line we mark three points. We know that at output zero variable costs are zero, so we have our first point: the point where the axes meet. The second and third point can be marked on the graph. For the second point we have selected an output level of 400 (we could just have easily chosen 500 or 600). We then calculate variable costs at this output level. To do this just multiply variable costs per unit by the chosen output level. So in this case we have 400 x £5 = £2000. For the third point we select an output level of 1000. So, 1000 x £5 = £5000. The variable cost line can now be drawn by joining the three points.

At every level of output (apart from zero), the business's costs will be a combination of fixed and variable costs – the two added together make total costs.

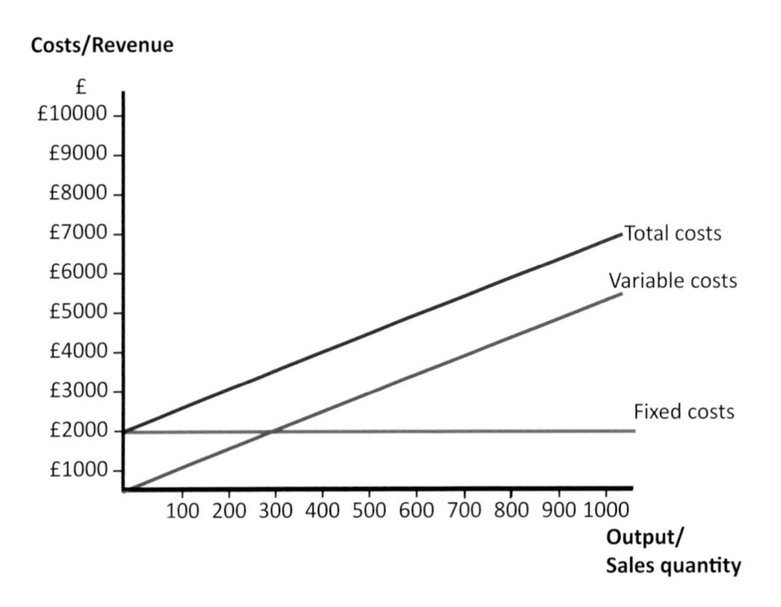

At output zero the business only has fixed costs, there are no variable costs. We must now draw the **total cost line** – this will always start where the fixed costs line meets the vertical (costs) axis. To mark the second point, choose a level of output and add together fixed and variable costs at that level. In this case, at an output of 400 boxes of fruit and veg, the fixed costs are £2000 and the variable costs are also £2000 (£5 x 400). So the total costs at an output of 400 = £2000 + £2000 = £4000.

At the third point, at an output of 1000, the fixed costs are £2000 and the variable costs are (£5 x 1000). So the total costs at an output of 1000 = £2000 + £5000 = £7000. The total cost line can now be drawn by joining the three points.

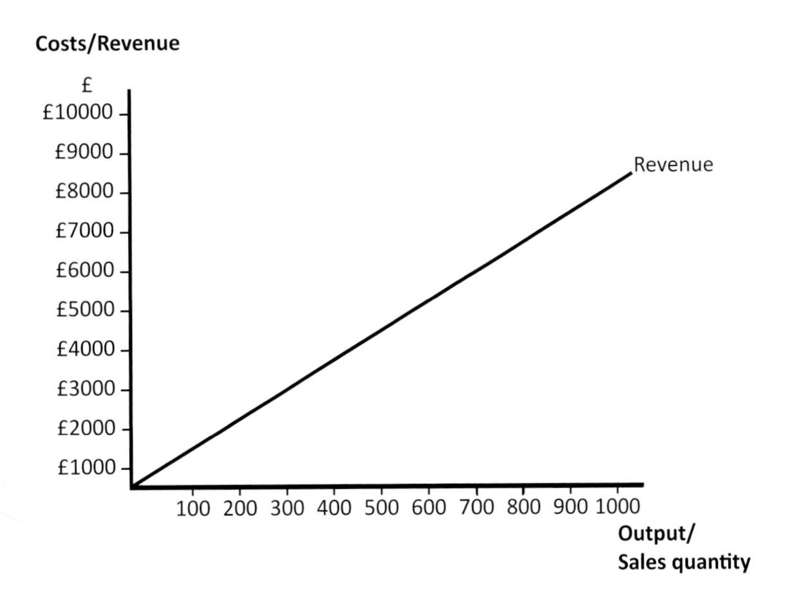

The last line that we need to add is the **revenue line**. This line tells us the revenue at any level of sales. Revenue is the number of sales multiplied by the selling price per unit. In this case the average sales price is £9. To draw the revenue line we again use three points. The first is straightforward. At sales zero, revenue is zero; so we can mark the start of our revenue line. To mark the second point we use a similar method to drawing the variable cost. If we choose sales of 600 units we have:- 600 (Sales) x £9.00 (revenue per unit) = £5400. To mark the third point at 1000 sales we have 1000 x £9.00 = £9000. Connect your points and you have the revenue line.

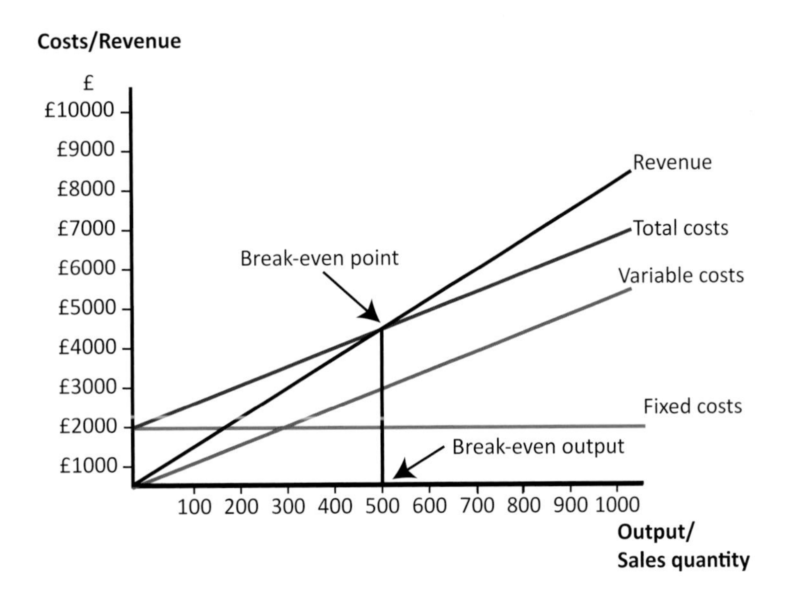

The point where the revenue line cuts the total costs line is break-even point. Draw a vertical line straight down from the break-even point; this will give you break-even output. A horizontal line drawn from break-even point to the costs/revenue axis will give you break-even costs/revenue.

Calculating profit and loss using a break-even chart

Using the break-even chart we can calculate the break-even point and profit and loss at various levels of output.

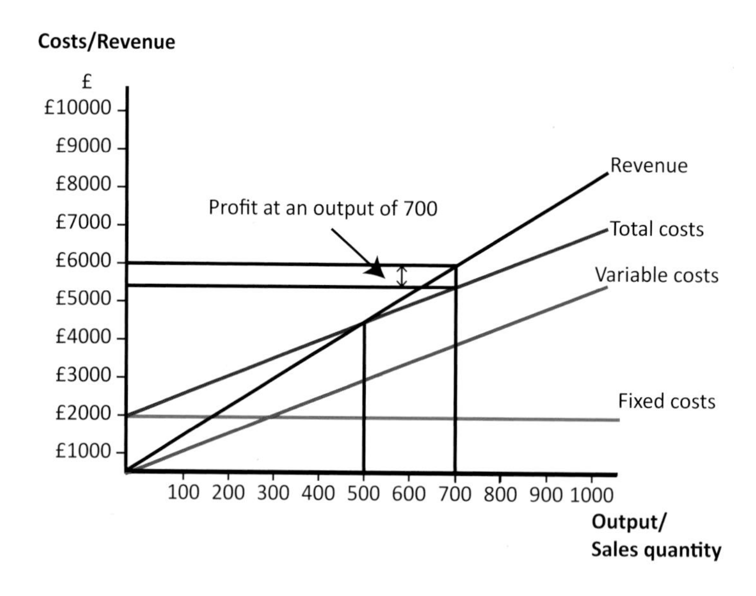

To find profit or loss at different outputs we must measure the difference between the revenue line and the total costs line at the given level of output. For example, to calculate profit at an output of 700 units you would firstly draw a vertical line up from the 700 output point. You would draw this so that it meets both the total costs and revenue lines (this has been done on the chart). At output 700 we are to the right of break-even point, so the business is making a profit. We can see this clearly because the revenue line is above the total costs line. To find out exactly how much profit is being made at this level of output (or any other output level), we measure the gap between the total revenue and total costs lines. In this case, profit is £700.

The margin of safety

A business's margin of safety is the difference between output level and break-even output, when output is above break-even. So if output is 900 units and break-even is 500 units, then the margin of safety is 400 units. The margin of safety indicates the amount by which demand can fall before a business incurs losses. The margin of safety can be identified on the break-even chart by measuring the difference between the break-even point and the actual level of output. Businesses will want to ensure that they have a healthy margin of safety just in case an unexpected drop in sales affects their business. A small margin of safety could put the business at risk if they experience a drop in sales.

Changes in costs and revenues

In business, costs and revenues are not fixed, and a break-even chart can be used to show the effect of an increase or drop in revenue and/or costs on the profitability of a business.

An increase in the price of the boxes from £9 to £11 will change the total revenue line (Revenue 2), it becomes steeper and will cut the total cost line sooner, resulting in break-even at a lower level of output. If the price was reduced then the opposite would happen and the break-even point would be at a higher level of output.

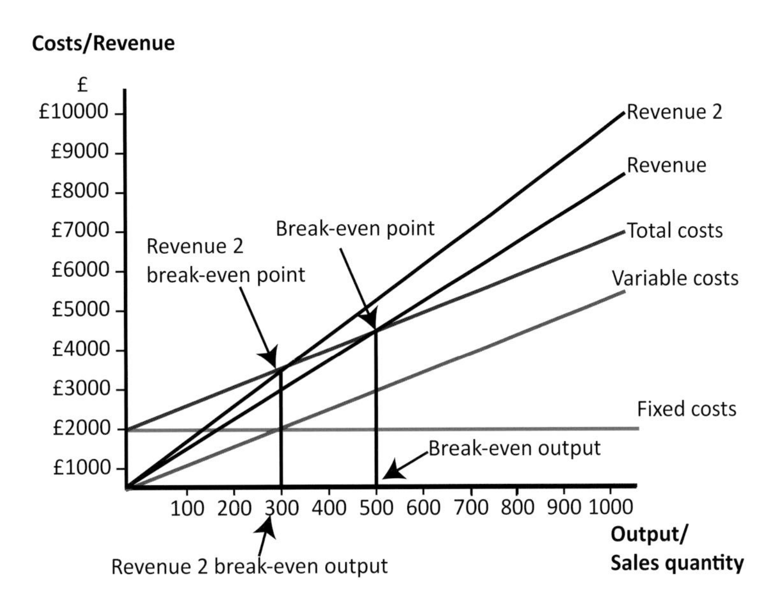

An increase in the variable cost will change the total cost line (Total costs 2). It becomes slightly steeper and will cut the revenue line at a higher output level, resulting in break-even at a higher level of output. If the costs were reduced then the opposite would happen. If variable costs remained the same but fixed costs changed then this would result in a parallel shift in the total cost line.

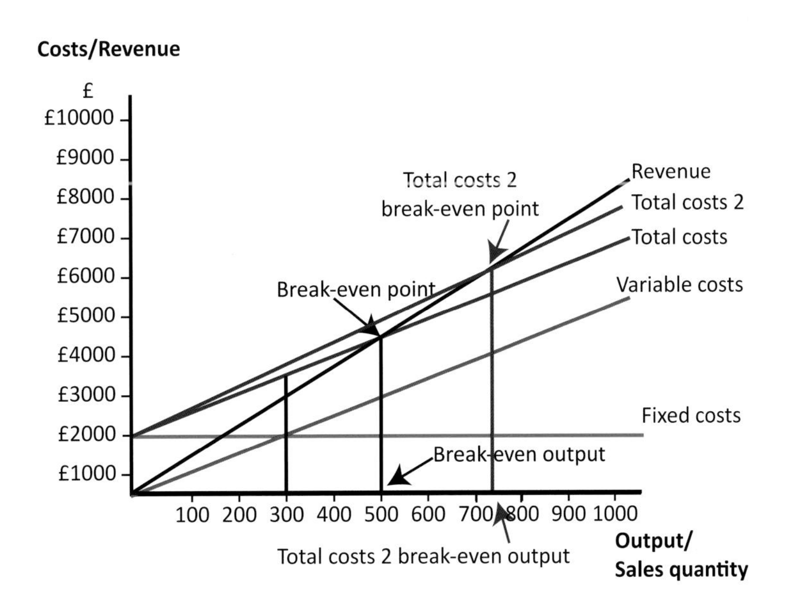

How useful is break-even analysis?

- Break-even does provide a simple and easily understood representation of costs, revenue and potential profit.
- Break-even is also useful as part of a business plan and can help when seeking a loan.
- It also allows use of 'what-if' analysis. Using 'what-if' analysis, business owners can judge the impact on profitability of a number of costs and revenue variables. For example, the effect of an increase in fixed costs by 10% could be quickly judged, and the same applies to potential changes in variable costs and revenues. Using this method the impact of the changes on break-even output, margin of safety and profitability can be measured.
- However, the use of 'what-if' does not fully overcome the weaknesses of break-even. The first problem is that the method assumes only one product is produced and sold, but this simple situation is rarely repeated in the real world of business. This initial problem can be overcome if the business (e.g. a sandwich shop) sells a similar range of products: then an average cost and revenue per customer can be estimated.
- The method also assumes that all goods produced are sold, and sold at the same price. Most businesses have wastage through damaged stock, poor quality stock etc., and it is likely that at least some products (end of line) will be discounted.
- The linear relationship of costs/revenue to output/sales can also be questioned. In each case economies of scale are likely to come into play, breaking down the relationship.
- Some fixed costs are stepped. This occurs when a business acquires more capacity, and costs, such as rent, may increase. This sharp rise in fixed costs makes it difficult to apply break-even analysis.

Break-even graph
http://bit.ly/1S1S6l4

Key terms
http://bit.ly/1StX9fC

Discussion themes
Test Question. 1. A small family ice cream business sells boxes of cones (ten in each box) and has the following costs. Rent £500 per month Electricity £200 per month Wages £1800 per month Equipment loan £210 per month Leasing charges £120 per month Ice cream 11p per cone Packing 30p per box of ten cones Wafer 2p per cone The revenue is £3.20 per box of 10 cones a. What is the break-even output in boxes of cones, per month? b. What will be the profit or loss at an output of 2100 boxes per month? c. What will be the profit or loss at an output of 1550 boxes per month? d. What would happen to the break-even output if wages increased by £300 per month?
Define the terms fixed and variable costs.
What is a semi-variable cost?
How does a business calculate profit?
What is contribution? If a product sells for £15 and the variable costs are £12.50 what is the contribution per unit?
Discuss the usefulness of break-even analysis to a business.
Explain how a business can analyse changes in costs and/or revenue through break-even.
What happens to the margin of safety for a business if its costs remain the same but their price is reduced?
Discuss the following statement: 'The failings and weaknesses of break-even analysis make it barely useful in the real world.'

Chapter 11
Functional departments

When a business has a traditional hierarchical structure, it will be typically structured by functional departments i.e. **departments with clearly defined roles and responsibilities**. This division into functional departments helps with communication as people know who to speak to if a problem arises. It also helps workers understand their roles and how the business works, setting out the responsibilities of each part of the business.

Although departments are separate from each other, their roles are connected. For example, the human resources department is responsible for making sure that the other departments have enough workers with the right skills; the finance department ensures that there is money available to carry out activities across all departments. Marketing works with production by providing information about the products that customers want, whilst purchasing has the job of making sure that there are enough materials for production to manufacture.

In most large companies the functional areas are as follows:

- Marketing (Sales and Marketing);
- Human Resources (Personnel);
- Finance (Accounts);
- Operations (Production).

They may vary in name but essentially they carry out the same functions. Depending on the type of business, there may be a range of other functional departments which specialise in performing a particular type of task. Typical examples are:

- Legal Department;
- Transport Department;
- Purchasing Department;
- Design Department;
- Technical Department.

Functional objectives

These are the **goals** of each of the functional departments and if a business is to be successful then these objectives must be closely tied to the corporate objectives. For example, if the marketing department sets itself a goal of achieving 10% more sales over the next year, whilst the human resources department is seeking to reduce staffing by 5% across the company in the same period, then they are likely to be working against each other. Goals must be carefully coordinated to ensure that they are consistent with the corporate objectives – in other words, all departments are working together to achieve the same overall objectives of the organisation.

Depending on the nature of the organisation in question, some departments are likely to be much larger than others. For example, in a car manufacturing business, operations management is likely to employ the majority of the workforce. Nonetheless, the other functional departments are essential to the success of the business. No matter how efficiently the production line is run, there is no point in producing thousands of cars per week if the sales and marketing department have not persuaded enough potential customers to purchase them. All functional departments must work in conjunction with one another in order to achieve a common set of objectives set out in the corporate plan.

Discussion themes
What is the purpose of the marketing department in a business?
Explain the main functions of the finance and human resource departments in a large business.
Why would the operations function differ for different types of business?
'Business functions have to work together to achieve the business objectives.' Using examples, explain this statement.
'The most important business function is marketing.' To what extent do you agree?

Chapter 12
Marketing

'Marketing is the management process involved in identifying, anticipating and satisfying customer requirements profitably.' Source: The Institute of Marketing.

There are many different definitions of marketing but it must be remembered that marketing is not simply about advertising and selling. Any definitions that imply this are incorrect. Marketing affects all aspects of a business and can be regarded as a philosophy – a way of thinking about how to satisfy customers' needs and wants. It is an ongoing process and businesses must be prepared to respond to any changes that take place which impact upon the market in which they operate.

Marketing involves a wide range of activities:

- Researching the market – this involves gathering and analysing information on consumers, the marketplace and competition.
- Analysing the market – this is an examination of market conditions to identify new opportunities.
- Setting of marketing goals – these must be linked to the business's overall objectives.
- Developing a marketing strategy – this involves constructing a plan which details how the marketing objectives can be achieved. This strategy should be based around the use of the **marketing mix**, the 4Ps of marketing:
    - product;
    - price;
    - promotion;
    - place.

Marketing involves a whole range of activities, starting with researching the market and setting objectives. It also includes developing new products, designing packaging, establishing the right marketing mix, etc. All these activities are aimed at providing goods and services which will satisfy the customer and at making a profit for the business. The better the marketing, the more desirable (or desired) the product or service which is provided for the customer and the more profits the business should be able to make.

Different types of markets

Businesses need to be aware of the type of market they operate in. The strict definition of a market is 'a place where buyers and sellers meet'. This meeting does not have to be physical; it can, for example, be on the phone or over the internet. The actual marketplace of a business can be small, local markets with a specific location. Other markets are national or international with no single location. For example, the world market for oil is a global market in which buyers and sellers are linked by telephones, faxes and the internet, and trading takes place in many locations.

Market orientation, product orientation and asset-led marketing

Market orientation	When a business bases its marketing mix on its perception of what the market wants.
Product orientation	When a business bases its marketing mix on what the business sees as its internal strengths.
Asset-led marketing	When marketing decisions are based on the needs of the consumer and the strengths of the business.

Market orientation/market-led

When a business is market-orientated, the business's marketing activities will be dictated by the market. It will at all times attempt to meet the needs of the market with little if any reference to internal strengths of the business. Any business that is market-orientated thinks that its most important 'asset' is its customers. The business believes that, as long as it is able to identify potential customers, find out what they want, and then produce that for them, it will remain successful.

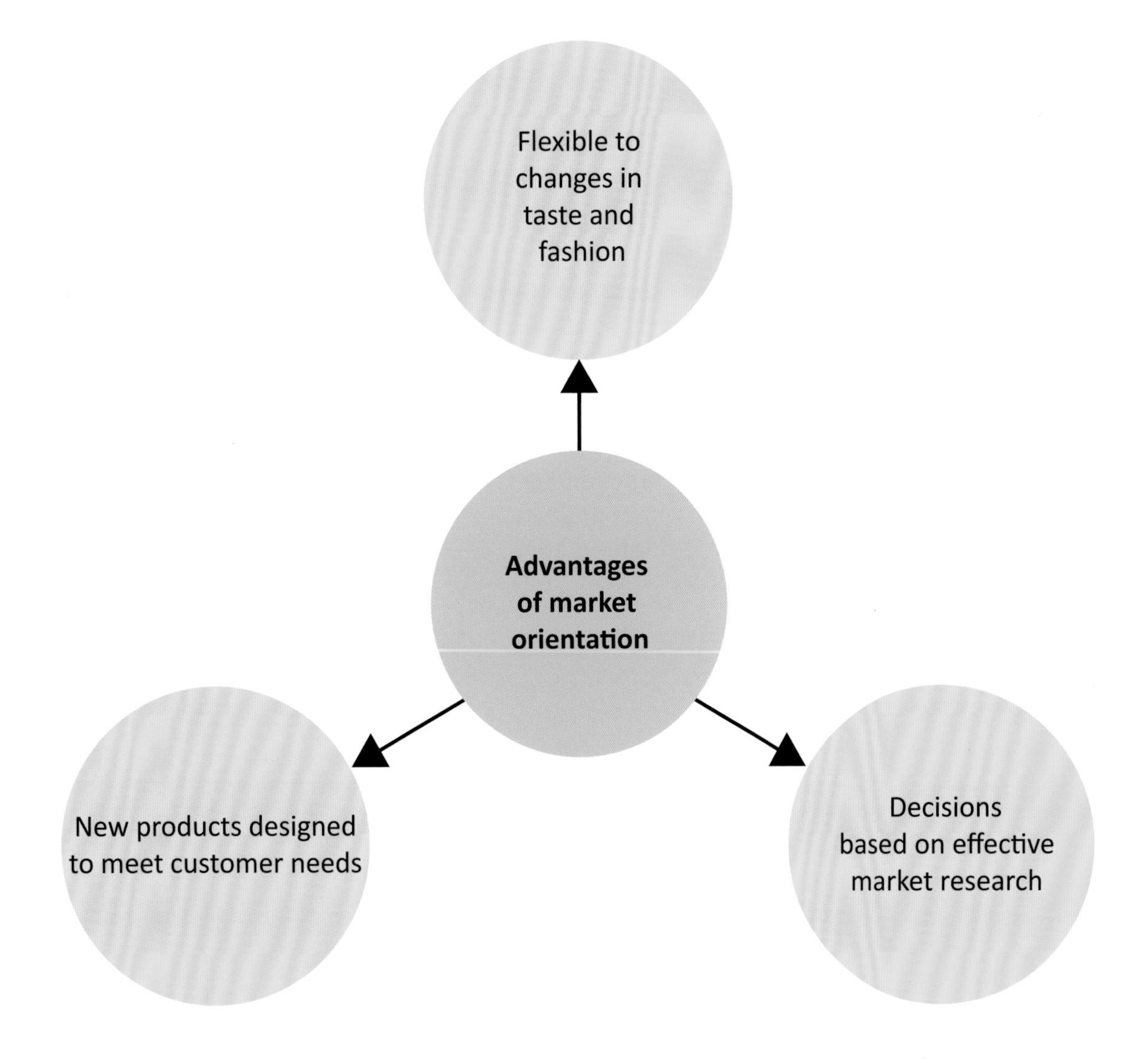

However, there can be disadvantages to being market-led. These disadvantages include:

- high cost of market research to understand the market;
- constant internal change as the needs of the market are met;
- unpredictability of the future, especially from the point of view of staff;
- abandonment of earlier product investment.

Product orientation

When a business is product-orientated, it will base its products or services on what it perceives as its internal strengths. Businesses with a product-orientated approach to selling try to sell whatever they can make, without trying to find out if it is what the customers want. Sony grew hugely successful using this policy. The clearest example was the Walkman cassette player, launched in the late 1970s. Marketing professionals said it would not sell because it had no recording facility – a generation of teenagers proved them wrong. McDonald's approach with its products is heavily product-orientated, with core products produced the same way in a range of very different international markets. The initial focus is on developing and making the product then trying to sell it to consumers.

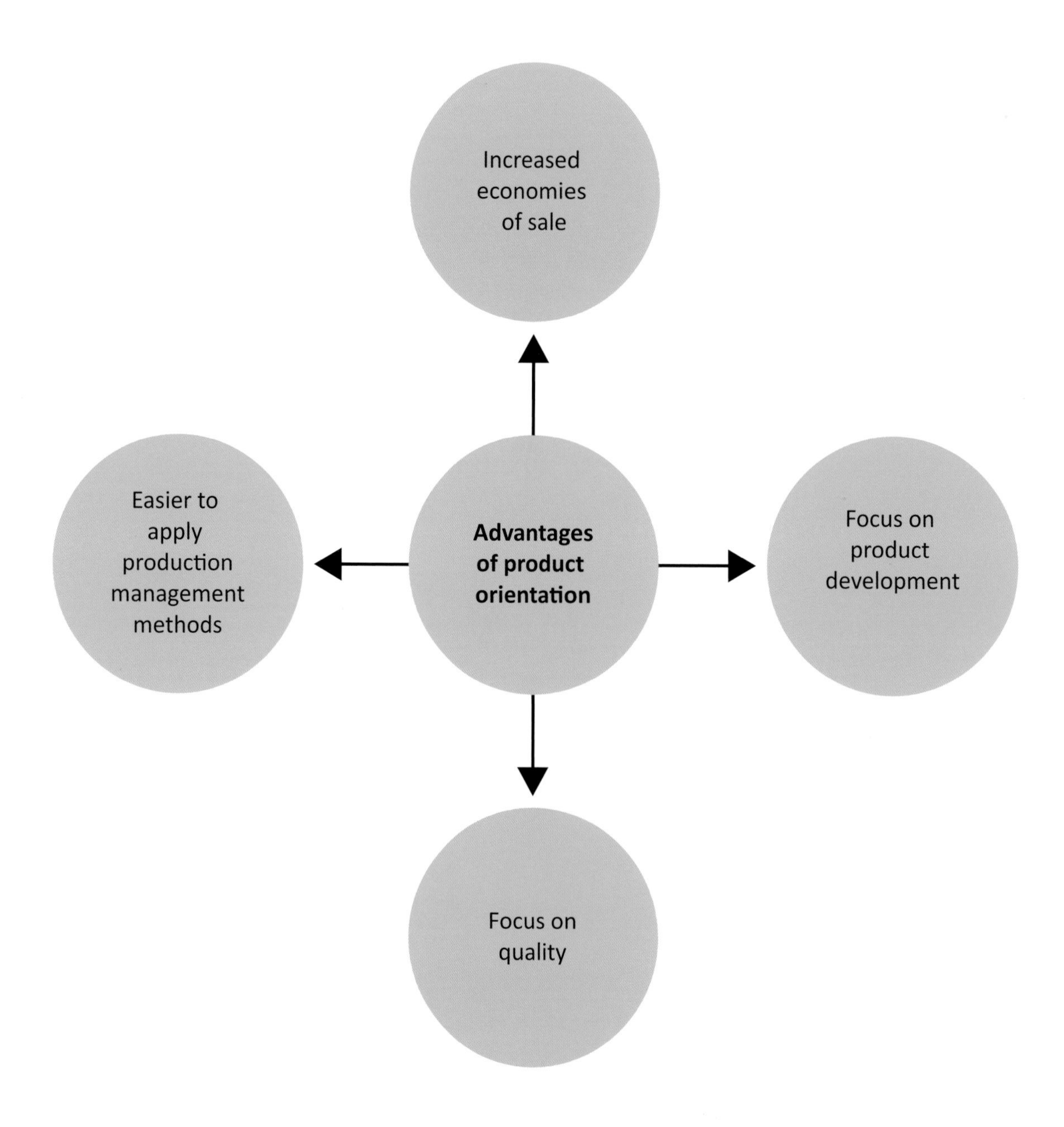

However, of course there are disadvantages as well. These disadvantages include:

- changes in market structure will not be responded to;
- fashion and taste are not accounted for in the product mix.

Asset-led marketing

The perfect situation is of course for a business to relate customer taste to the business's own strengths. Therefore, a business should find out what the market wants, and then ask the question, 'How using our skills, knowledge, assets and brands, can we meet these customer needs?'

Asset-led marketing tries to achieve this – the key word here is 'led'. Assets such as labour force skills, management skills, patents, recognised brands or capital, should be used to help satisfy consumer demand. Identify what you are good at and relate this to customer needs.

This relating of internal strengths to market needs should be one of the basic rules of any business's marketing strategy as this approach focuses on the most appropriate opportunities, given the business's assets.

How to effectively combine these two factors (internal strength and market needs) can be demonstrated by examining the use of database marketing.

The growth of store loyalty cards has allowed the development of database marketing. Using this form of marketing, businesses develop a database of their customers' activities, shopping habits and tastes. They then use this database to target sectors of their market with different offers, promotions etc. This targeted marketing improves the effectiveness of marketing spend.

A simple example of this would be Tesco sending details of their back-to-school children's clothes promotions to customers on their database who spend money on fish fingers and burgers (these customers are likely to have young children). The business has targeted a market segment that is most likely to buy the promoted product. In this example we see that the internal strength of the business is the effective application of IT; this is then related to seasonal market demand, increasing product sales.

When a business applies asset-led marketing it will benefit from several advantages. These advantages include:

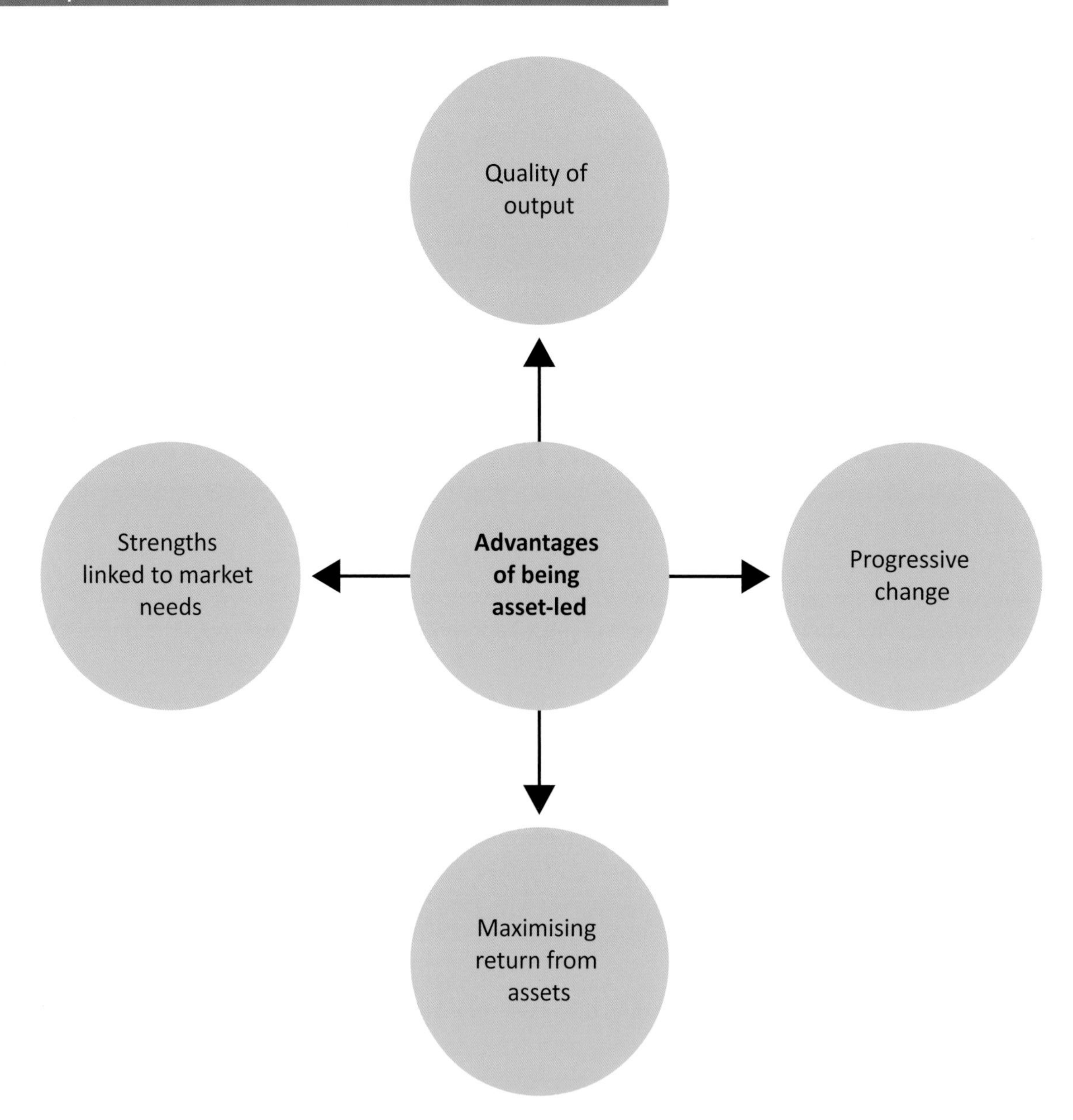

Marketing
http://bit.ly/1QlcrBM

Discussion themes
Explain what is meant by marketing.
'A business that has an effective marketing strategy will always be profitable.' Discuss this statement.
Why do businesses who offer a high quality product sometimes fail in the marketplace?
'Market orientation has more costs than benefits.' Do you agree with this statement?
'All businesses should adopt an asset-led marketing approach.' Do you agree with this statement?
Watch the two adverts. Discuss whether the products shown are product or customer-orientated. What advantages come from the orientation adopted? Wiltshire Farm Foods (2014) https://www.youtube.com/watch?v=kSmrdxNPvIg Sony Walkman commercial (1983) https://www.youtube.com/watch?v=7lipckhgG5g

Chapter 13
Product

The product is any good or service offered for sale to customers. A product can be quite simple such as a biro or a pair of socks; but often there is more to a product than just the item itself. For example, a jar of coffee is not just a jar of coffee – it is a gateway to a more exotic life, or a method of ensuring that friends come round for a chat in the morning. Some products are purchased to show personal style or to pretentiously demonstrate wealth. Products often come wrapped in add-ons, such as service packages or free delivery and installation on electrical goods. Do not just think of a product as a purely functional item: consider its personality and what it says about the consumer too.

Product portfolio

The product portfolio is the mix of products the business produces and sells. Having a product portfolio makes a great deal of sense in a number of ways. A product portfolio:

- spreads fixed costs;
- allows for greater economies of scale;
- allows the targeting of wider markets;
- reduces risk;
- smoothes out overall sales;
- creates opportunities for growth.

The product portfolio of Proctor and Gamble includes:

Product breadth and depth

Breadth is the number of product lines a business produces or retails: its depth is the number of product varieties within each product line. The product portfolio of Proctor and Gamble is made up of over 20 brands (product breadth), but is also made up of the varieties within each branded product (product depth). For example, there will be a number of sizes of Duracell batteries, but also different sizes of packs. We can multiply the 20 products by the number of varieties to measure the complete product portfolio. Having depth increases the number of repeat buyers looking for variations of the product and also allows targeting of different market niches (rechargeable, alkaline and quantum batteries, for example).

Branding

A brand can be defined in several ways – examples of different definitions are given below:

- 'A brand is the name given to a product to help differentiate it from other similar products.'
- 'A brand is a product consumers rely on, for quality, value and service.'
- 'A brand involves a distinctive identity for a product with which users can identify.'
- 'A brand is a name, term, sign, symbol or design which identifies a seller's products and differentiates them from competitors' products.'
- 'A brand is a product which can be identified easily by consumers and, in the eyes of consumers, has value, properties or an image that separates it from the competition.'

Marketing is often brand driven – the objective is to establish a product with a separate identity in consumers' minds, making the product desirable, wanted, even needed. Brands are important for customers because they represent attributes, values, benefits and personality. Brands can offer long-term profitability to businesses, offering a degree of predictability to sales and revenues. However, brands do not just happen – they must be developed carefully, and when mature, the development must continue so that full long-term value is extracted from the brand.

Why use branding?

Advantages:

- To create increased consumer loyalty – this is important when competition is intense.
- To separate the product from the herd – especially in markets where there is otherwise little differentiation and products are marked by their similarities rather than their differences.
- To increase price inelasticity of demand – this gives greater control over pricing strategies.
- To increase value of the business – brand values are often higher than other asset values of a business.
- To ease customer choice – brand identity makes recognition of products easier, making purchase more likely.

Disadvantages:

- High cost of advertising – brands must constantly be kept in the consumer's eye.
- Loss of brand value for one product can affect a whole range of similarly branded products.
- Brands invite competition – often from copycat manufacturers.
- High cost of research and development in ensuring that the brand continues to develop and lead the market.

Unique selling point/proposition (USP)

By unique selling point, we mean that the product or service has a feature or features that can be used to separate it from the competition. This could be the result of a technological advantage. A good example of this is the Dyson range of vacuum cleaners. Dyson is now the market leader, with vacuums selling at around £250. Before Dyson, with its bagless system and bright colours, the market leader was priced at £90.

USP can also result from some feature of the product and its design. For example, the hole in Polo mints or the design of the iPad.

Product differentiation

Making your products different from the competition is important. This separates your brand from competitor brands. Products might be very similar in the way that they are made or how they are used but may be perceived quite differently by consumers. Products can be differentiated from the competition by:

- methods of promotion – creating a personality for the product;
- packaging – eco-packaging;
- form – making your products look different from the competition;
- the provision of add-ons – Kia cars have a seven year warranty;
- quality and reliability – these are features which can be emphasised (for example, BMW and Rolls Royce cars).

Product differentiation helps create customer loyalty and gives a business more control over the pricing strategies used.

The product life cycle

This represents the different stages in the life of a product and the sales that are achieved at each stage. For some products the life cycle can be short – for example, one-hit wonder bands or this summer's fashion. Others appeal for a longer period and then go out of fashion or are replaced by newer, more up-to-date or technologically advanced products. However, there are some products that are unique: for these the life cycle goes on and on. Coca Cola, the VW Golf and Mars bars are examples of products with impressively long and ongoing life cycles. Whatever the product, it will have a life cycle of some sort.

The stages of the product life cycle

Marketing experts have divided the product life cycle into five stages:

- Introduction
- Growth
- Maturity
- Saturation
- Decline

Introduction

The product is new to the market and few potential consumers know of its existence. Price can be high and sales may be restricted to early adopters (those that must have new technology, gadgets or fashions first). Profits are often low as development costs have to be repaid and advertising expenditure can often be high.

Growth

The product is becoming more widely known and consumed. Advertising tries to establish or strengthen the brand and develop an image for the product. Profits may start to be earned but advertising expenditure is still high. Prices may fall.

Maturity

The product range may be extended. Competition will increase and this has to be responded to. Advertising should be used to firm-up the image of the product in the consumers' minds. Sales are at their peak, profits should be high.

Saturation

Very few new customers are gained, replacement purchases are the trend. Businesses should try to reduce their costs, so that prices can be more flexible. The battle to survive is beginning and the market for the product is 'full'. Profits may start to decline.

Decline

Sales can now fall fast and the product range may be reduced, with the business concentrating on core products. Advertising costs will be reduced, with attempts made to mop-up what is left of the potential market. Overall profits will fall. Price is likely to fall, but by concentrating on remaining market niches there may be some price stability.

Businesses will try to make the product stay in the maturity stage as long as possible as this will maximise profits and help the business gain the greatest return on the money invested in the product. To do this, the business will need to use extension strategies.

Example life cycles

Below we see a typical, or classic, product life cycle:

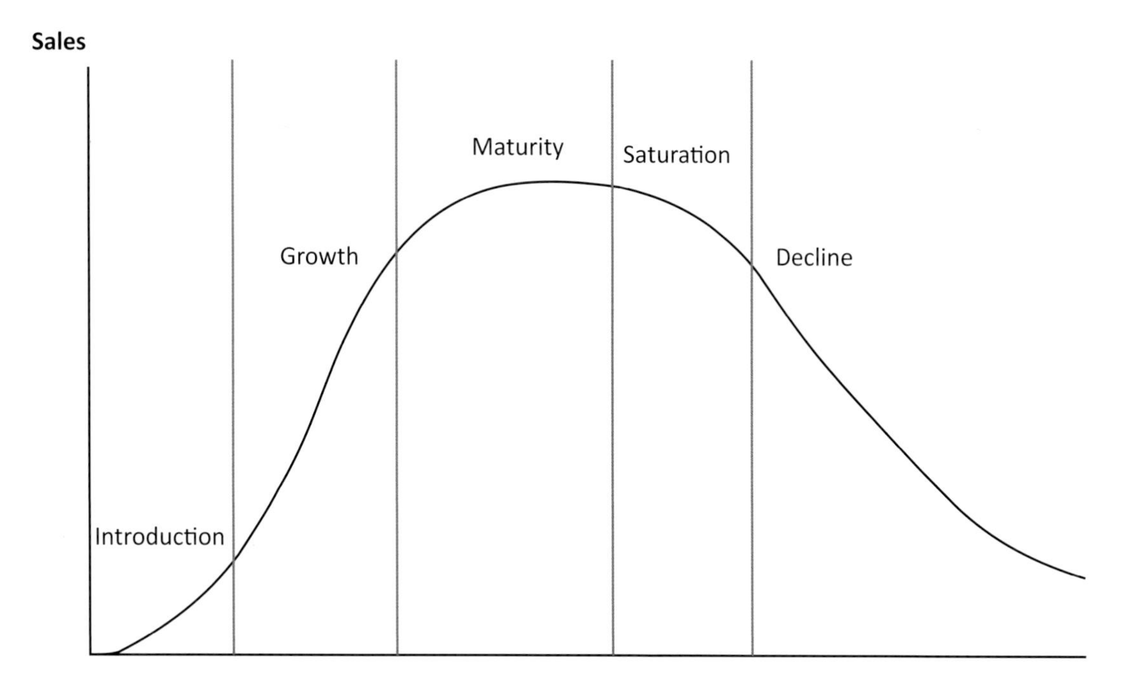

In this example we see the five stages, starting with introduction, through growth, maturity, saturation and finally decline. The product life cycle measures the change in sales of the product that occurs over time. We can see that sales increase through introduction, growth and into maturity until we reach the saturation stage of the product life cycle. Sales now start to fall and the product moves into decline.

Profits can be plotted against a life cycle. The red line below shows the likely change in profitability of the product over its life. Initially losses are made as research and development costs have to be recouped and advertising costs are likely to be high. As the life cycle moves through growth into maturity, profits are made. Profits are likely to continue to be made through to the end of the cycle, though at a lower level.

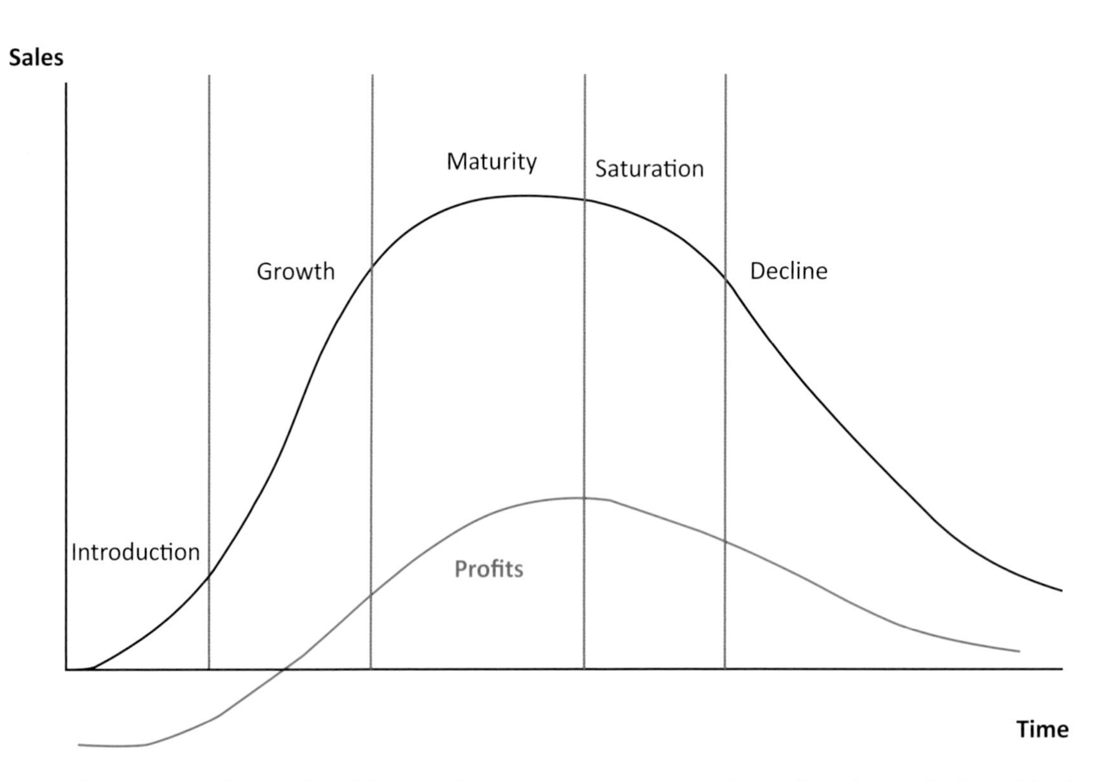

This is a typical structure of a product life cycle but there are many products that do not fit into this classic model.

In the 'Straw on Fire' life cycle, the product quickly moves through all the stages. Introduction is short and market saturation may be reached in a matter of months. During this time sales can become incredibly high and products with 'Straw on Fire' life cycles can dominate the market for a short period. Some of the best examples of this type of life cycle can be found in the children's toy market: there have been many over the years including Furbies, Cabbage Patch dolls, hula hoops, yo-yos, loom bands etc.

The 'Extended' product life cycle demonstrates that some products remain in the marketplace for a long time – often much longer than competitor products. These products stay in maturity and seem to avoid decline. Consider the shape of the life cycle of Coca Cola or Rice Krispies. Are these products in decline, or are sales being maintained?

Extension strategies

These are used to extend the life cycle of the product. They may be necessary because a new product has not been developed to replace an ageing product. They may also be used as a product has a declining market share in a large or growing market.

Extension strategies could include:

- repositioning the product in the marketplace;
- relaunching the product, aiming at a different segment, e.g. promoting the healthy aspects of consuming the product;
- using the 'now with' policy – this tactic is often used with limited edition cars.

Successful extension strategies can transform the position of a product in the marketplace. Lucozade was once a drink for children who were unwell – now it is marketed as a sports drink. Other extension strategies do little more than delay the end of the life cycle. Hopefully the delay will be long enough to allow a new profitable product to become established, replace the product in decline and help the business keep a balanced product portfolio.

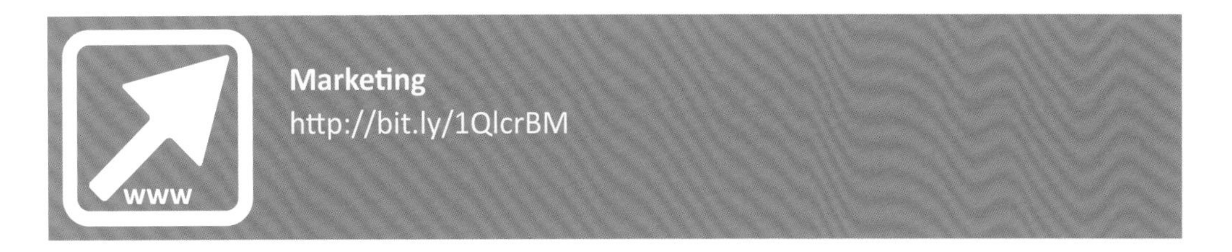

The Boston Matrix

The Boston Matrix was devised by the Boston Consultancy Group in the 1960s and it allows the analysis of a business's products by dividing the products into four categories. The categories the products are placed in depend on their market share and the level of growth that is occurring in the market. In the diagram below we see the structure of the Boston Matrix. This structure can be used as a guide to product mix management.

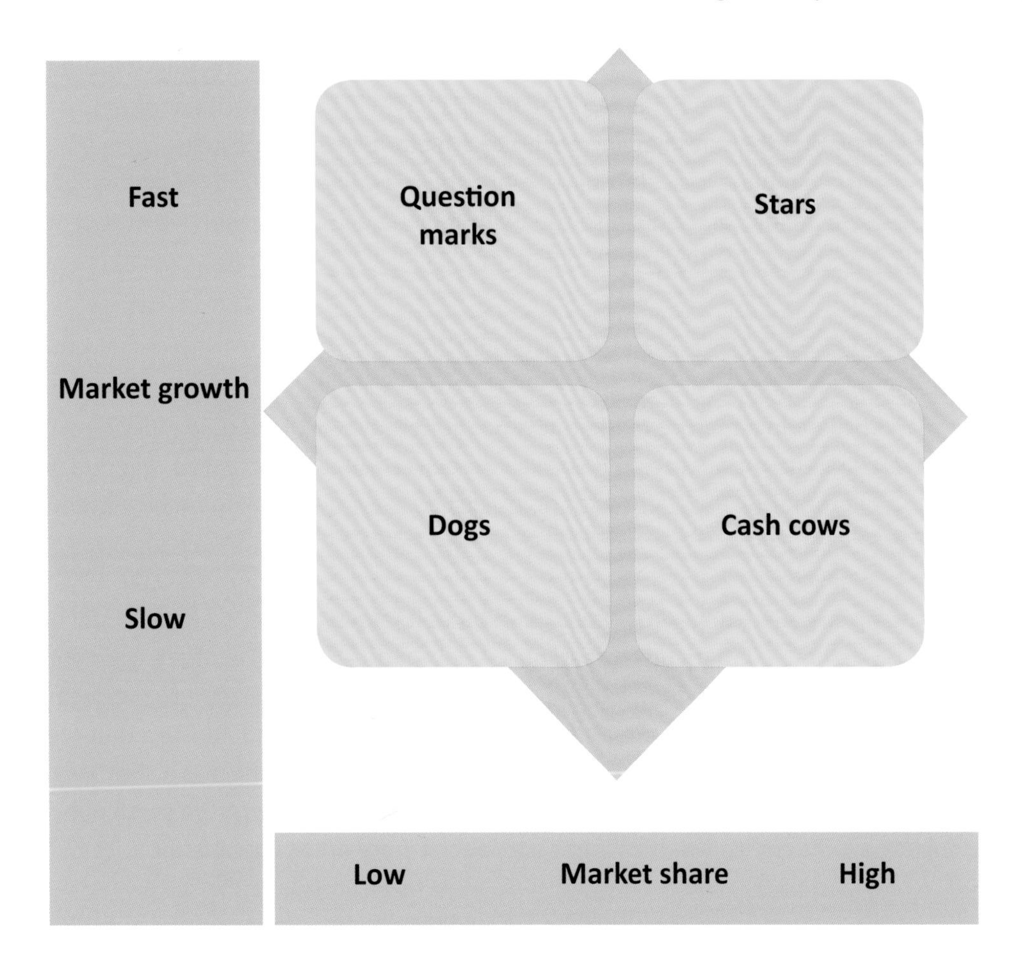

Cash cows (High market share – slow market growth)

Cash cows are very profitable products and expenditure on such things as advertising is relatively low. Customers know and understand the product, and brand value has been established. It is also likely that development costs have already been recouped, increasing profitability further. Examples of such products would be the Ford Focus, Kellogg's Corn Flakes and Cadbury's Dairy Milk.

Stars (High market share – fast market growth)

The market may be somewhat immature, with new customers being attracted to the marketplace and new competitors being tempted by potential profits and market share. Competition is high – businesses are fighting for a share of potentially huge profits. Stars are products that have a high market share in a fast growing market. Star products have high levels of revenue, but also have high levels of costs. Advertising and marketing expenditure is high. Brands have to be established and hopefully the products will develop into cash cows. The classic example of a recent product that was a star and has become a cash cow is the Apple iPad.

Question marks/Problem children (Low market share – fast growing market)

This is one of the worst situations for professional marketing people. They have a product in a fast growing market but the products are not selling. They are being beaten by the competition. They are failing, but it is likely to be worth doing something about it. After all, it is not good business for businesses to have products that fail to capture market share in markets that are growing in importance, especially when the new market may eventually replace an existing market.

For products which are question marks, a product relaunch may solve the problem or a basic redesign may increase sales. In the mid 1980s jeans were out of fashion but the market for teenage clothes was growing fast. Levis relaunched their jeans, led by advertising for 501s, which had never been a style of jean worn for fashion. Within a few months sales had increased by a factor of 10 – the product became a star. The TV adverts used pop songs as soundtracks, starting a trend which is still popular in marketing 30 years later. In contrast, there have been many competitors to the iPad since launch and most have ended up as question marks, heavily discounted and eventually withdrawn.

Dogs (Low market share – slow growing or shrinking market)

Dogs have low market share in a mature market. It is not generally worth spending money on redeveloping, redesigning or advertising the products as it is unlikely to be recouped in increased revenue. Even so, dogs may still be marginally profitable. Problems with dogs exist as they may take up management time, tie up assets and give very low returns.

The issues surrounding so-called 'dog' products can be quite complex. Some businesses still sell hand push carpet sweepers. You do not see them advertised on TV, competing for market share against the Dyson, but they still produce profits for niche businesses. The development costs of this type of product were paid back long ago, marketing is virtually non-existent and they are profitable enough to ensure that manufacture continues. Currently sales of alcohol through public houses are falling and there is a shrinking market. Businesses with a portfolio of bars and pubs sell off the less successful ones (often small pubs with no food facilities) and focus on large city centre bars and gastropubs where profits are higher.

It can be worth holding on to dogs especially if they provide synergies – for example, a company may boast that it provides a complete range of products, which can help attract customers who may occasionally wish to buy the dog. A business may also subsidise loss-making products in order to appear ethical – thereby winning customers and enhancing their reputation. If a business has dogs that are unproductive or do not provide synergies for the whole organisation, one solution is to sell off the dogs to small specialist niche businesses and use the money raised to invest in developing new products.

How to use the Boston Matrix

Businesses must ensure that they use the Boston Matrix in the way intended:

- to judge how to manage individual products and the product range, given market conditions;
- to recognise the importance of using successful, profitable products to fund the development of the stars and cash cows of the future;
- to see whether they have products in fast growing and potentially very profitable market sectors.

The Boston Matrix can help businesses analyse whether they have the portfolio that they want and whether it matches the objectives of the organisation. From analysing their product portfolio using the Boston Matrix, managers can then establish their marketing strategy in order to obtain the desired portfolio.

Most businesses would like to have a product mix or portfolio which has no problem children, many cash cows and plenty of stars that look like developing into cash cows. However, in the real world there are very few businesses that are that successful. Even Microsoft, the world's largest software company, is struggling in some sectors including tablets and mobile phones.

Discussion themes
Explain what is meant by a product portfolio.
Why is branding important for a business?
What costs are involved in establishing and maintaining a brand?
'Every product should have a USP.' Discuss this statement.
'Product life cycles can help a business create an effective product portfolio.' Discuss this statement.
'Extension strategies are a waste of money.' Do you agree with this statement?
How can a business use the Boston Matrix to manage their product portfolio?
Product life cycle extension strategies: Read the article and summarise how a business can use extension strategies to prolong the life of a product. http://smallbusiness.chron.com/product-life-cycle-extension-strategies-3280.html
Sales Director Samantha Fernando explains how an understanding of the product life cycle has helped when developing new products: https://www.nibusinessinfo.co.uk/content/heres-how-understanding-product-life-cycle-has-helped-my-business-flash-video
The Boston Matrix on You Tube: http://www.youtube.com/watch?v=TXKU7gVnBqs http://www.youtube.com/watch?v=1gZmmlKl6uk

Chapter 14
Price

There are a wide variety of pricing strategies available to businesses. Before they can consider which to adopt, businesses must take into consideration the effects of supply and demand in the marketplace. This interaction of supply and demand is known as the market mechanism.

Price takers

The market mechanism, through the interaction of supply and demand, will set the price of products and also determine the quantity supplied. The whole marketing mix is used to influence the pattern of demand in the marketplace, so businesses can have some control over price. However, in certain circumstances, businesses will have to accept the price set by the market. This type of business is known as a price taker. Accepting the market price (being a price taker) is the only option under perfect competition.

Perfect competition occurs when goods are undifferentiated (cannot be told apart), there are a large number of producers, and buyers have complete information about what is available on the marketplace. When a good produced is indistinguishable from the competition and there are a large number of suppliers, then a situation nearing perfect competition can arise. We can see near perfect competition in the markets for some fresh produce (lettuces, cucumbers, tomatoes etc.). In these circumstances the producer has little or no control over price, and so must accept the going market price. The producer is a price taker.

Price makers

When a business is not a price taker, which is the case in the majority of markets, then it has the opportunity of using pricing strategies. Not all pricing strategies are available to all businesses, but there are still choices to be made. Pricing strategies fall into two broad groups:

1. **Market-orientated strategies** – businesses are market-orientated when they produce what the market wants. With regard to price, this means that a market-orientated business will set a price at the level the market is willing to accept.
2. **Cost-based strategies** – businesses are product-orientated when they produce goods without in-depth reference to the needs of consumers. With regard to price, this means that a product-orientated business will set a price related to the cost of producing or supplying the product.

Market-orientated pricing strategies

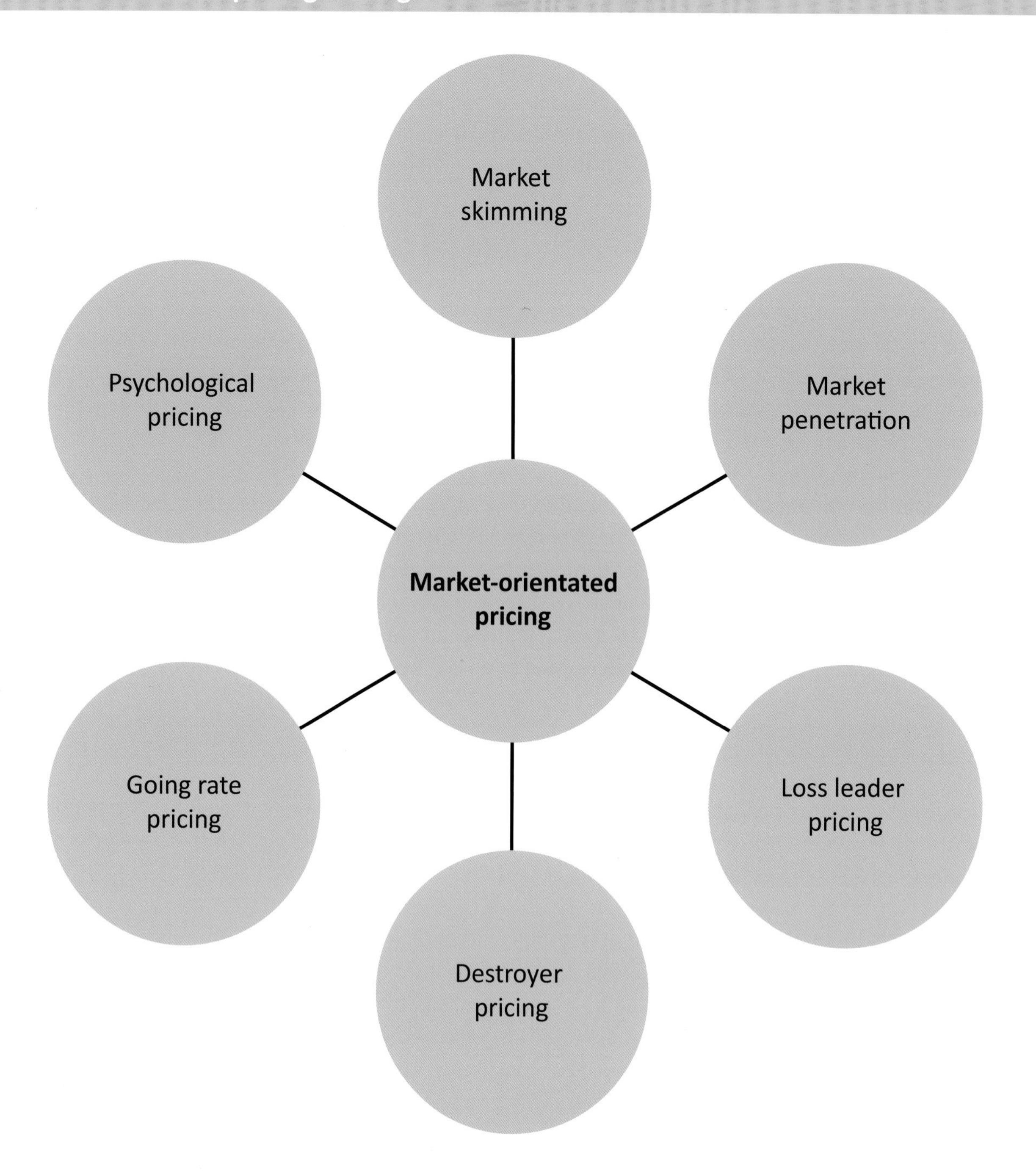

The type of strategy used will depend upon several factors. These may include the type of product, the product range, economic circumstances, the financial strength of the business and the levels of competition in the market.

Market skimming

Market skimming means charging a high price to maximise profits on each item sold for a limited period. The aim is to gain as much profit as possible for a new product while it remains unique in the market. The ability to skim depends on having either a technological advantage or an advantage based on brand image. If technological advantages exist, then some consumers, known as early adopters, are willing to purchase products so that they can be the first to own these products. Digital watches are a good example of this. When they were first launched, digital watches may have sold for around £500: similar watches today might sell for £25. Each generation iPhone initially 'skims' the market when first released.

Brand image can also allow market skimming to occur. Products from brands such as Armani or Chanel will be at the top of the market price band. Businesses will work hard to protect, develop and increase the value of their brand image to allow skimming strategies to continue.

Market penetration

In this case the objective is to gain market share. It involves pricing a product at a low level so that retailers and consumers are encouraged to purchase the product in large quantities. This pricing strategy can help establish brand loyalty – when the price of the product does rise from the initially low level, customers will continue to purchase it. However, if the price is set too low, customers may take the view that the product is low quality and therefore they will not purchase it in the first place. Businesses using this policy to break into a new market may initially lose revenue. If the life cycle of the product is relatively short this policy should be avoided, as the business will not have enough time to recover the cost of this strategy. There must be enough time for market share to grow and then the price can be gradually raised and the initial cost of the penetration strategy can be recovered.

Going rate pricing

For many small businesses accepting the current market pricing structure is all they are able to do. When this is the only option there is a strong element of being a price taker. They must sell their goods or services at a price broadly in line with the price charged by their competitors. Normally as new entrants enter the market, the price charged will have to be similar to that of the market leader.

Psychological pricing

Using this strategy, prices are set at the level that matches what consumers may expect to pay. Consumers perceive that they are receiving value from the price paid. For example, a producer of shirts which has established a reputation for quality and style would set a price well above what a high street store such as Marks and Spencer might charge, even though the difference in quality may be marginal. This will help to reinforce the image of the company and will be in line with the advertising messages that the business has put in place.

The policy of pricing goods just a little below a round figure, such as £19.99, is also an example of psychological pricing. Businesses using this tactic hope to convince potential purchasers to buy their goods in the belief that they are getting value for money.

Loss leader pricing

This strategy involves the selling of products at a loss, with the expectation that this will generate further sales of some form, elsewhere in the business. The additional sales that occur will hopefully recoup the initial loss and subsequently make a profit for the business. The classic example of this has been supermarkets selling goods like bread at a loss in order to attract customers into their stores. An increasingly common example, which is much more controversial, is supermarkets selling heavily discounted beer and wines. Other examples of loss leader pricing include free mobile phones, where profits will be made on line rentals. Most mobile phones are now sold on a loss leader basis.

Destroyer pricing

This is also known as predatory pricing. This involves setting a price low enough to drive competitors out of the market. This type of pricing is not only used by the largest businesses on a national scale, but it can also appear in battles between local businesses. Destroyer pricing is often seen as anti-competitive and therefore illegal. Microsoft has been investigated by competition authorities in the US and Europe for allegedly using destroyer pricing strategies through the bundling of free programmes (such as Windows Media Player) within its operating systems.

Cost-based pricing strategies

Businesses which concentrate on internal costs when pricing products are known as product-orientated businesses. Pricing strategies used are based around the costs of production.

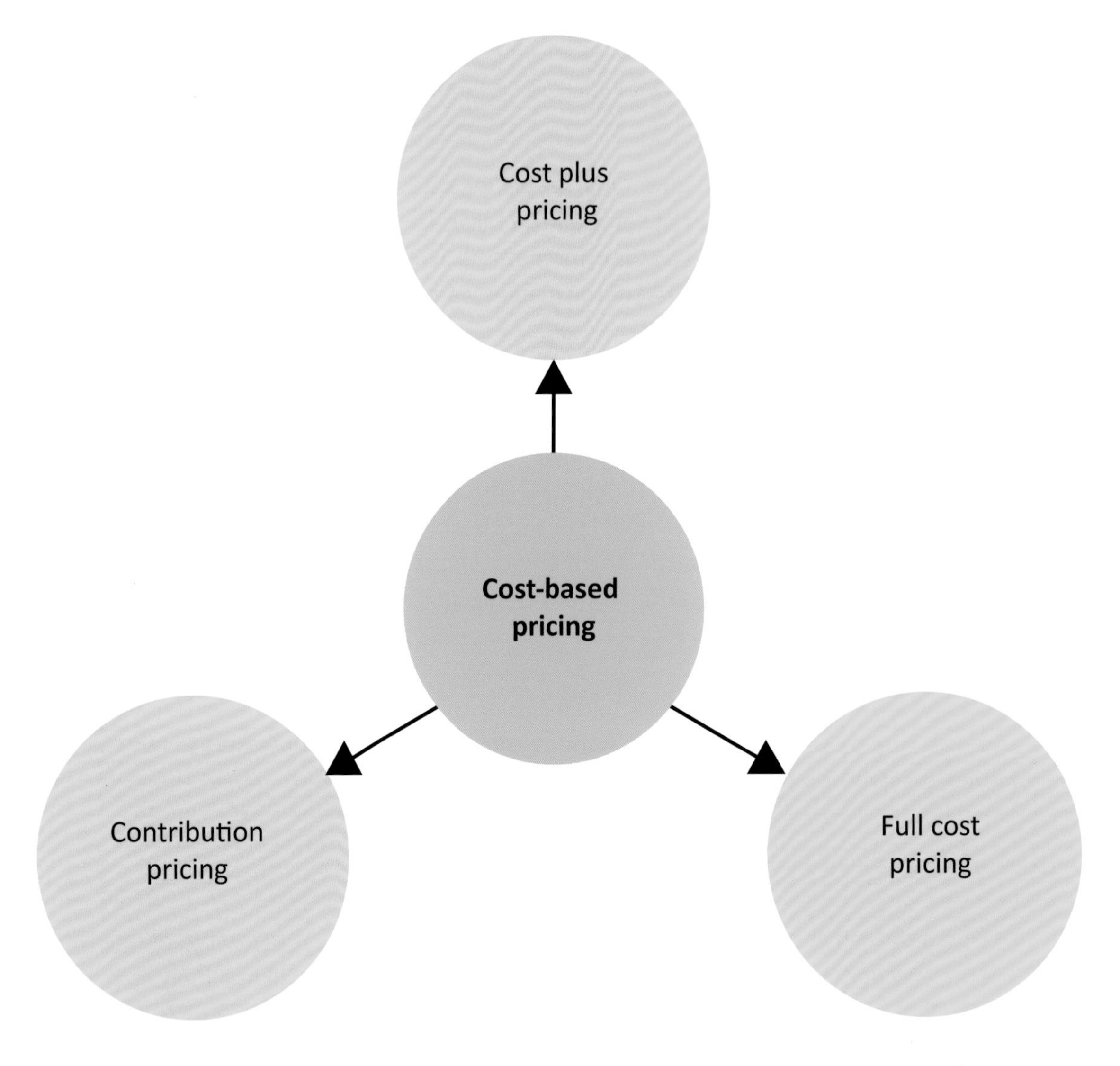

There are three main types of product-based pricing, and each uses the costs of production/supply as the basis of deriving price.

Cost plus pricing

Using this method, a profit percentage is added to the average cost of producing the good. This is known as adding a **mark-up**. Therefore, if the production costs of the good are £1, and the business adds a profit percentage of 40%, then the business will sell the good at £1.40. This simple method of pricing does have advantages: firstly changes in costs can be passed directly on to the buyer and secondly, every good sold is sold at a profit. However, there are disadvantages too. Actions of competitors are often totally ignored. This can lead to loss of sales or loss of profits if a higher price could be charged because of little or no competition. Also, for exporters, this method makes no allowance for currency changes that will affect the price of goods and order levels.

Full cost pricing

This is similar to cost plus pricing but it takes the concept further. Now all the costs of the business are taken into consideration. This means that each good will bear its proportion of overhead costs such as marketing and administration. The advantages and disadvantages are similar to cost plus pricing but there is the added disadvantage of the complexity of apportioning overhead costs.

Contribution pricing

This is another variation on the same theme, but in this case price will be based on the variable costs plus a contribution towards overheads and profits. This method can give flexibility because orders can be accepted on a different contribution basis for different products. This flexibility allows pricing strategies, such as price discrimination between different buyers, to be used.

Criticisms of cost-based pricing

As a result of its product-orientated approach, cost-based pricing takes no account of customers' needs or wishes. If prices are set too high then sales will inevitably suffer. Using these methods means that a further increase in prices must occur as overheads are redistributed. Also, when a business produces a large range of products, allocating overheads is a complex and time-consuming procedure. Cost-based pricing takes no account of the situation in the marketplace and is too rigid when the pattern of demand changes.

It can still be argued, however, that businesses using cost-based pricing methods concentrate more on their strengths and do not waste time, energy and money on futile price wars or price-based competition.

Discussion themes
Explain the difference between a price maker and a price taker.
Identify the types of products that would use penetration pricing.
'Cost-based pricing is ineffective in today's marketplace.' Discuss this statement.
'Effective pricing strategies are the best way to win customers.' Discuss this statement.

Chapter 15
Promotion

Promotion is the attempt, through various forms of media, to draw attention to a product and thereby gain and retain customers. All types of promotion try to communicate with the public in an attempt to encourage them to purchase a business's products or services. As consumers we are surrounded by promotion. We cannot get away from it – whether it is on TV, on buses, on the packaging of food we eat, or in the mail we receive almost every day. Promotion allows us to find out about products and provides us with up-to-date information about those products. It also allows us to make educated choices about the goods we consume, provides free-to-view TV and internet and keeps thousands of people employed. However, it can encourage a waste of resources, pushing up prices and encouraging greed and envy when wants cannot be satisfied.

Objectives of promotion

The general description of the overall objective of promotion to gain and retain customers can be extended to include the following specific objectives:

- **To provide potential customers with readily available information** about the product so that the consumer knows the benefits of using the product and where to access the product. This is often the objective for new product launches.
- **To increase sales or market share** by targeting both existing customers and new customers.
- **To give the products an image, or to establish a brand identity.** A great deal of promotional activity which takes place is done to keep the product in consumers' minds. This reminds consumers why they bought the product and why they should continue using it over rival brands.
- **To establish a corporate image**. Some advertising does not sell a specific product or range of products; instead the objective is to establish the right image of the producer or retailer within the mind of the consumer.
- **To enable long-term business planning to take place**. Promotion is part of the whole process of bringing a product or service to market. Effective promotion allows life cycles to be developed and prolonged. This then enables production and investment to occur with greater confidence.

It must be remembered that most products are not purchased on impulse: before purchases are made the consumer moves through a series of phases or levels of commitment to the product. These phases can be outlined as:

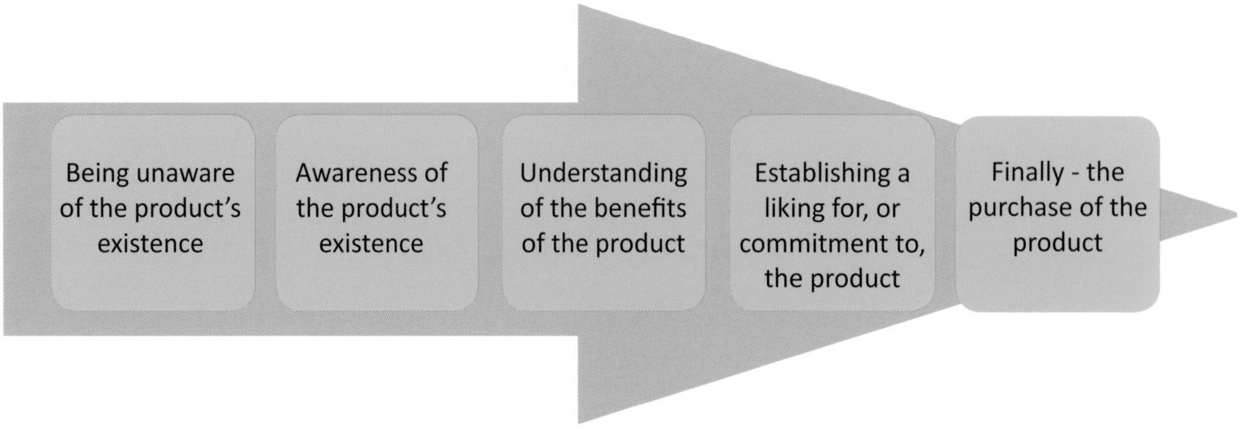

Being unaware of the product's existence

Awareness of the product's existence

Understanding of the benefits of the product

Establishing a liking for, or commitment to, the product

Finally - the purchase of the product

Types of promotion

Promotion can be above-the-line, or below-the-line.

Above-the-line promotion

Above-the-line promotion is what is generally called **advertising**. It is used to reach a mass audience. It is worth noting that advertising and promotion are not the same. Above-the-line promotion (advertising) is carried out through various independent media – the most important being TV, magazines, newspapers, radio, posters and, of increasing importance, the internet.

The choice of media used depends on a number of factors:

- Target market – who is the business trying to sell to?
- Whether the objective is to convey information or another type of message – will the product sell only when consumers fully understand its function, or do people buy on impulse?
- Cost – for many small businesses this is the first question they ask about any form of promotion.
- The reach of the media – who reads the magazine or watches the adverts? Are they likely to buy the product?
- The product itself – is the product suited to a certain type of promotion? For example, is the best way to promote plastic food containers through personal selling door to door or by an advert in the local paper?

For most mass market products a combination of the above media will be used, each of which will be used to deliver a different message about the product. For example, when promoting a car, the manufacturer may use national television adverts to project the image of the car to a wide market and appeal to the aspirations of the potential buyers. Magazines may be used to reinforce this image, whilst local radio might be used to tell customers about local price and finance deals and which garages in the area stock the car. In this example of promoting the car, we can see a division of the type of advertising message. One type of message sells the product through image, style and the aspirations of the potential buyer – this is known as **persuasive** advertising. The local radio promotion is much more **informative**.

Most products will use a combination of the two types of advertising. The type of media used in advertising will, to a large extent, determine whether the emphasis is on persuasion or information. Also certain products lend themselves to one or the other type. For example, the promotion of ice cream brands will tend to be more persuasive, while the promotion of computers will tend to be more informative.

Below-the-line promotion

Below-the-line promotion offers a wide range of alternative promotional strategies and these are often used to support above-the-line promotion. Below-the-line promotion targets consumers directly. Examples of below-the-line promotion are:

- personal selling;
- packaging;
- sales promotions;
- direct mailing;
- exhibitions and trade fairs;
- public relations.

For many consumer products, below-the-line promotion is used only for short-term periods. Offers and promotions come and go quite quickly. However, for other products, such as industrial goods, producer goods and financial services, personal selling plays a long-term strategic role in establishing a relationship with the customer.

Promotion is a complex issue. The type of promotion used will differ between products, the markets targeted and throughout the various stages of a product's life cycle.

Factors impacting on the promotional strategy

- **Product differentiation** – many markets are highly competitive. It is important that promotion provides a method of product differentiation. The role of promotion is to differentiate its product in the market and make it stand out from the crowd. The focus here remains on those features, functions or benefits that may not be offered by a competitor or may not be offered so well. Products, like Innocent smoothies, differentiate through an ethical approach to their products. Coffee brands can be differentiated through types of user – value for money or luxuriously expensive.
- **The marketing budget available** – it is normal to set a total budget for promotional activities based on the objectives of the business, the availability of cash and actions of competitors.
- **The stage in the product life cycle** – during the introduction and growth stages of the product life cycle there may be a more informative approach, in order to raise customer awareness. During the maturity and saturation stages a more persuasive approach may be adopted to reinforce customers' allegiance.
- **Cultural sensitivity** – if a product is to be launched in a new international market or translated across markets, it becomes imperative to take into consideration local affiliations and sensitivities. These include both cultural and religious considerations. Often, these issues may even present themselves within one country.
- **The target market** – the people who make up the target market need to be considered before committing to a promotional strategy. If a market is not tech-savvy (technically aware), then more traditional means may need to be employed. Conversely, the younger generation, used to accessing information on a daily basis via their iPhones, may be targeted via the internet.
- **Competitor actions** – the promotional strategies a competitor uses need to be taken into account as well. If a competitor is about to launch a campaign which targets a segment of the population not previously targeted, then perhaps a business needs to react in order to protect market share.

Promotion methods
http://bit.ly/1NiDvez

Discussion themes
The five most common advertising techniques http://smallbusiness.chron.com/5-common-advertising-techniques-15273.html
Video showing a range of promotion methods Explain how promotion can be altered to appeal to different target markets. https://www.youtube.com/watch?v=MmQndanKkRI
Innovative examples of 'guerrilla marketing' What is guerrilla marketing and why is it used by small and large businesses? https://www.youtube.com/watch?v=nJ4uCOJjDF8
The top ten misleading marketing tactics https://www.youtube.com/watch?v=M-HrTC8QCbM
Explain the difference between above-the-line promotion and below-the-line promotion.
'Promotion is the most important aspect of the marketing mix'. To what extent do you agree with this statement?
'Businesses that use persuasive advertising are unethical'. Discuss this statement.

Chapter 16
Place

Place is all about where businesses sell their products and what methods are used to distribute the goods to the customer. Place is 'the marketplace', where buyers and sellers meet and exchange payment in return for goods and services. The marketplace does not have to be 'physical', such as a shop – it could be online, over the phone or through mail order.

The two key questions businesses ask in relation to place are:

1. Where shall we sell our products?
2. What methods shall we use to distribute the goods to the final consumer?

For some goods choosing the right 'place' is obvious: baked beans are traditionally sold on supermarket shelves, chocolate bars in newsagents, sun cream in chemists and so on. However, choosing a place to sell a product can be more complex and may be part of an overall strategy in an attempt to achieve an image or develop a brand.

Why 'place' is important

The place where a product is sold can be used as part of a strategy to establish a certain brand identity. When Häagen-Dazs ice cream was launched in the UK, it was only available through upmarket outlets such as Harrods and Covent Garden coffee bars. The objective was to establish a super-premium ice cream brand. Only when this perception was established in consumers' minds was the product offered for sale through a wider range of outlets. Today it can be found in supermarkets all across the UK.

Some goods are now sold through a wider range of outlets than ever before, which encourages higher levels of consumption. A good example of this widening of the number of places where a product is sold can be seen with some soft drinks. Go into any train station, airport or leisure centre and you will see soft drinks vending machines. Premium prices are often charged because demand is high – participants are thirsty and hot after a game of squash and 90p for a can of Coke is acceptable.

Prime selling space can be jealously protected. Manufacturers offer retailers discounts if their brand is given pride of place on supermarket shelves. Wall's ice cream has fought through the courts to prevent other brands being sold in fridges they have supplied to local supermarkets and independent shops.

Distribution

Distribution is all about how to get the goods to the customer. Traditional methods have relied upon the 'manufacturer – wholesaler – retailer – consumer' chain. However, for many goods and services this relationship has broken down. Direct selling, whether through the internet, or through magazines, catalogues or junk mail, can allow businesses to supply their customers more readily – and often at much lower prices.

With the growth in size of retailers and improvements in stock ordering methods, there has been a reduction in the need for the 'middleman' – wholesalers are often cut out of the equation. This use of a direct supply relationship between manufacturer and retailers cuts costs for large businesses. This puts increasing pressure on smaller retailers, who still rely on wholesalers to supply them with their goods for sale.

Methods of distribution

- **Using a wholesaler**

Traditional methods of distribution have relied upon the 'manufacturer – wholesaler – retailer – consumer' chain.

The wholesaler has a role in breaking bulk – this means buying large quantities from the manufacturer and selling smaller quantities to the retailer. This relationship is useful to all parties concerned. The manufacturer has the convenience of selling in bulk to the wholesaler. Single drops of very large quantities lower distribution expenses. The small retailer, who buys in quite small quantities, benefits because they do not have to store large quantities of stock and can buy at their own convenience.

- **Manufacturer to retailer**

For many goods and services the use of wholesalers has declined significantly. With the retail market now dominated by big businesses the role of the wholesaler has become much less important. Manufacturers supply most of their produce direct to the big retailers, each of which buys massive quantities. This growth in the size of retailers, and improvements in stock ordering and handling methods (EPOS systems), has led to a reduction in the need for the middleman – wholesalers are cut out of the chain. This reduction in the length of the distribution chain cuts costs for large businesses and represents a good example of a purchasing economy of scale.

- **Direct selling – manufacturer to consumer**

Direct selling, whether through junk mail, magazines and increasingly through the internet, has allowed manufacturers to charge much lower prices. Books bought over the internet can be 40% cheaper than high street prices. More singles are now sold as downloads from online music retailers such as iTunes than as CDs through record shops. Traditional catalogue shops, such as Index, have been replaced by B2C – Business to Consumer internet shopping. Selling direct allows manufacturers to keep more of the profits and attract customers through competitive prices and convenience.

Internet marketing

Internet sales are increasing massively. During November 2014 online sales were over £7 billion in the UK, up 9% on the previous year. Tesco, the UK's largest grocery retailer, have a full range of products for sale on the internet and their major competitors, such as Sainsbury's, Asda and Morrisons have all followed their example. The internet retailer Amazon.com, which started as an online bookseller, has opened up distribution centres all over the UK, employing thousands of previously unemployed people. 'Click and collect' is becoming more and more popular. John Lewis reported that 40% of its online sales over Christmas 2014 were through 'click and collect'. Business to business trade on the internet, where shopping around for best value is so important, looks like becoming the new method of cost reduction.

E-commerce can offer a low-cost way for small businesses to compete against much larger rivals: products can be marketed and sold worldwide with an internet e-commerce enabled shop. To actually set up an internet based shop can cost just a few hundred pounds and the cost can be further reduced through the use of auction sites such as ebay. There are several entrepreneurs who have become millionaires by selling through ebay. Although some potential customers are still wary of using the internet to buy goods because of issues related to fraud or non-delivery, the majority of UK households have purchased goods online and the proportion using e-commerce continues to grow significantly.

Multi-channel distribution

It makes sense to try to use a combination of distribution channels. For example, Apple sets up its own shops (with carefully designed brand values) in major cities. It also sells through a huge range of retailers and, of course, has an online presence. In adopting such a strategy Apple is maximising as many of the advantages as it can from each distribution channel chosen.

Discussion themes
Explain what is meant by a distribution channel.
'Businesses without an internet sales presence are doomed to failure.' To what extent do you agree with this statement?
What is multi-channel distribution?
How important was place in Mars' marketing mix? Mars ice cream http://luiscabral.net/economics/teaching/mars.pdf http://news.bbc.co.uk/1/hi/business/141928.stm

Chapter 17
Decisions related to the marketing mix

All businesses have choices to make when it comes to marketing their products:

- What shall the price be?
- What is the best design for the product?
- Where should it be sold?
- How should the product be promoted?

These decisions and how they relate to each other are known as the marketing mix, often referred to as the 4Ps of marketing – price, product, place and promotion.

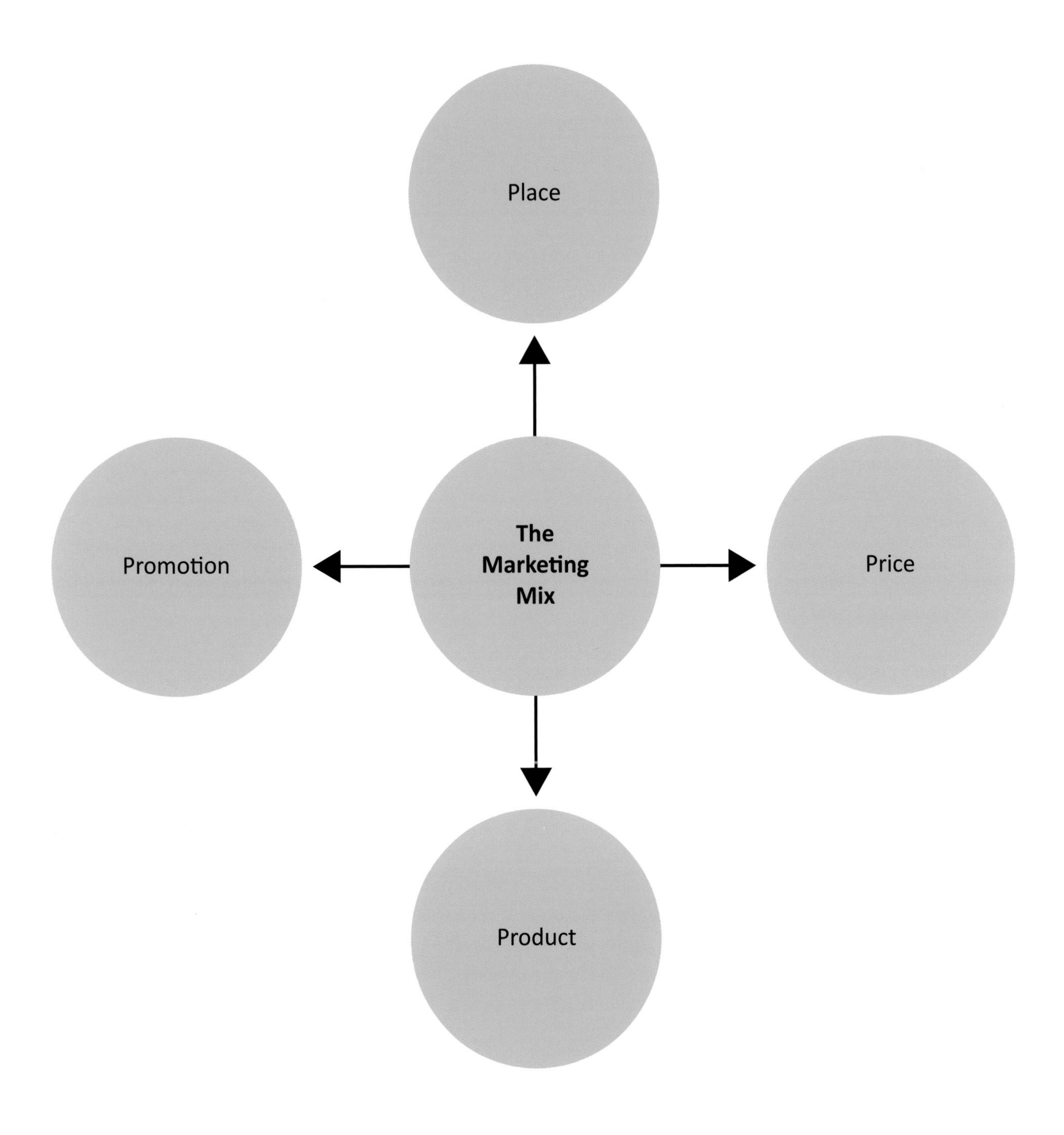

Every product sold will have different combinations of these four factors and these combinations will change over time. None of the 4Ps can be ignored, but priority will be given to different combinations of the four factors. The priorities a business will decide upon will depend as much on the needs of consumers and the actions of competitors as upon the nature of the product or service itself. The elements of the marketing mix which have priority will vary over time, depending on the nature of the market in which the product or service is being sold.

Global brands and marketing

The development of global brands has been one of the most important changes in how products are marketed across the world. Brands that cross international borders are like gold dust to companies. Businesses that are able to make their products appealing to consumers in many different countries can benefit from significant marketing and production economies of scale. Reaching millions of potential consumers around the world with a marketing strategy that differs very little from one country to another can drive down costs and increase profit. Global superstars can be used to promote a product throughout the world because they have universal appeal. Getting the likes of David Beckham to promote your product can boost global sales massively, fully justifying the enormous fee such a superstar may command.

The marketing mix in different contexts

How the marketing mix is applied will differ in a variety of contexts:

- local markets;
- national markets;
- global markets;
- goods or services markets;
- niche markets;
- mass markets.

Local markets allow specific marketing tactics to be used, adapting the 4Ps to local taste and incomes.

National markets need more consistency. A national marketing strategy needs to be developed, allowing the brand to become known and understood.

With **global markets** we have seen the need to establish an identifiable global brand – making promotion as homogenous as possible. Utilising the same advert with a local voiceover is typical of many global marketing campaigns. Where global marketing often differs is in relation to pricing. The level of income of the target market may vary from country to country and pricing needs to reflect this. In some circumstances penetration pricing needs to be used in order to establish a product or service, especially when strong domestic brands dominate the market.

Goods are perhaps easier to market than services. With goods there is a tangible product, but with services it is perhaps more difficult to identify what the customer needs. The focus on marketing for many services, for example insurance, holidays, car hire, professional services (healthcare) is often based on simplicity and clarity. 'This is what we do, we do it effectively and quickly, and we will make clear the benefits'. We see this with a range of TV adverts, for example BUPA healthcare, Hertz car hire, the marketing of financial comparison websites etc.

Often for businesses **mass marketing** is not an option – after all appealing to and developing products for a mass market is an expensive business. There are huge product development costs, massive expenditures on promotion and constant competition. Smaller businesses will therefore have to accept that aiming for specific niches may be their only option. With **niche marketing** a business will target a single niche within the market, ignoring the rest of the marketplace.

Niche marketing is based on designing goods or services specifically tailored for the needs of a relatively small target market. Therefore, there must be a full understanding of the desires and needs of the niche. This understanding can be gained through market research, but is often based on an understanding of a particular market that comes through personal experience. The internet has allowed businesses selling niche products to access markets far more readily. In the past, one of the major problems facing niche product businesses has been being unable to economically target customers who are likely to be geographically dispersed. Now the internet removes this problem and raising awareness is much simpler. There is no need to list in local *Yellow Pages* throughout the country or use magazine ads that may be irrelevant to most readers. Instead, potential customers can access the niche product/service providers by quickly searching websites.

New technology and marketing

The development and widespread use of the internet over the last twenty years has had a huge impact on marketing. Each of the 4Ps has had to change and evolve to meet the demands of this new method of reaching customers.

Clicks and bricks	Clicks and bricks is a marketing term which means that businesses need to have a web presence (clicks), plus a physical presence on the high street or in shopping centres (bricks). Examples of businesses using this form of widening of distribution channels include PC World, Argos and Tesco. Each of these businesses has been very successful in using a web presence to increase sales and customer loyalty.
Social media	Zoella, the hugely popular fashion and lifestyle blogger, has just bought a £1 million house. She has seven million YouTube followers and each video she posts is topped and tailed with adverts aimed at the demographic of her followers. This is a typical example of how social media is used to market products. Viral advertising is another form of social media advertising, with funny or stylish ads being sent from person to person. This form of marketing is of growing importance as fewer young people consume traditional media (TV and newspapers) and instead consume entertainment and information online.
M-commerce	M-commerce (mobile commerce) is the buying and selling of goods and services through wireless handheld devices such as mobile phones. This means 'having your retail outlet in your consumers' pocket'. Through mobile technology it is now possible to reach your customer 24 hours a day. M-commerce does not just mean buying: it is about providing your customers with product information, promotions and all other aspects of the marketing mix. Consumers use M-commerce to compare prices online, take photos for future reference and research their potential purchases online.

Pricing and the internet	A comparison of prices has become a great deal easier for customers. Using the web, individuals can carry out their own research or use comparison sites, such as Money Supermarket, to find the best deal across a huge range of products. This access to pricing information has had an impact on prices charged by businesses. It has been argued by economists that the increase in internet shopping has had a direct impact on lowering inflation rates.
E-tailing	Online shopping (sometimes known as E-tailing, from 'electronic retail' or E-shopping) is a form of electronic commerce which allows consumers to directly buy goods or services from a seller over the internet. The internet has changed buying habits and E-tailing is now a very important part of the retail industry, and is continuing to grow. The internet, and the use of search engines, has made accessing customers a great deal easier than in the past. All a business needs to sell its products is a decent website, some form of payment processing and 'shop' software. All of this can be created for less than £500. In fact, there are 1000s of entrepreneurs running their businesses through auction sites such as Ebay, with hardly any fixed costs at all. All of these businesses mean extra competition for existing traditional businesses – as well as lowering prices for customers.

Discussion themes
Article in The Drum: M-commerce has grown 63% in the last 5 years. http://www.thedrum.com/news/2014/02/11/m-commerce-has-grown-63-last-5-years-average-199-spent-mobile-purchases-2013
A 40 minute BBC programme on selling to India. It covers many of the problems with branding worldwide and many themes of international marketing. Theo's Adventure Capitalists – India https://www.youtube.com/watch?v=wDVAmeh5S9U
Explain the impact of new technology on the use of the marketing mix.
How might the marketing mix be adapted to meet the different needs of consumers in the global marketplace?
'Product will always be the most important aspect of the marketing mix.' Do you agree with this statement?
How has new technology changed the way that businesses carry out their marketing activities?

Chapter 18
Budgeting

A budget is a financial plan of action normally covering a specific time period, for example, six months or one year. A budget will describe expected levels of expenditure and revenues of a business. Large businesses will prepare budgets on a departmental basis or in relation to business functions. For example, a business will have an overall budget based upon the budgets of departments such as marketing, purchasing and human resources.

All budgets should be objective driven. This means that the expected revenues and expenditures of each department will be ultimately based on what the business is trying to achieve. Therefore, if a business has the objective of increasing sales by 20%, then the overall budget and departmental budgets should reflect this.

The budgeting process

Budgeting and monitoring of budgets is an ongoing procedure in large businesses. Budgets should be continually evolving to adapt to changes.

Typically the budgetary process will involve the following procedure:

1. Establish the aims and objectives of the business – what are the profit and market share targets? What is the targeted turnover?

2. Set production, marketing and financial budgets. These are the three main functional budgets and each is dependent upon the objectives of the business.

- Production budget – the objectives of the business have established the output levels required. The production budget attempts to put these output levels into practice. This will involve costs of purchasing raw materials and components, direct labour costs and other costs of production. This is an expenditure only budget.
- Marketing budget – both revenues and costs are combined. Revenues are from sales predicted and costs are from operating the business's marketing strategy.
- Financial budget – this will be based upon the business's cash flow forecast. Will income be able to cover expenditure or will there be a need to examine methods of raising funds to finance other budgets?

3. Next the budget should be further broken down. Within each of these budgets, there is the opportunity to break budgets down further, so there may be a training budget, a health and safety budget, a direct selling budget etc.

4. Procedures for monitoring budgets should be established. For example, the monitoring may involve activities such as collecting feedback, checking targets and communicating regularly with budget holders.

5. Any variance from predicted budgets should be examined and reacted to.

6. The experience and knowledge gained from setting one period's budgets should be applied to the setting of the following period's budgets.

Benefits of budgeting

The budgeting process has important benefits for a business. These benefits include the following:

- Improved management control of the organisation. Managers know who is spending what, and why they are spending the money.
- Improved financial control. Part of the budgeting process is the monitoring of expenditure and revenues. Any changes from (variances from) budgeted amounts need to be explained and reacted to.
- Budgeting allows managers to be aware of their responsibilities. Managers who are in control of their budgets are aware of what they should be achieving and how their role fits in with organisational objectives.
- Budgeting ensures, or should ensure, that limited resources are used effectively. The budgeting process allocates resources to where they are most likely to help achieve the firm's objectives.
- Budgeting can motivate managers. When managers at all levels are involved in the budgeting process they will have a commitment to ensuring that budgets are met.
- Budgeting can improve communication systems within the organisation. The budgeting process itself will involve communication both up and down the hierarchy. This will help to establish formal methods of communication, which can be used for purposes other than setting and administering budgets.

Problems with budgets

The budgeting process can cause problems. These include the following:

- Those excluded from the budgeting process may not be committed to the budgets and may feel demotivated.
- If budgets are inflexible, then changes in the market or other conditions may not be met by appropriate changes in the budget. For example, if a competitor starts a major new advertising campaign, and the marketing budget does not allow for a response to this, sales are likely to be lost.
- Also an effective budget can only be based on good quality information. Many managers overstate their budgetary needs to protect their departments. This can lead to lack of control and poor allocation of resources.

Zero budgeting

Zero budgeting involves managers starting with a clean sheet – they have to justify all expenditure made. This does the following:

- improves control;
- helps with allocation of resources;
- limits the tendency for budgets to increase annually with no real justification for the increase;
- reduces unnecessary costs;
- motivates managers to look at alternative options.

Budgetary control

The basis of budgetary control is variance analysis. A variance is any unplanned change from the budgeted figure.

Variances can be favourable (F) or adverse (A):

Favourable variance occurs when:	**Adverse variance occurs when:**
expenditure is less than expected;	expenditure is higher than expected;
revenues are higher than expected.	revenues are lower than expected.

Budgets must be monitored for variances in order that they can be reacted to. Each budget has a budget holder (the person responsible for the budget) who will be expected to take appropriate action.

Calculation of variances

Calculation of variances is relatively simple. The actual figure must be compared with the budgeted figure and the difference shown as either favourable (F), or adverse (A). These variances should then be totalled, to gain an overall favourable (F) or adverse (A) figure.

	Budgeted	Actual	Variance
Sales revenue	£163 000	£179 000	£16 000 (F)
Raw materials	£73 000	£81 000	£8000 (A)
Labour	£41 000	£43 000	£2000 (A)
Total variance			£6000 (F)

Remember – a favourable variance occurs when expenditure is less than expected or revenues are higher than expected.

Summary

Budgets are an important management tool. They help with financial control and in co-ordinating business activity. They can also assist in motivating staff. However, a poorly-prepared budget is valueless: it wastes time, can demotivate staff and may restrict business activities so that management cannot react to changes in the market place.

Discussion themes
Better business through budgeting http://www.businessweek.com/stories/2006-01-18/better-business-through-budgeting
Benefits of budgeting that relate to business management http://www.dummies.com/how-to/content/benefits-of-budgeting-that-relate-to-business-mana.html Summarise the benefits described.
Watch the video. Discuss why having a budget for a small business is so important. https://www.youtube.com/watch?v=Qu3YkLzl_7k
Explain the purpose of budgets.
Discuss the following statement: 'The benefits of budgeting will always outweigh the problems of setting budgets.'
Explain what is meant by zero budgeting. Why is this approach to budgeting better for some areas of business?
What is meant by adverse and favourable variances?

Chapter 19
Business finance

For many businesses there are potentially a wide range of ways of raising funds. These are needed to help set up the business, to keep the business going when cash is short and to help the business expand and grow.

Whether any money for investment is actually available will depend upon a number of factors:

- how well established the business is;
- the amount of profit previously made;
- how much security the business can offer (like buildings or other assets);
- the type of business (sole trader, partnership, private limited companies, public limited companies).

Businesses can raise finance from internal sources and/or external sources.

Internal finance

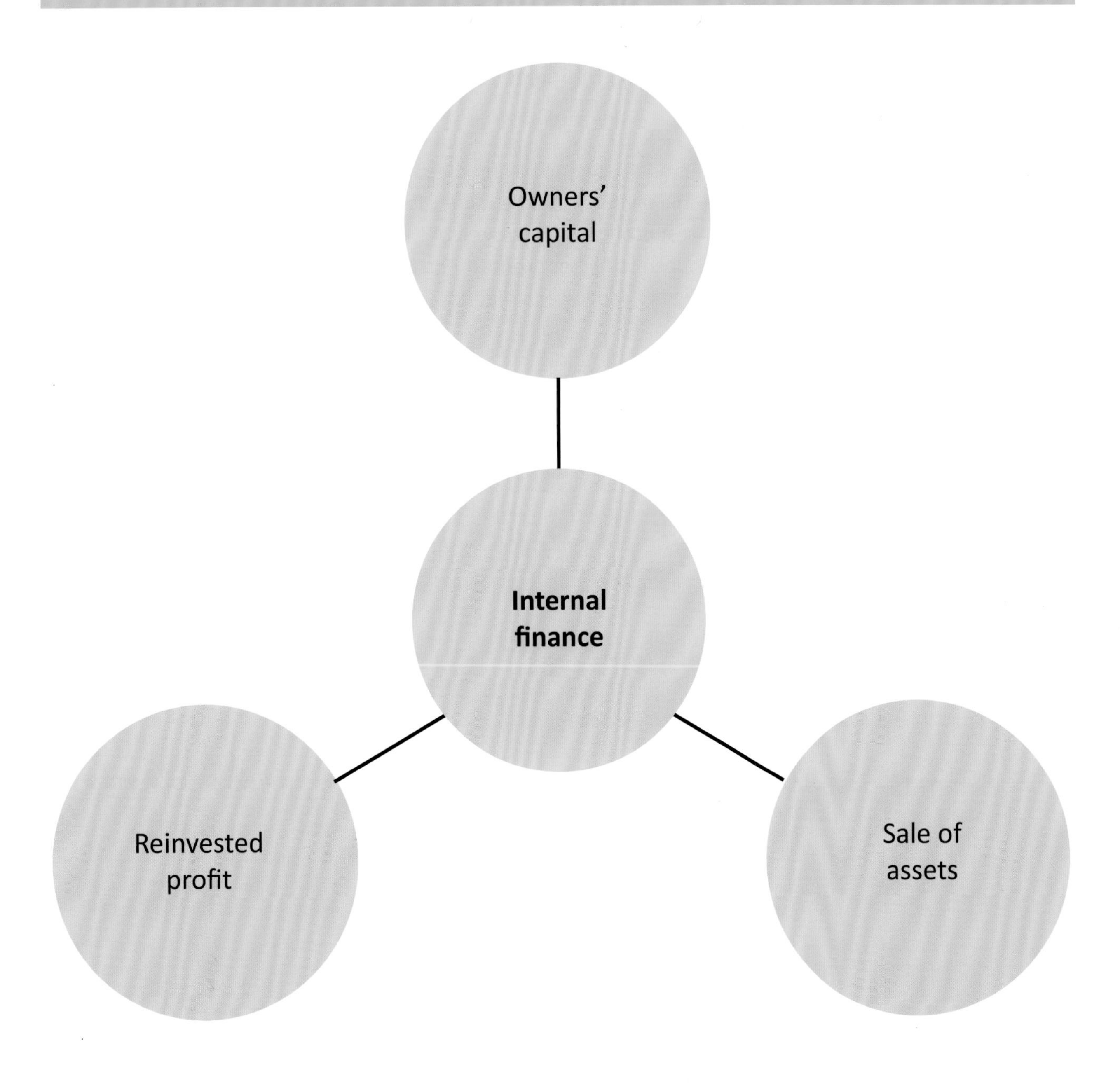

Sale of assets

A business can sell some of the assets it owns to raise finance. Businesses may have assets they no longer need, such as an old factory site, which can be sold. Often the selling of assets only happens when other ways of raising money have failed. In some cases the business may lease back the asset, so that it still retains its use. Big businesses often do this – e.g. the sale and lease back of office blocks. Selling assets and leasing the asset back improves cash flow in the short term. If the cash raised from the sale of the asset is used effectively by the business, cash flow and profitability can also improve in the long term.

Owners' capital

For small businesses, further investment of the sole trader's or partners' own capital (savings) may be the only method of raising money. Risk-taking entrepreneurs may sell their own assets (e.g. house) to raise money to invest.

Reinvested profit

When a business makes a profit it can pay out the profit to owners or shareholders or it can reinvest the profit back in the business. Often both may occur, with some profits going to owners or shareholders and the rest reinvested in the business.

Reinvesting profit is a good idea as there is no interest to pay on the money invested (there would be interest to pay if all the profits had been given to the owners, and the money for investment had come from loans). Also the owners should be happy to reinvest profits as the growth of the business will increase the value of their share of the business, and hopefully lead to higher profits in the future. However, there is a short-term cost – less profit to be shared amongst owners and lower dividends for shareholders of private limited and public limited companies.

External finance

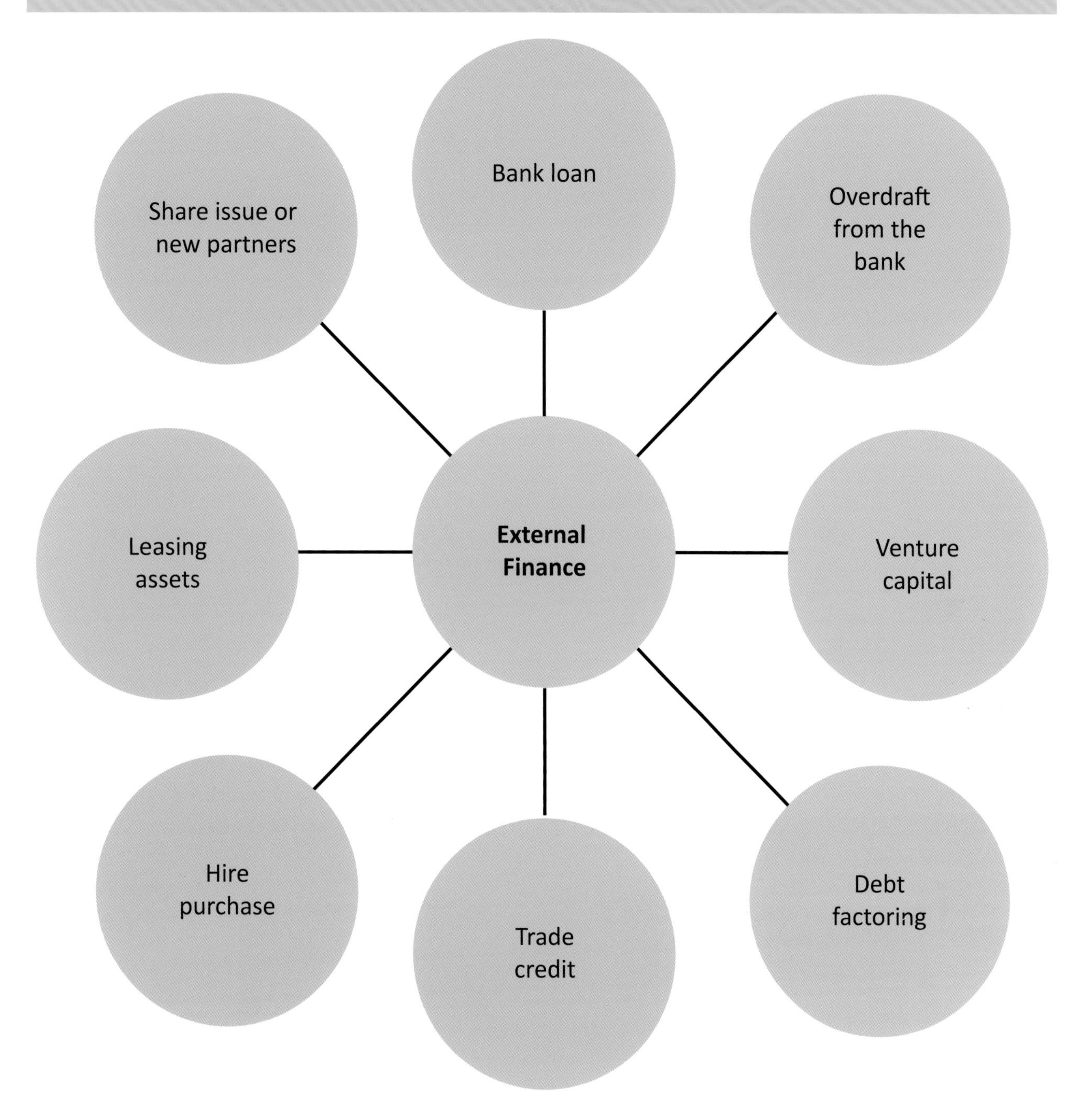

Share issue or new partners

For a sole trader, taking on a partner is a good way of helping fund investment. New partners not only bring in more capital (money) for investment, but can offer new skills which help a business grow. For existing partnerships new partners are also an effective way of funding growth. New partners 'buy in', and will be given part-ownership of the business. Their share of ownership, responsibilities and profits should be made clear in a new Partnership Agreement.

A share issue is the offering for sale of new shares in a business. For the largest businesses like BP, Vodafone and Tesco, there are literally billions of shares in issue, with some shareholders owning perhaps a few hundred shares and other big investors (like pension funds) owning millions. The money raised from share issues can be used for investment in the business or for expansion into new ventures. Shares can be sold by both Private Limited Companies (Ltd) and Public Limited Companies (PLC), and can be issued at any time in the life of the business, not just when the business is starting up. For the largest PLCs hundreds of millions of pounds can be raised through issuing shares. The major problem with share issues is that ownership is spread over a larger number of existing shareholders and new shareholders. If new shareholders have purchased enough shares they may try to change the way a business is run, or even attempt to take over the business.

Overdraft from the bank

An overdraft is a form of bank borrowing. A business becomes overdrawn when it withdraws more money out of its account than there is in it, so the business will end up with a negative bank balance. Once an overdraft limit (perhaps £5000) is agreed with the bank, the business can use as much of the overdraft as it needs at any time, up to the agreed overdraft limit. The bank will of course charge interest on the amount overdrawn, and will only allow an overdraft if they believe the business is creditworthy (capable of paying the money back). Interest rates on overdrafts tend to be very high.

Unfortunately a bank can demand the repayment of an overdraft at any time. Many businesses have been forced to cease trading because of the withdrawal of overdraft facilities by a bank. Even so, for short-term borrowing, an overdraft is often the ideal solution and many businesses often have a rolling (ongoing) overdraft agreement with the bank. An overdraft is often the best way of solving short-term cash flow problems, e.g. funding purchase of raw materials, whilst waiting for payment on goods produced.

Bank loan

This is lending by a bank to a business. A fixed amount is lent for a fixed period of time and normally for a specific purpose. The bank will charge interest on the loan and the interest, plus part of the capital (the amount borrowed), will have to be paid back each month. The bank will only lend if the business is creditworthy, and it may require security. If security is required, this means the loan is secured against an asset of the borrower. If the loan is not repaid, then the bank can take possession of the asset and sell the asset to get its money back.

Trade credit

If a shoe retailer buys on credit from a shoe manufacturer, it may not have to pay the manufacturer for a month after delivery. This means it could sell the shoes at a profit and have the money at the end of the month ready to pay its bill to its creditor – the manufacturer.

Extending a credit period will help short-term cash flow. Credit could be extended by delaying paying bills for an extra 14 days, meaning there will be more cash in the bank for this period. Unfortunately if a business delays payment of money it owes to its suppliers it would be no surprise if the supplier becomes somewhat upset – after all they have their own cash flows to think of. Also the next time the business requests credit from a supplier, they may be turned down and asked to pay cash.

Leasing assets

When leasing, a business pays monthly for the use of an asset but will never own it. Think of a partnership setting up a business as a parcel delivery service. They could lease a van from a leasing company. They will have to pay a monthly leasing fee, say £250, which is very useful if they do not wish to spend £8000 on buying a van. This will free up other money the business has, which can now be used for other purposes.

A business looking to purchase equipment may decide to lease if it wishes to improve its immediate cash flow. In the example above, if the van had been purchased, the cash flow out of the business would have been £8000. When leasing, the cash flow out of the business over the first year would be only £3000, leaving a possible £5000 for other assets and investment in the business. Leasing also allows equipment to be updated on a regular basis. However, in the long run, it may well cost more than outright purchase and the business does not have the van as an asset on its balance sheet.

Hire purchase

This is similar to leasing, but at the end of the hire period the asset belongs to the business that hires it.

Venture capital

Venture capital is money invested in a business by professional investors (venture capitalists).

When venture capitalists invest, they expect a say in how the business will be run and they also expect to make a good profit on their investment within two to three years.

The normal method of investment is for the venture capitalists to take an 'equity stake' – this means that in exchange for their investment they will be given a shareholding in the business. The percentage share will depend upon the amount invested relative to the value of the business.

The amount invested can be relatively small – perhaps £100 000, or quite large – say £20m. Of course the amount invested depends upon the size of the business and what it is trying to achieve. The venture capitalist expects quick growth, and potentially large profits.

From the business's point of view this form of finance comes with no interest payments and ongoing professional advice, so it often makes a great deal of sense. However, it does mean the current owners can potentially lose control of the business they have built if the shares are sold on.

Debt factoring

Debt factors are finance companies that will pay the selling business part of the value of an invoice issued as soon as sale has been made. So if company X sells goods on 30 days credit to company Y for £5000, the debt factor will pay company X a percentage of this debt (say 90% – £4500). The debt factor will hold the invoice and will collect the full value of the invoice (£5000) from company Y after 30 days. Company X benefits because cash flow is improved and they can use the £4500 to purchase raw materials and pay wages straightaway. Also, some aspects of debt management are moved outside the company. Of course, the full amount received by company X will be £500 less than the original invoice value. Debt factoring is normally only available to well-established businesses and the factor will carefully examine how creditworthy the debtors are before making any payment.

External finance
http://bit.ly/23cspnb

Suitable sources of finance
http://bit.ly/1n7SK4C

Discussion themes
Are you a financially savvy small business owner? http://www.smallbusiness.co.uk/financing-a-business/alternative-business-finance/2475372/are-you-a-financially-savvy-small-business-owner.thtml
Finance guide for small businesses. This includes a short video guide http://www.simplybusiness.co.uk/knowledge/articles/2013/05/small-business-finance-guide/
Identify the main reasons why businesses may seek extra finance.
Describe methods of finance available to small business owners.
What are the advantages of internal forms of finance over external forms?
Discuss the following statement: 'Venture capitalists offer the best form of external finance for a business that wishes to expand.'

Chapter 20
Cash flow

It is often said that in business 'cash is king'. This is because cash, at least in the short term, is the most important asset a business can have. Without cash, neither employees nor suppliers can be paid and, therefore, the business will grind to a halt. Cash is the oil in the machine of business and a cash flow forecast tells us how much cash is predicted to be available to the business.

A forecast cash flow statement shows the expected flows of cash into and out of a business over a trading period in the immediate future – e.g. the next six months or year.

A cash flow forecast predicts how much cash is, or will be, available in a business, or how much cash will be needed to keep the business running.

The cash flow forecast is made up of three parts:

- revenue/income;
- expenses/outgoings;
- balances.

To obtain a picture of what is included in a cash flow forecast we will examine the cash flow forecast of Good Wood Trading. Good Wood is a sole trader who is just setting up in business manufacturing wooden garden furniture. The items made will be sold through gardening exhibitions, and to local garden centres on a credit basis. The predicted cash flow forecast for the first six months of trading is shown below.

Predicted/forecast cash flow statement for Good Wood

	January	February	March	April	May	June
Revenue	£	£	£	£	£	£
Cash sales	600	1200	1750	2300	2600	3000
Debtor payments	0	600	850	1300	1490	1430
Total revenue	600	1800	2600	3600	4090	4430
Expenses						
Raw materials	970	1200	1350	1380	1670	1500
Wages	800	800	800	900	900	900
Loan repayments	220	220	220	220	220	220
Rates	40	40	40	40	40	40
Electricity	60	60	60	100	100	100
Travelling	80	80	150	150	150	150
Sundries	130	80	80	80	80	80
Exhibition charges	150	150	250	250	300	300
Total expenses	2450	2630	2950	3120	3460	3290
Net cash flow	–1850	–830	–350	480	630	1140
Opening balance	750	–1100	–1930	–2280	–1800	–1170
+/– Net cash flow	–1850	–830	–350	480	630	1140
Closing balance	–1100	–1930	–2280	–1800	–1170	–30

Parts of the cash flow forecast

Revenue

Revenue is the income received by a business for goods sold or services provided. It is the cash flow into a business. For Good Wood it is sub-divided into cash sales and debtor payments.

	January	February	March
Revenue	£	£	£
Cash sales	600	1200	1750
Debtor payments	0	600	850
Total revenue	600	1800	2600

Cash sales are created when sales are made and payment is immediate. This payment can be by cash or with debit and credit cards. In all of these cases the money is immediately available for use by the business.

Debtor payments occur because many businesses sell goods on credit – payment for the goods may not be due for 30 days or more. When goods are sold on credit, a debtor is created. We only enter the revenue from these sales when payment is made.

All the payments received by a business within the time period are known as total revenue.

Expenses

Under expenses or expenditure all of the money spent by a business within a time period is shown. This is the money flowing out of the business. There are many different types of expenditure – some of the more common types are shown here.

In a cash flow the expenses of a business are broken down so we can see exactly where the money is going. In January, Good Wood will spend £800 on wages, £60 on electricity and so on. All of these are examples of money flowing out of a business.

Total expenses is the total of all categories expenditure for the time period. For Good Wood the total expenditure for January is predicted to be £2450. This means that the total of cash flowing out of the business is expected to be £2450.

Expenses	January	February
Raw materials	970	1200
Wages	800	800
Loan repayments	220	220
Rates	40	40
Electricity	60	60
Travelling	80	80
Sundries	130	80
Exhibition charges	150	150
Total expenses	2450	2630

Calculating net cash flow

As explained above total revenue is the total of cash flow into the business and total expenses is the total spending by the business.

Net cash flow is calculated by taking total expenses away from total revenue. If revenue is greater than expenses then this figure is positive (+): if expenses are greater than revenue, then the net cash flow is a negative (–).

	January
Total revenue	600
Total expenses	2450
Net cash flow	–1850

	June
Total revenue	4430
Total expenses	3290
Net cash flow	1140

Closing balances

Once calculated, net cash flow can then be used to obtain the closing balance for the period. To find the closing balance, if the net cash flow is a negative we deduct this from the opening balance, or if it is a positive figure we add net cash flow to the opening balance. The opening balance is the amount of cash available at the beginning of the period.

	January	February	March
Opening Balance	750	–1100	–1930
+/– Net cash flow	–1850	–830	–350
Closing balance	–1100	–1930	–2280

Closing balance: for January there is a closing balance of –£1100, i.e. a predicted cash shortage of £1100. This was calculated by taking the net cash flow –£1850 from the opening balance £750. The closing balance for one month or period becomes the opening balance for the next month or period.

In this case the closing balance for January of –£1100, becomes the opening balance for February.

Cash flow forecast problems

Forecast cash flow statements are a prediction of the likely flows of cash into and out of a business. They will be based on past experience (when the business has a previous trading history), current and likely future economic and financial trends, along with the knowledge and understanding of the managers/owners and the future plans of the business.

As with all forecasts the further we look into the future the less certainty we have. Because of this, and because businesses operate in a world with changing fashions, changing economic climate, and changing competition, a business' actual cash flow statement can be very different from its cash flow forecast.

Typical reasons for cash flow forecast problems

Sales are not at the expected level

Increased/decreased competition
Economic growth/decline
Changing spending patterns of consumers/changing fashions
Government influences, e.g. increased or decreased taxation

Costs increase

Raw materials cost increases
Higher than expected level of inflation
Interest rate increases
Increased labour costs

Internal factors

Poor initial predictions of income and expenditure
Late payment of debtor
Poor budgeting and lack of control of spending

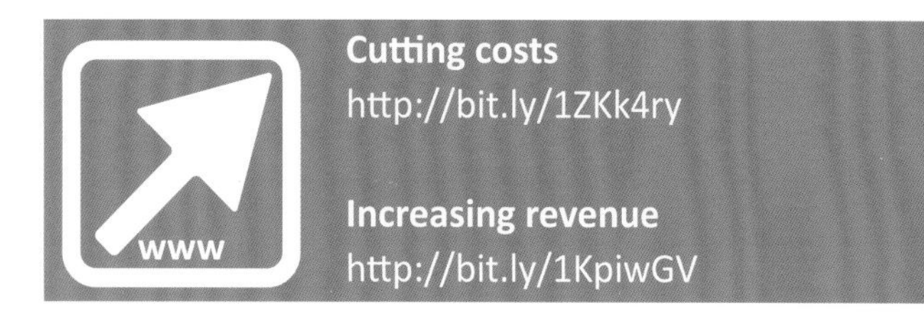

Making use of a cash flow forecast

All businesses should monitor cash flow and examine any differences between actual and forecast figures. This will allow action to be taken before a real business crisis arises. As experience is gained in managing and monitoring cash flow, business owners and managers will be able to improve the accuracy of their forecasts. The forecast cash flow is also used to tell us if the business is likely to have enough money coming in to pay all of its expenses. If the forecast cash flow tells us that the business is unlikely to have enough money coming in to cover costs, then the business must arrange to obtain the required amount of money. Perhaps the most popular method of funding a shortage of cash is to borrow from a bank (external) and this borrowing can take the form of loan or an overdraft. However, there are other methods of funding, each of which has an important part to play.

So what happens when a business needs cash, or liquidity? Up to now we have just referred to cash, but the fact is we are talking about the liquidity of a business. Liquidity is a measure of the availability of working capital. If managers of a business say they have a liquidity or working capital problem, this means that they will have a problem meeting all their immediate or near future expenditure demands. In other words, they do not have enough cash in hand, or do not expect enough cash to be flowing into the business and cannot convert enough assets into cash in the short term to be able to pay all their bills. This is important as businesses do not always (in fact rarely) need to keep enough immediate cash on hand to meet likely future expenditure. What they must do, however, is keep enough 'liquid assets' available, in order that cash flow can be effectively managed. So if there is a predicted cash shortage, what can managers/owners do?

Solutions to a predicted cash shortage

- Increase revenue – this is much easier said than done. A business may try to increase prices but this is likely to reduce demand. Alternatively, new methods of distribution (places to sell) may be found; but in the short run this will increase costs and worsen the cash flow situation.
- Reduce costs – wages are often a major cost. Reducing staff will cut costs, but will impact on output or service provided. Looking for cheaper suppliers makes sense, but there could be an impact on quality.
- Delay payment – if the business has creditors then delaying payment will improve immediate cash flow. However, the impact could be delayed deliveries, interest charges on debts, as well as demand for cash on delivery for future supplies.
- Extra funding – this could be a new injection of capital from the owner, or perhaps a business loan. However, if cash flow is predicted to be poor, then loans become unlikely. Outside investors could possibly be interested, but are unlikely to act quickly and will want a share of the business. An overdraft is possible if the business has a good account management history with the bank. Finally, using an invoice factoring service can bring creditor payments forward, but there are related costs and provision of the service will depend on the quality of debtors and trading history.

Benefits of preparing a cash flow forecast

- An accurate cash flow forecast will allow a business to get a clear idea of how it is performing (although it does not provide an accurate statement of profitability), and how it is likely to perform in the future.
- The forecast allows managers to be able to specify times when the business may need additional funding, such as when cash outflow exceeds inflow.
- In addition, inconsistencies in future performance can be identified and remedied.
- Also, when there is predicted to be a large positive cash flow, businesses can plan ahead on how to use this money – perhaps by investing or paying off debts.

Limitations of using a cash flow forecast

- Drawing up cash flow forecasts takes management time that might be more productively used completing other tasks in the business.
- Cash flow forecasts need to be accurate to have value: this may be especially difficult to achieve if the business has little or no trading history to base the predicted cash flow on.
- The longer the timescale the less accurate the forecast is likely to be.
- Inflation can impact on the accuracy of figures.
- Cash flow forecasts needs to be monitored to have ongoing usefulness.

Discussion themes
What is a cash flow statement? – MoneyWeek Investment Tutorials film https://www.youtube.com/watch?v=GkGdlgX3xYI
What is the difference between a cash flow statement and a cash flow forecast?
Explain why cash flow forecasts can be sometimes just a rough estimate.
Describe methods of solving short-term cash flow problems. Are there any disadvantages to these methods?
How can a business improve its cash flow in the long term?
Discuss the following statement: 'Spending time and effort on producing cash flow forecasts is a complete waste of time.'

Chapter 21
The trading, profit and loss account

Profit and loss accounts are said to give a 'historic view' of the business's trading income and expenditure over the previous 12 months. The account will show all income and expenditure received and incurred over the previous year.

The first section of a profit and loss account is sometimes referred to as the trading account. The trading account shows what the sales of the business have been and the direct costs of making those sales – known as the cost of sales.

When we take the cost of sales away from the sales of a business, the figure we are left with is known as gross profit. This is the first figure of real importance.

A simple profit and loss account

The profit and loss account for Frying Tonite (a takeaway) for the year 2013–14 is shown to the right. It is normal practice for profit and loss accounts to be produced for 12 months trading. However, the 12 months do not have to run from January to December – they can cover any 12 consecutive months.

The profit and loss account of Frying Tonite shows the income the business has received from its trading activities over the last 12 months, and all the money it has spent performing these business activities over the same 12 months.

Because the profit and loss account looks back over the past twelve months the first line always gives the business's trading income for the year: i.e. the revenue gained from the goods the business has sold, or the services it has provided. Trading income can be called different things: 'sales' or 'revenue' or 'income' or 'turnover', but they all mean the same thing.

	£	**£**
Sales		96 500
Less **Cost of sales**		
Opening stock	3900	
Purchases	28 600	
Less **Closing stock**	4700	
		27 800
Gross profit		68 700
Less **Expenses**		
Wages	27 880	
Rent	4600	
Rates	2350	
Travel	2600	
Sundries	860	
Electricity	300	
Total expenses		38 590
Net profit		30 110

The trading account

The extract on the right shows the trading account for Frying Tonite.

The total income received by Frying Tonite for their sales of chips, fish, pies etc. during the year 2013–14 is £96 500.

Cost of sales – these are the direct costs of purchasing the stock that is used in sales. For Frying Tonite this would include fish, oil, potatoes etc.

	£	£
Sales		96 500
Cost of sales		
Opening stock	3900	
Purchases	28 600	
Less **Closing stock**	4700	
		27 800
Gross profit		68 700

To calculate the cost of sales, we must first add opening stock (i.e. the stock the business has at the beginning of the year) to purchases the business has made during the year. Once we have done this we take away closing stock (i.e. stock left over at the end of the year). We take away closing stock as it has not yet been sold or used, so it is not part of the cost of sales.

Cost of sales =

opening stock + purchases – closing stock

So for Frying Tonite the calculation would be:

£3900 + £28 600 – £4700 = £27 800

The figure for the cost of sales is placed in the second column, below the sales figure.

Gross profit is calculated by taking the cost of sales away from sales.

For Frying Tonite sales are £96 500, the cost of sales are £27 800, so:

£96 500 – £27 800 = £68 700

Gross profit explained

Gross profit is an indicator of how efficient the business is at making and selling its product. However, the figure for gross profit on its own does not help us judge the level of efficiency: after all, a large business is likely to have a much higher gross profit figure than a small business, but the small business could be better run or have less stock damage.

The profit and loss account

Net profit is often referred to as 'the bottom line' in business. This is for two reasons. Firstly on a simple presentation of a profit and loss account, it is the actual bottom line. Secondly, the net profit figure tells us the actual profits of the business after all costs have been paid.

How we calculate net profit is shown below.

Less **Expenses**		
Wages	27 880	
Rent	4600	
Rates	2350	
Travel	2600	
Sundries	860	
Electricity	300	
Total expenses		38 590
Net profit		30 110

The gross profit for Frying Tonite has already been calculated in the trading account.

Now we have to allow for expenses. Expenses are the indirect costs that the business incurs. These expenses are not direct costs of production. Examples of expenses include rent, interest payments and electricity. The total expenses figure is placed in the second column, beneath the figure for gross profit. To find Frying Tonite's net profit we will have to total these expenses and take them away from the gross profit.

To calculate net profit, we simply take the figure for total expenses away from the gross profit figure.

For Frying Tonite, gross profit is £68 700, expenses are £38 590. So:

£68 700 – £38 510 = £30 110 net profit.

Net profit explained

Net profit is an indicator of how efficient the business is overall, this is because all the business's revenues and expenses are included in the calculation. Like the figure for gross profit, net profit on its own does not help us judge the level of efficiency. A large business is likely to have a much higher net profit figure than a small business because it manages its expenses better.

The appropriation account

This final section of the profit and loss account shows how the profit or loss is distributed. However, before the profit is distributed the business will have to pay tax on its profits.

Frying Tonite will have to pay £6000 in corporation tax – deducting this figure will give the profit after tax.

As a private limited company Frying Tonite will have to pay out dividends to its shareholders – this is then deducted from the profit after tax figure to give the final retained profit figure of £16 110.

The retained profit can then be reinvested into the business to help the business grow.

	£	£
Net profit		30 110
Tax		6000
Profit after Tax		24 110
Dividends		8000
Retained profit		16 110

The presentation of profit and loss accounts for unlimited and limited business can vary greatly – there is no one correct way of presenting this financial information. Sole trader accounts tend to be more straightforward and may not include an appropriation section as all the profit will go to the sole trader.

Private and public limited companies tend to be more complicated and can take a number of different layouts. Limited companies have to provide an income statement, which shows the same information as a profit and loss account: a financial statement that measures a company's financial performance over a specific time, including the net profit or loss incurred.

Other names used include the 'profit and loss statement' or 'statement of revenue and expense.'

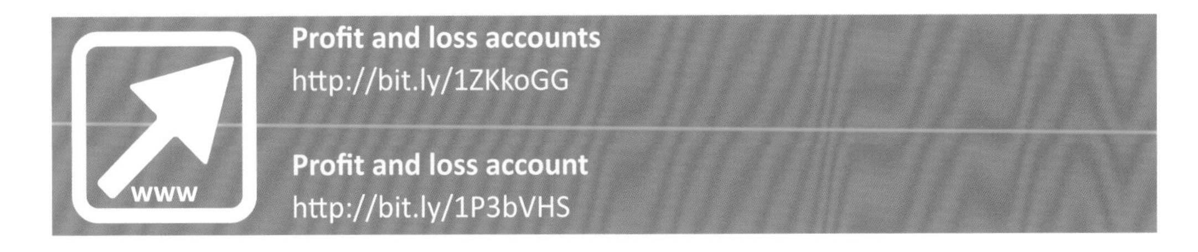

Discussion themes
Money Week video – 'what is profit'? http://moneyweek.com/videos/beginners-guide-to-investing-what-is-profit-04914/
What is the difference between gross and net profit?
What are the calculations for gross profit, net profit and retained profit?
'A profitable business should always pay a high dividend to its shareholders.' Discuss this statement.
How can a business improve its profit?

Chapter 22
Ratio analysis

Accounting ratios allow managers and other stakeholder groups to make judgements on how efficiently a business is being run. Profit is the main indicator of how well a business is performing.

Gross profit explained

Gross profit is an indicator of how efficient the business is at making and selling its products. However, the figure for gross profit on its own does not help us judge the level of efficiency: after all, a large business is likely to have a much higher gross profit figure than a small business. Consequently, a calculation is used to help us judge the efficiency of the business. This calculation, known as an accounting ratio, is called the gross profit margin (GPM). The better the performance the higher the gross profit margin percentage will be.

Calculating the gross profit margin (GPM)

To calculate the gross profit margin two figures are needed – these are gross profit and sales (also known as sales turnover or sales revenue).

The formula is quite straightforward:

$$\frac{\text{Gross profit}}{\text{Sales}} \times \frac{100}{1} = \text{GPM\%}$$

Example: if we had a gross profit of £438 700 and sales of £956 500:

$$\frac{438\ 700}{956\ 500} \times \frac{100}{1} = 45.8\%$$

Commenting on the gross profit margin

When the GPM has been calculated, a business or stakeholder cannot just say if it is good (high) or bad (low) without considering the type of business involved.

Variations in the GPM between businesses are caused by both internal and external factors. Internal factors include the size of the business, the quality of stock control, management of expenses etc. External factors include the level of interest rates, the type of industry the business operates in and the target market. The influence of both sets of factors becomes clearer if we look at two examples.

A large supermarket chain will have a relatively low gross profit margin. It may buy a can of beans from the manufacturer for 20p and sell it at 25p. Many supermarket chains have GPMs of around 18%. However, a corner shop may have a relatively high gross profit margin: it may buy a can of beans from the wholesaler at 25p and sell it at 40p. The supermarket can trade with a lower GPM because it can spread its other costs (expenses) over a large number of sales. On the other hand, the corner shop will have relatively high expenses in relation to sales and these have to be covered by a high GPM.

Between different industries GPM can vary a great deal. Jewellers may have a very high GPM (60–80%). They may sell their goods at two or three times the price they paid their supplier. A dairy farmer, however, might find that the price they receive for their milk is little more than the cost of producing it.

Nonetheless, even with these influences on GPM, a judgement can still be made. Low GPM businesses may include supermarkets, manufacturers of mass production goods and food manufacturers; whilst high GPM businesses will include restaurants and retailers of upmarket goods. Therefore, looking at the accounts of a fast-food outlet the GPM is 25% – this is likely to be poor, but if the accounts relate to a manufacturer of tinned vegetables, this level of GPM may be totally acceptable. Overall, an improving ratio over two years' accounts is always positive and the higher the ratio, the better.

Net profit explained

Net profit is an indicator of how profitable the business is overall: this is because all the business's revenues and expenses in its calculation are included. Like the figure for gross profit, net profit on its own does not help judge the level of efficiency – after all, a large business is likely to have a much higher net profit figure than a small business. However, the small one could manage its expenses more efficiently. A second calculation is used to help judge the efficiency of the business. This calculation, again known as an accounting ratio, is called the net profit margin.

Calculating the net profit margin (NPM)

To calculate the net profit margin two figures are needed – these are net profit and sales. The following formula is used:

$$\frac{\textbf{Net profit}}{\textbf{Sales}} \times \frac{\textbf{100}}{\textbf{1}} = \textbf{NPM\%}$$

Example: if we had a net profit of £136 500 and sales of £956 500:

$$\frac{\textbf{136 500}}{\textbf{956 500}} \times \frac{\textbf{100}}{\textbf{1}} = \textbf{14.2\%}$$

Commenting on the net profit margin

When the NPM has been calculated, commenting and judging whether it is good (high) or bad (low) is easier than when examining the GPM. The type of business involved must still be considered, but the NPM does not vary by quite as much as the GPM over different industries and sizes of business.

A business with a high GPM often has proportionately higher expenses, whilst a business with a low GPM often has proportionately lower expenses. Knowing what to expect will help to make a critical comment on the NPM and, importantly, the difference between the NPM and the GPM. One important factor that will lower the NPM is if the business is relatively new. A newly established business, in its first years of trading, may have high expenses as it tries to establish itself. A good example of this would be high expenditure on advertising. As a result of these relatively high expenses, a new business could have a low NPM; but this low NPM may not necessarily indicate problems.

How do we judge a good or bad NPM and how do we comment?

Perhaps the easiest way to judge NPM is to construct bands of performance. Therefore:

- A NPM of 18% + may be regarded as good, indicating effective business management of costs and expenses.
- A NPM of 10–17%, might be viewed as satisfactory, but cost or expenses management could be improved.
- A NPM of less than 10% could be regarded as poor, indicating that there are real opportunities for improving cost and expenses management.

Remember that when commenting on accounts an allowance for the type and age of business should be considered. Walmart, the world's largest retailer, has one of the lowest NPMs in the business, at below 3%! On the other hand, Microsoft has a NPM of around 48%.

If the figures that have been calculated do seem low, businesses and stakeholders should look for the main causes of poor performance. Are costs of sales high? This would lead to a low GPM, which in turn may lead to a low NPM. By working through the profit and loss account, individual costs and expenses can be analysed to see what the cause of the low NPM is.

When assessing the performance of the profitability ratios it is important to make comparisons with other businesses in the same industry as well as making comparisons over time.

By comparing with similar size businesses in the same industry the profitability of the business can be compared 'like with like'. The businesses would be expected to have similar features and therefore the comparison is more valid when judging the significance of their gross and net profit ratios.

When evaluating the GPM and the NPM it is important to compare these over time. This can be by just comparing the business's performance over, for example, a five-year period, or even better, comparing the business against similar businesses in the same industry over the five years.

One year's figures may be misleading and not a true reflection of the profitability of the business over a longer period of time. By analysing data over a longer period of time patterns can be identified and a more accurate evaluation of the profitability of the business may be carried out.

Discussion themes
What is profit? MoneyWeek investment tutorials – includes GPM and NPM. https://www.youtube.com/watch?v=lQuYnADhuwo
Explain the purpose of calculating profit ratios.
'A low NPM is not always an indicator of poor performance.' Discuss this statement.
'Profitability ratios are the only way to judge business performance.' Do you agree with this statement?

Chapter 23
Changes in working practices

Working practices have been changing rapidly over the last 30 years. Employment practices are very different now than in the 1970s and before. This is due to the following factors:

- the decline in trade union power;
- the end of demarcation (a process that separated different types of work and assigned them to members of different trade unions);
- the loss of employment in heavy industry;
- the increasing number of women in the workforce.

Throughout this period we have been moving towards a pattern of employment and contractual arrangements that has led to a greater degree of flexibility in employment practices.

A more flexible workforce is one designed to provide labour in the quantities required at the time that businesses need it. Every business has changing demands for labour. This can be related to changes in the economy, seasonal changes or even as demand fluctuates from day to day. The flexible workforce is designed to meet these changing demand patterns and provide labour specifically when it is required.

Key features of the flexible workforce

Flexible hours	A worker on flexible hours has an agreed number of working hours. These are made up of core hours which must be worked – the remainder of the contracted hours can be worked on a flexible basis. For example, a worker has a contract for 35 hours with core hours of 10am–3pm over five days. The remaining 10 hours can be worked in non-core time (say between 8–10am, and 3–6pm over the 5 days). This can work well for parents who may need to collect children from school.
Home working	Many jobs of professional status (e.g. design, accountancy, IT programming), can include homeworking time as part of each working week. A good PC and broadband connection can mean that many tasks can be fulfilled by working from home. Those who do these sorts of jobs from home benefit from time saved and the stress of commuting. Businesses benefit by a reduction in overheads if less office space is required.
Part-time employment	Part-time working is becoming increasingly common. Parents with young children and students find that it particularly suits their requirements, and businesses benefit from the flexibility it offers. During busy periods, part-time workers are employed to meet the needs of the employer. At quieter times the core full-time staff are sufficient. Clearly this has cost-saving implications.

Temporary employment	Employment for a specific period of time, for example six months to cover maternity leave. Some temporary work is arranged through employment agencies which provide workers to employers who are seeking workers with specific skills for a set period of time. The growth in temporary contracts has been much criticised by trade unions as it offers little security or career development to those employed.
Job-sharing	Job-sharing means that two people share the same job, often on a fifty-fifty split. Job-sharing often lets professional workers continue in employment, when otherwise they may have had to take a career break. The best example of this happens with new mothers, who, through job sharing, can combine work with bringing up children. Job-sharing may last a number of years.
Multi-skilling	This involves businesses training their workforce to be able to work effectively across a wide range of tasks. This offers a greater degree of flexibility. No longer do manufacturing firms have to wait for a specific tradesperson to come and fix a fault – it can be done by the production staff who have been trained to spot and resolve problems with machinery. Multi-skilled workers are likely to be better motivated and change will be far easier to implement with a flexible workforce.
Zero-hours contracts	This type of contract means that an employee has to be available for work but is not guaranteed any work. This provides employers with total flexibility. If the employer is busy, those on zero-hours contracts may find that they are on nearly full-time hours. However, if demand for labour falls, workers may find themselves sent home. Workers on these contracts have virtually no income security at all. These contracts are being increasingly criticised as they are deemed to be exploiting workers.
Hot-desking	Hot-desking means that an employee has no fixed work space within an office environment. Hot-desking cuts down the need for office space – if a business has a sales team that spends little time in the office, supplying permanent desks for the team is a waste of resources. Also it is supposed to allow greater innovation and encourages new networks to be established in the workplace. Some workers who are forced to hot-desk complain of the breakdown of workplace relationships, and can feel disconnected from the organisation.

Possible benefits to businesses of flexible working practices

- Businesses can expand and contract their workforce quickly in response to a rise or fall in the demand for their product or service. Permanent staff are not easy to dispose of in comparison to temporary workers on zero-hours contracts.
- Temporary staff and subcontractors may be cheaper to employ as they are unlikely to get any of the benefits that may be available to permanent staff. For example, employers are responsible for training permanent employees, which can prove very expensive. Temporary sub-contracted workers will have acquired their skills elsewhere at no cost to the business currently employing them.
- A flexible workforce is likely to make a business more efficient. This may result in lower costs and make the business more competitive, especially for those businesses operating in sectors that are labour intensive.

Possible drawbacks to businesses of flexible working practices

- Temporary workers are less likely to have the same commitment to a business when compared to permanent workers. They will take a short-term view and may not carry out their work to the same standard as those who see their long-term future within the business. This may damage the company's reputation and result in the loss of customers.
- Communicating with a workforce which works largely from home can be an issue and the benefits of teamwork may be lost. Workers may feel isolated and the cross-fertilisation of ideas which springs from meeting with colleagues on a regular basis may result in less innovation.

Discussion themes
Using examples, explain what is meant by the flexible workforce.
Flexible working practices bring more advantages to employers than employees. To what extent do you agree with this statement?
Read the article on zero-hours contracts and give the reasons why employers use them and why some people dislike their use. http://www.bbc.co.uk/news/business-23573442

Chapter 24
Workforce planning

At its simplest, workforce planning is about 'trying to predict the future demand for different types of staff and seeking to match this with supply'. Therefore, workforce planning involves looking to the future and judging the level of demand for skills within the business. In other words, it means ensuring that there will be the right number of workers, with the right skills, doing the right jobs, at the right time and in the right place.

A comparison between the present workforce and the desired future workforce will highlight shortages, surpluses and skills gaps. This can be done by carrying out a skills audit of the current workforce to see what skills and experience the existing workforce have. If any gaps are identified then these gaps become the focus of a detailed workforce plan. The workforce plan will develop and implement strategies that will build the relevant skills and capacity needed for business success.

Long-term staffing problems can arise for a number of reasons. These may be internal staffing issues (staff loss, retirement, training, promotion, flexibility) or external factors (these include changes in the population structure, government policy, the changing nature of industry, competitors, unemployment, availability of skills).

Workforce planning does not always mean recruitment – it may also mean shedding workers. This can be done through redundancy, both voluntary and compulsory, early retirement schemes and allowing natural wastage to occur (workers who leave for other employment or retire and are not replaced). One criticism of mass redundancy schemes is that the workers who choose to leave are often those who find it relatively easy to find a new job; whilst those who stay have less marketable (and useful) skills. Early retirement schemes can remove the most experienced managers whose skills will be lost to the business forever.

The main factors that influence workforce planning are:

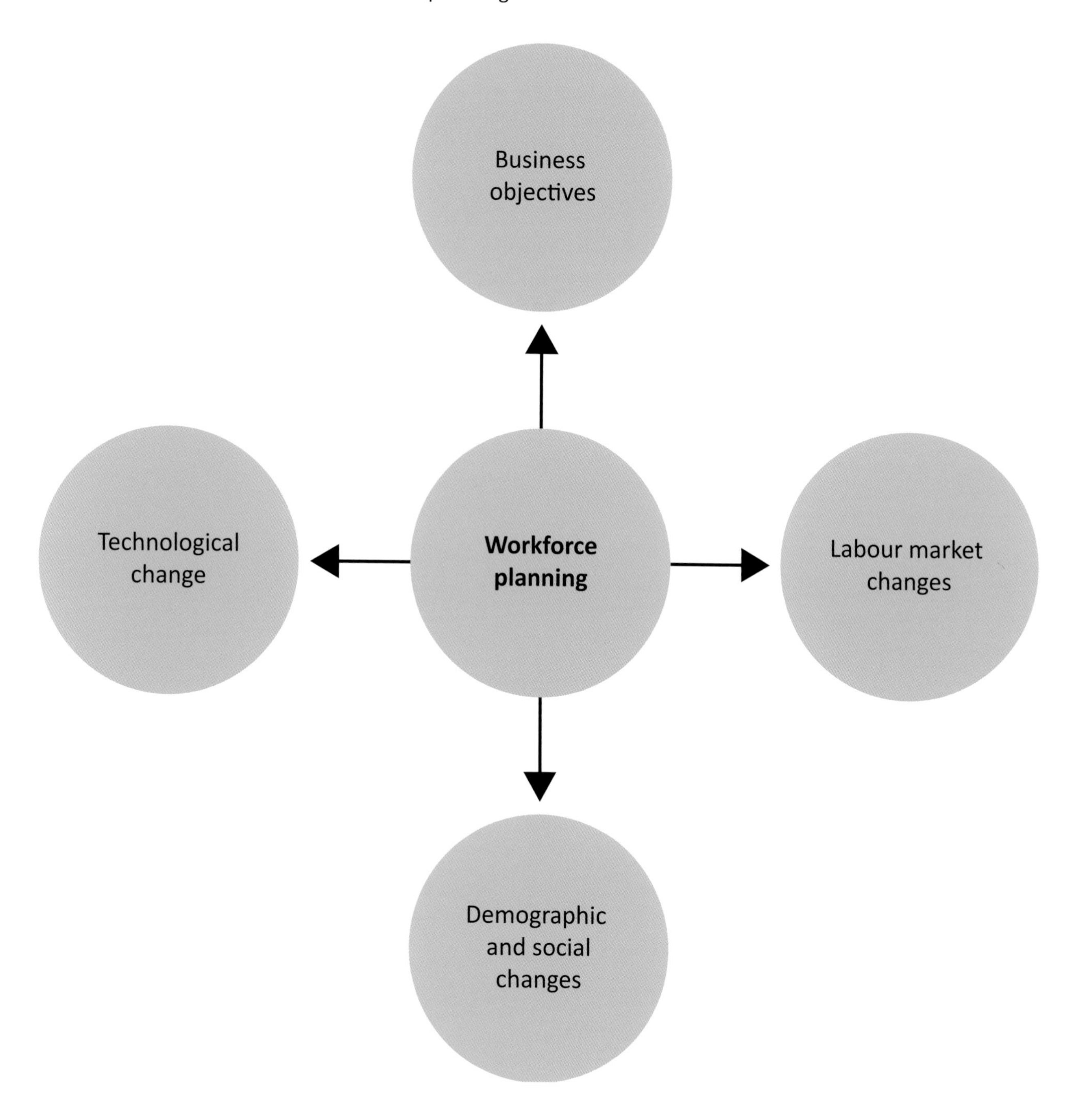

- Business objectives, such as increasing output or opening new branches, will invariably require more employees.
- Labour market changes – labour market trends have implications for the recruitment and retention of staff. Engineers are in increasingly short supply as less undergraduates are choosing to study in this discipline.
- Demographic and social change – demographic change, such as the ageing population in the UK, is affecting both the demand for products and services required by this age group, as well as workforce supply.
- Technological change – technological change is leading to large change in ways of working and the skills needed in the workforce. Many manual tasks can now be carried out by robotic technology, reducing the demand for certain types of labour.

Benefits of workforce planning

There are a number of important benefits to businesses who have effective workforce planning programmes. Workforce planning is vital in helping businesses to tackle problems such as staff shortages and the control of staffing costs. It can help to ensure the production of quality products and services.

Workforce planning will also help a business:

- decide how many employees are and will be needed;
- manage employment expenditure by anticipating changes;
- ensure that sufficient and appropriate training and development is provided;
- cope with peaks and troughs in supply and demand for different skills;
- deliver an improved service to customers;
- reduce employee turnover;
- implement diversity policies;
- manage staff performance and sickness absence.

Discussion themes
What is a skills audit?
'Workforce planning is only needed by big businesses.' Discuss this statement.
Explain why Barclays is cutting its workforce. What are the consequences of undertaking a radical workforce plan? https://uk.finance.yahoo.com/news/barclays-planning-slash-workforce-075134891.html

Chapter 25
Recruitment

Vacancies in a business can arise for a number of reasons. These include: expansion, retirement of existing workers, workers leaving for a new job elsewhere, workers having promotion or temporary reasons such as maternity leave. For small businesses recruitment is often a simple process. Managers and business owners often understand in detail what tasks are involved in a job and will know the type of person required to perform the job well. Often finding someone to fill a vacancy can also be relatively simple, with word of mouth or the job centre sufficient to find suitable applicants.

The formal recruitment process

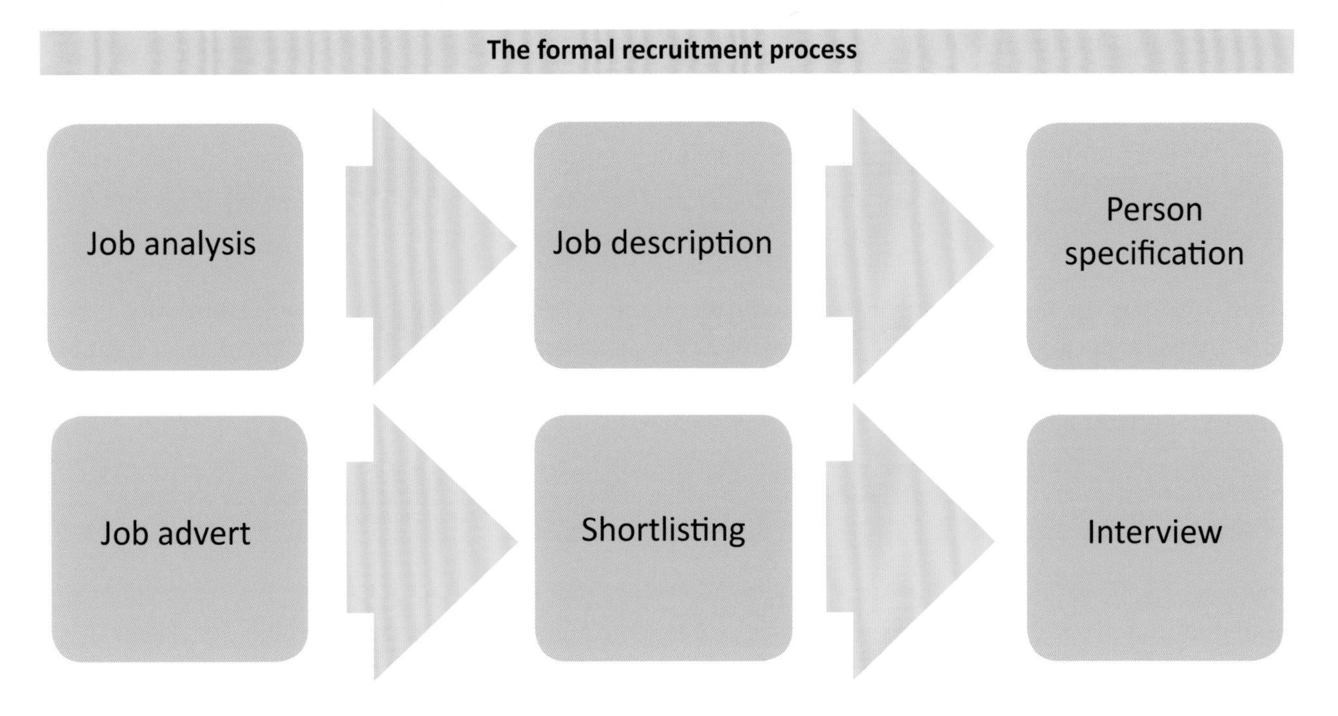

For larger businesses there is a more formal recruitment process that needs to be followed.

The first stage is the completion of a job analysis. A **job analysis** is the process which identifies and determines in detail the particular duties and requirements of the job, and also what the position requires in terms of aptitudes, knowledge, and skills.

The job analysis allows the completion of a **job description**. Every job should have some form of job description. This explains the tasks involved in the job, the job title, responsibilities attached to the job, place of work, and employment conditions (holidays, salary etc.). Job descriptions need to be updated regularly, as jobs often evolve, as those doing the job become more experienced and skilled.

The next stage in the recruitment process, after preparing or updating a job description is the preparation of a **person specification**. This describes the skills, knowledge and experience needed by an individual to complete the job. It will detail educational requirements, experience and skills needed, perhaps physical attributes (e.g. for a fireman) and important aspects of personality required.

Once the job analysis, job description and person specification have been prepared the business can start to look for the right candidate.

Internal methods of recruitment

This method involves finding someone already employed by an organisation to fill a vacancy. Internal vacancies may simply be placed on a notice board, published on an intranet or advertised in an in-house magazine. Therefore the cost of recruitment is reduced: there will be no need for external advertisements and all the administrative costs and time involved in dealing with applications. There are several other advantages too. These include the fact that the applicants will already know the business and its methods of working and are therefore likely to settle into the job a great deal easier than external candidates. Another benefit is that internal recruitment may increase motivation of the workforce.

There are, however, problems with using internal recruitment. Firstly, there will be a limited range of applicants and the potential of finding new talent will be reduced. There is also less likelihood of an input of new ideas and methods of working into the organisation. As one person is promoted then another vacancy is created, which then has to be filled.

External methods of recruitment

There are a wide variety of methods that businesses can use to find suitable candidates. The actual method or methods used will depend on the type of vacancy and the number of vacancies available. For skilled and professional workers it may be appropriate to use recruitment agencies that are specialised in finding specific workers for specific tasks. Headhunters can be used when very senior management positions arise. Headhunters will use their knowledge of the employment market to find suitable candidates. For semi-skilled workers advertisements in local and national newspapers may be appropriate. The job centre can be used for administrative and unskilled workers. Where people are needed to enter management training programmes, often the most suitable method for finding a good pool of candidates is to use recruitment programmes at universities. Many of these recruitment methods are expensive but can help ensure that the right candidates are found.

Applications

Applications are normally made through the use of the business's own application form, often backed by a letter of application and a CV. It will be the job of the personnel department to initially sort through the applications and to produce a shortlist for interview.

Interviews

Interviews are best carried out by a panel consisting of a specialist personnel manager, a manager from the department the person is applying to and an independent member. This would allow an all-round picture of the candidate to be determined. The objective of an interview is for the candidate to be able to explain their suitability for the job and for the interviewers to gather as much relevant information about the candidate as possible.

Telephone interviews

Telephone interviews are interviews held over the phone rather than face-to-face. They will usually be carried out by a member of the company's human resources team. A telephone interview will usually be given to candidates who have passed the online application and/or psychometric test stage of the recruitment process, and are used to select applicants to be invited to a face-to-face interview. Telephone interviews are normally used by the large corporate recruiters rather than small or medium-sized businesses. Telephone interviews are used by all kinds of employers – banks, accountancy and law firms, consultancies, retailers, manufacturing companies etc.

Advantages of telephone interviews:

- They are time and cost-effective – most last about 20–25 minutes.
- They test the candidate's verbal communication skills and telephone technique.
- They can test the candidate's commitment – they often involve questions to check if candidates have researched the employer.

The actual choice of candidates may not just depend on interview but the application process can also contain tests for personality and aptitude.

Work trials

A work trial is a way of trying out a potential employee before offering them a job. They are the ultimate extended interview. Work trials can last up to 30 days (but normally perhaps a week), and during the trial the potential employee will be introduced to the core tasks of the job and try to complete them effectively. Work trials are often used to help people back into employment, and are commonly used for unskilled work. A successful work trial is expected to lead to employment.

Selection exercises – personality tests and aptitude and ability tests

Personality tests – psychometric testing

A psychometric test is a way of assessing a person's personality in a measured and structured way. This type of test is used by employers to help them identify candidates with suitable personality traits for the job. They help employers decide whether candidates have the enthusiasm and motivation that the employer is looking for and whether they are likely to fit in with the organisation's culture and methods of working.

It is common for graduate employers to use psychometric tests as part of their selection process. Organisations believe tests help them recruit the right people with the right mix of abilities and personal qualities. They are also useful for 'sifting out' a large number of applicants at an early stage and so saving the employers both time and money.

Aptitude and ability tests

Aptitude and ability tests can take a variety of forms. However, whatever type is used they are designed to test the ability of the candidate to complete the core tasks of the job. Within a manufacturing workplace the test is likely to take the form of work sample tests. These involve completing a sample of the work that the candidate will be expected to do. Alternatively, for a job in accounts, suitability is more likely to be checked through the use of a numeric ability test. This test will include basic arithmetic, number sequences and simple mathematics.

Selection methods
http://bit.ly/1nilBTu

Induction

Once candidates have been selected and before they formally start their job of work they should go through an induction process. Induction involves introducing a new employee to the workplace. They will become familiar with the administrative systems of the employer and be introduced to work colleagues and direct line management. The objective of induction is to familiarise new employees with their place of employment and to make them feel more comfortable in their new employment. A successful induction programme will motivate staff and reduce the risk of staff leaving at an early stage.

Discussion themes
Explain the recruitment process.
'The advantages of internal recruitment outweigh the disadvantages.' Discuss this statement.
Describe the different selection exercises a business can use to select the right candidate for a job.
Evaluate the importance of having good recruitment and selection procedures to a business and its stakeholders.
The pros and cons of internal recruitment (PDF). http://www.msubillings.edu/BusinessFaculty/larsen/MGMT321/Recruiting%20-%20internal%20v%20 external%20hiring.pdf

Chapter 26
Training

Training provides workers with knowledge and skills which enable them to perform their jobs more effectively. Modern theories of motivation argue that training is one of the keys to successful motivation of workers. Without training, workers are unlikely to reach their potential and feel let down by their employers.

Most large organisations now have structured training programmes, designed to satisfy both the organisation's needs for skilled workers and employees' needs for advancement and achievement in work.

Types of training

Training can be on-the-job, learning by doing – with on-the-job training an employee is shown or taught how to complete tasks by a more experienced worker. This takes place in the workplace.

Mentoring, job rotation, apprenticeships and graduate training schemes can all be regarded as forms of on-the-job training.

Training can be off-the-job – where the employee attends college to study for qualifications such as NVQs or MBAs, or through the use of internal (in-house) courses structured directly for the needs of the business.

Benefits of on-the-job training

- no disruption to the workplace through worker absence;
- low cost;
- training is directly relevant to the job.

Costs of on-the-job training

- management time is spent planning the training;
- management or supervisor time is spent doing the training;
- potential reduction in the quality of output as trainees complete work.

Benefits of off-the-job training

- a wider range of skills are gathered;
- input of new ideas into the workplace;
- employees gain worthwhile qualifications.

Costs of off-the-job training

- lost production and disruption to workplace when employees are absent;
- actual costs of courses;
- workers may seek to use their qualifications to seek better employment elsewhere.

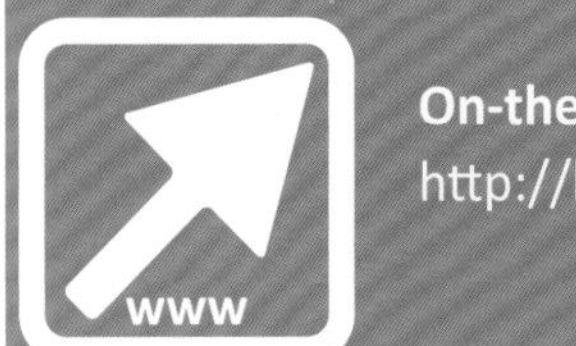

On-the-job, off-the-job training
http://bit.ly/1JfKGtf

Why businesses train

- all businesses need to have workers with skills to ensure that production or provision of service is of the best **quality** possible;
- training workers creates **flexibility** – workers are now able to adapt to change more easily and contribute more to the business;
- training **motivates**, thereby allowing workers to reach their potential and contribute fully to the business;
- **job enrichment** and **job enlargement** can be implemented if workers are given the right training;
- training can assist in **retaining high-quality staff** who might otherwise leave;
- training can also be helpful when **recruiting** as potential employees might be attracted by the opportunities offered.

Retraining

Training is an ongoing process. Employees often need to be retrained to cope with the changing working environment. Changes in the working environment can be due to:

- new health and safety requirements;
- new working practices;
- new technology;
- new government training schemes.

Apprenticeships

Apprenticeships are formal agreements between an employer and a young employee that commits the employer to facilitate training and workplace experience for the employee. This will lead to a recognised qualification that is accepted throughout the relevant industry. All apprentices are paid a wage which is dependent on age.

Below is a link to government information about the benefits of apprenticeships and the opportunities they provide:

https://www.gov.uk/government/publications/a-parents-guide-to-apprenticeships

In-service training
http://bit.ly/1JfKKZX

Discussion themes
How can employees be trained?
Why is training an expense businesses are prepared to pay?
What are apprenticeships? What are the benefits to the employee and the business of participating in an apprenticeship scheme?
Use the website to summarise the benefits to businesses, the employee and the economy of effective training. What services do they offer? http://www.skillstraininguk.com/overview-1

Chapter 27
Appraisal

Built into the principle of effective Human Resource Management is the idea that staff should be regularly appraised by their direct line manager. This means there will be regular meetings (once every six months or on an annual basis) in which the staff member's performance is analysed, normally against performance targets. An employee may be judged on a range of tasks completed: for example, number of complaints, performance of subordinates and management of budget. As well as these measures of performance, training needs are discussed and career prospects examined. Within the staff appraisal interview bonus earnings may also be set. Staff appraisal is sometimes referred to as performance appraisal or performance management.

Staff appraisal does have both supporters and critics.

The supporters argue that staff appraisal:

- motivates;
- improves performance;
- allows the setting of achievable targets;
- identifies training needs;
- identifies potential;
- allows those who understand the job (i.e. the line managers) to give a value to the work done;
- enables achievable bonuses to be earned.

Critics argue that the staff appraisal system:

- can cause tension in the workplace (especially in relation to the allocation ofbonuses);
- puts workers under tremendous pressure to keep improving performance;
- places too much power in the hands of line managers who may be ill-equipped to use the system effectively or, alternatively, abuse the power the system gives them.

Also managers can have conflicting roles. At one time a supporter and developer of staff, at other times responsible for reprimanding and disciplining staff.

The success of staff appraisal in the workplace also depends on acting upon staff problems which are highlighted – if problems are not followed up, and feedback provided, demotivation can quickly occur. To be successful, appraisal systems must be based on clear criteria for appraisal (set, agreed and understood targets) and managers must be trained to solve problems that can arise as a result of any poor performance indicated in appraisals. Employees must be encouraged to fully participate in the system by talking about their problems, their own failings and adopting methods of resolving problems and improving performance.

Self and peer assessment

Self-assessment is the process of having the employee:

- critically reflecting upon their own performance;
- recording their progress;
- suggesting targets for the future.

Perhaps the most important benefit of self-assessment is that the process encourages self-reflection: 'Am I doing the best job I can and how could I improve?'

Peer assessment refers to the process of having employees of a similar level of responsibility critically comment upon the performance of a co-worker and perhaps suggest methods of improvement. This method helps employees learn from each other and it may be less critical (softer) than appraisal by managers. This is useful when large groups require appraisal and may be helpful as workers naturally compare their performance with that of their co-workers.

360 degree appraisal

360 degree appraisals involve the appraised staff member receiving feedback from people (named or anonymous) whose views are considered helpful and relevant. This could come from staff or other stakeholders who are in a position to make judgements on performance – fellow workers, line managers, junior staff, team members, customers and suppliers. It could also include self-assessment to give a complete appraisal of the individual. The method should provide a full (360 degree) picture of performance and may help a business when making decisions related to the promotion of individuals.

Discussion themes
'The best person to appraise an employee is the employee's line manager.' To what extent do you agree with this statement?
How can performance appraisal help the employee in their job?
What are the possible dangers to a business of operating an appraisal system?

Chapter 28
Workforce performance

It is important for a business to measure the effectiveness of its workforce. When managers examine workforce performance they are examining the effectiveness of human resource management (HRM) policies. Some elements of workforce performance cannot be directly measured – such as motivation and commitment. However, there are a number of ways of more precisely measuring the effectiveness of HRM policies and workforce performance. The most popular of these are:

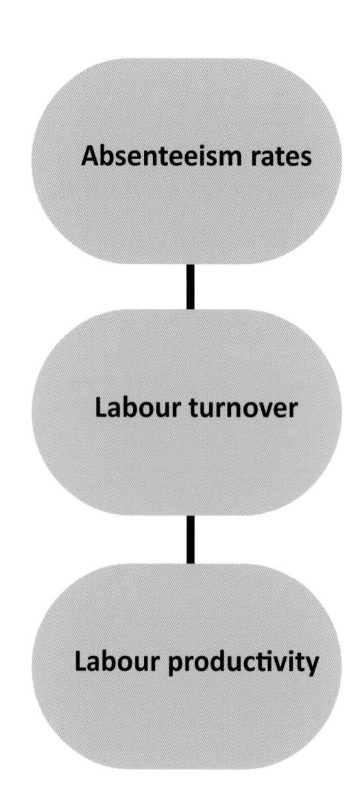

Absenteeism rates

Absence from the workforce can occur for a wide variety of reasons. Whatever the reason it is a problem for businesses of all sizes and it needs to be carefully monitored. If an employee misses 13 working days out of 253 working days in a year, the absenteeism rate for that individual would be over 5%. To calculate a business's absenteeism rates take the total number of workers (say 300 workers) and multiply by the number of working days in a year (this varies from job to job, but is typically 253 days per year) – this gives the total number of working days as 75 900. If there was a total of 980 sick days taken in the year, the business's absenteeism rate would be 1.29%. A high level of absenteeism may be an indicator of dissatisfaction and demotivation in the workplace. Whatever the reason, a business needs to address the issue as the impact of absenteeism is never positive. Absenteeism also increases costs for a business and may impact on the performance of the business, such as missed phone calls or poor quality service.

$$\frac{\textbf{Total number of staff absence days over a year}}{\textbf{Total number of working days that should have been worked}} \times 100$$

Approximately 40 million days are lost each year in the UK due to workplace absenteeism. A total of 93% of employees say that colds and flu are the reason for being away from work. However, research indicates that in reality at least half of all workplace absence has absolutely nothing whatsoever to do with health. In fact workers may decide to stay away from the office for a variety of work, personal or domestic issues. These include bullying in the workplace, responsibility for children or elderly relatives, job demotivation, low pay and the occasional hangover.

Labour turnover

This is a measure of the rate at which employees are leaving an organisation. Some businesses will have a naturally high level of staff turnover – these might include direct sales organisations and fast-food outlets, where staff turnover might be as high as 60% per annum. In other types of businesses staff turnover is much lower; for example, banks generally experience an annual staff turnover of around 5%.

The percentage staff turnover can be measured by dividing the number of leavers by the average number of full-time employees over a given period.

$$\frac{\textbf{Number of staff leaving}}{\textbf{Average number of staff employed}} \quad \textbf{x 100}$$

A business has 11 000 staff of whom 550 leave in one year. What is the rate of staff turnover?

$$\frac{550}{11\ 000} \times \frac{100}{1} = 5\%$$

A refinement of this measure would be to examine staff turnover among core workers: i.e. those who are regarded as critical to the success of the company. The same formula as above would be used, but now we only measure turnover in a specific group. The advantage of this method is that it focuses on the important members of staff, whilst examining turnover in the whole organisation might be a less meaningful exercise.

The 'call centre' industry is one of the worst for both staff turnover and absenteeism, with a staff turnover rate of 25% and an absenteeism rate of 35% (one in three days missed from work compared to a national average of 3%.

Labour productivity

Productivity is a measurement of the efficiency with which a business turns production inputs into output. Labour productivity is the most common measure – output per worker. It is a very important measure because of the impact on labour costs per unit produced. Higher productivity means lower labour costs and, as a result, greater competitiveness. For example, the automobile industry measures the output of cars per worker per year. If HRM policies are working, productivity should improve; assuming that capital investment is on par with competitors, productivity should be as good as, or better than, competitors.

$$\frac{\textbf{Total output per period of time}}{\textbf{Average number of employees per period of time}}$$

Discussion themes
What is the difference between labour turnover and labour productivity?
How could a business reduce a high absenteeism rate?
'A business should always be concerned if it has a high absenteeism and labour turnover rate.' Discuss this statement.

Chapter 29
Organisational design

All but the smallest businesses will have a recognisable internal structure and there are a wide variety of structural types that could possibly be adopted by any business. The form that a business's internal structure takes will depend on a number of factors.

These factors include:

- the views and philosophy of management;
- the need for different communication systems;
- the industry within which the business operates;
- the traditions of the business;
- the skills of the workforce.

Whatever the influence and interaction of each of these factors, the outcome will always result in the creation of a structure made up of layers of hierarchy, spans of control, chains of command, communication pathways and levels of responsibility. It is these component parts that make up organisational design.

Factors that determine internal structure

- **Views of management**. The type of manager that operates within the business will have a large impact on the internal structure of the business. Managers with a democratic leadership style will encourage workers to take responsibility; whilst managers with an autocratic leadership style will prefer a recognisable hierarchical structure.
- **Communication systems**. Where communication is controlled and closely monitored, the business structure is likely to contain many layers with narrow spans of control and definite paths of responsibility. However, where more open and free communication is encouraged, the business structure is likely to be less hierarchical and more flexible.
- **The industry**. Retailing encourages a hierarchical structure, with clear-cut responsibilities and chains of command. In other industries, such as software development, the boundaries of responsibility are less clear and the chains of command tend to be much shorter.
- **Traditions of the business**. The standard pyramid-shaped hierarchical structure is one that many businesses develop as they grow. Often businesses that have been owned by the government for many years have a traditional structure: when privatised these businesses find many difficulties in changing this hierarchical structure. Other businesses, often in the 'new economy', work towards achieving a less rigid organisational structure, consisting of fewer layers of hierarchy.
- **Skills of the workforce**. The more highly skilled the workforce, the more likely they are to need less supervision. This results in a flatter, more open structure where involvement in the decision-making process is encouraged at all levels.

The component parts of internal structure

Layers of hierarchy

This is the management structure of an organisation and indicates who is responsible to whom. For example, in the police force, there is a chain of command all the way from Chief Constable down to Constable. In between we have Assistant Chief Constable, Deputy Assistant Chief Constable, Chief Superintendent, Superintendent, Chief Inspector, Inspector and Sergeant. There are nine layers or levels of hierarchy in this organisation.

Chains of command

These are the paths along which communication takes place and instructions or orders are passed down. Using the police force as an example, the Chief Constable may make a decision to stamp out begging. This instruction is passed down through the layers of authority and decisions will be made as to what methods will be used to carry out the policy. The constables, who will have responsibility for carrying out the task of removing beggars from the streets, will eventually be ordered to carry out the policy using the methods devised by their superiors in the chain of command.

Levels of responsibility

Each layer of the hierarchy will have its own level of responsibility. The amount of responsibility and the freedom to make decisions based on this responsibility will depend on the amount of control that has been delegated from above. The amount of delegated control will depend on business structure, style of management and the type of business involved.

Span of control

The span of control tells us how many workers are directly responsible to a manager or supervisor. When there has been a high level of delegation the span of control is often wide. Workers are trusted to achieve quality and complete their tasks without constant supervision or monitoring. A narrower span of control operates in strictly hierarchical organisations where control is tight and centralised.

Typical organisational structures

Traditional hierarchical structure

The hierarchy below is an example of the traditional pyramid-shaped hierarchy. Although only three layers are shown, there are many levels or layers to the hierarchy and the span of control is narrow at the top, but will widen somewhat at the bottom where supervisors' key role is to monitor performance. The path in red is one typical chain of command. At the top of the hierarchy are the senior management. At the bottom of the hierarchy are the shop floor workers; in between there are layers of middle management and supervisors. Functional departments in large organisations have been typically organised in this way. This type of organisational structure is often referred to as a 'tall' structure.

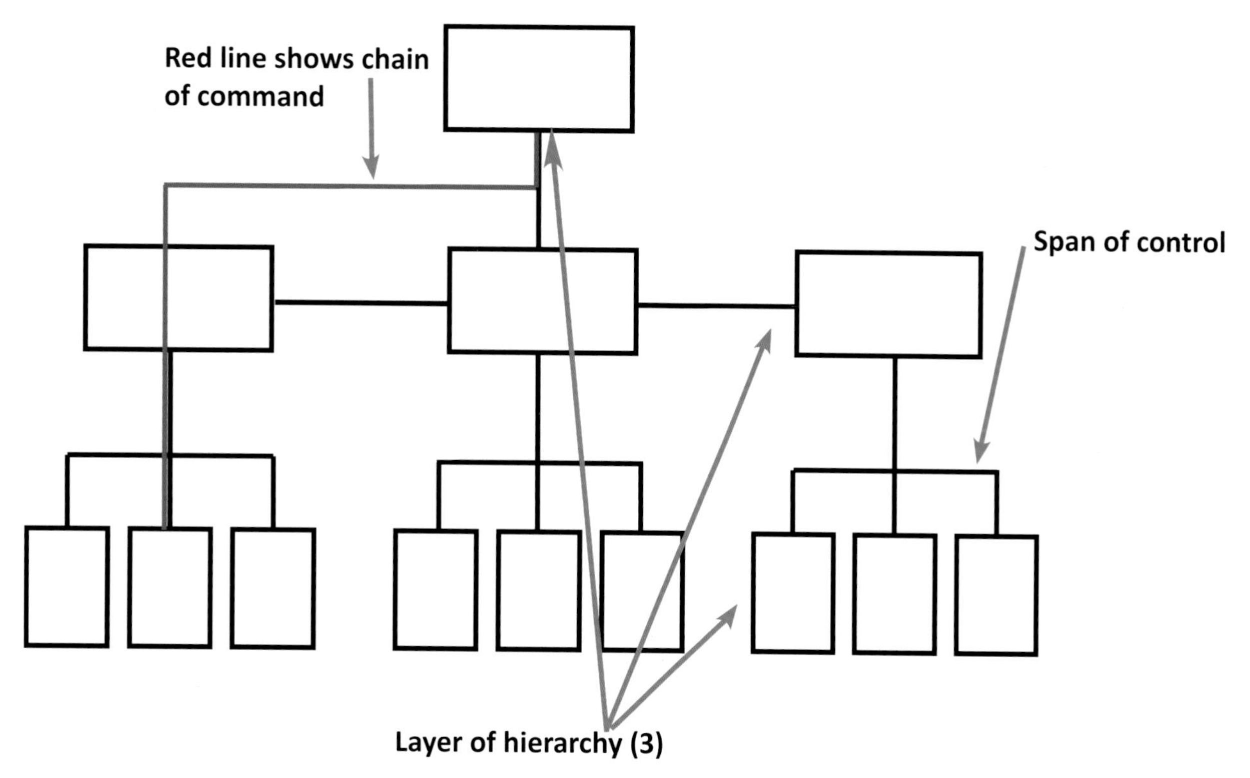

This form of hierarchy does have advantages:

- Control is at the centre, and senior management fully understand exactly who does what, and what their responsibilities are.
- Paths of communication and responsibility are clearly defined.
- Departments understand their position in relation to other departments within the organisation.
- Each worker knows how they fit into the organisational structure.

Possible disadvantages:

- Senior management are distanced from those who implement decisions. What senior managers perceive as being the case may, in reality, be very different.
- Vertical communication is difficult, with information that is received by management distorted by the layers it must pass through. Very long chains of communication could even mean that instructions are out of date by the time they are received.
- Communication between different departments is hampered by the lack of direct contact between departments.

Flatter hierarchical structure

Below is an example of a flatter organisational structure. The span of control is wider, the chain of command is shorter and there are fewer layers in the hierarchy.

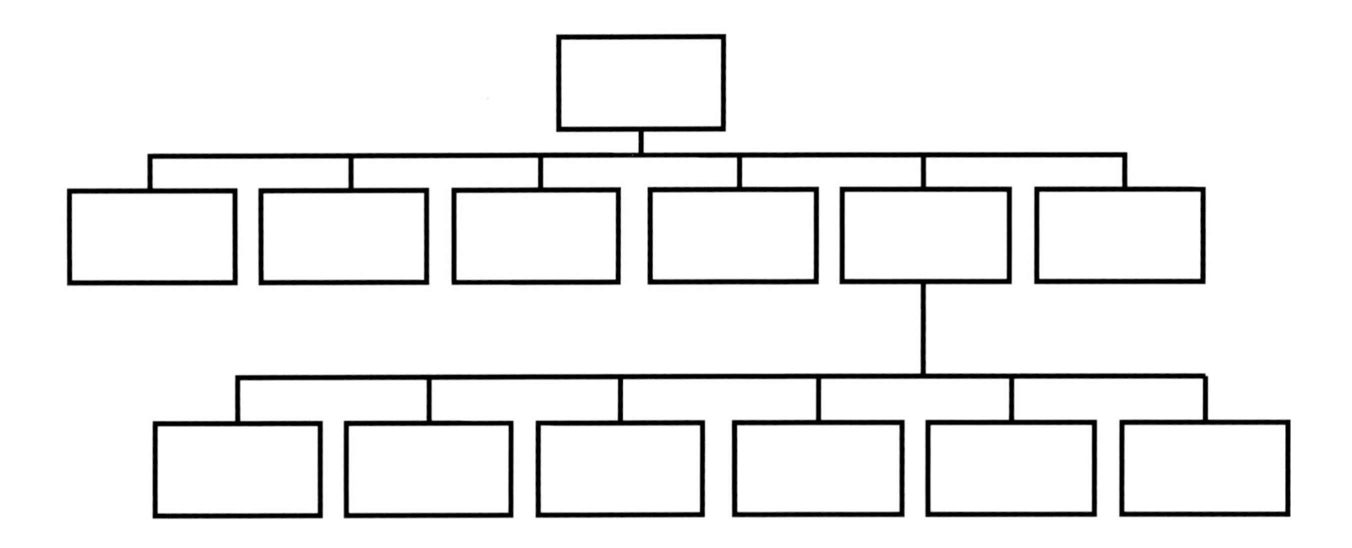

If existing traditional businesses wish to achieve this structure, **delayering** must occur. Delayering means the removal of whole layers of hierarchy and management. This is normally achieved through compulsory redundancy programmes.

Advantages of a flatter organisational structure:

- increased motivation as a result of the delegation of authority;
- decisions are made more quickly by those nearest the 'ground';
- communication is quicker and suffers less distortion;
- empowerment of workers.

Disadvantages are:

- loss of central control of the workforce;
- different departments may not be working to the same objectives.

The matrix structure

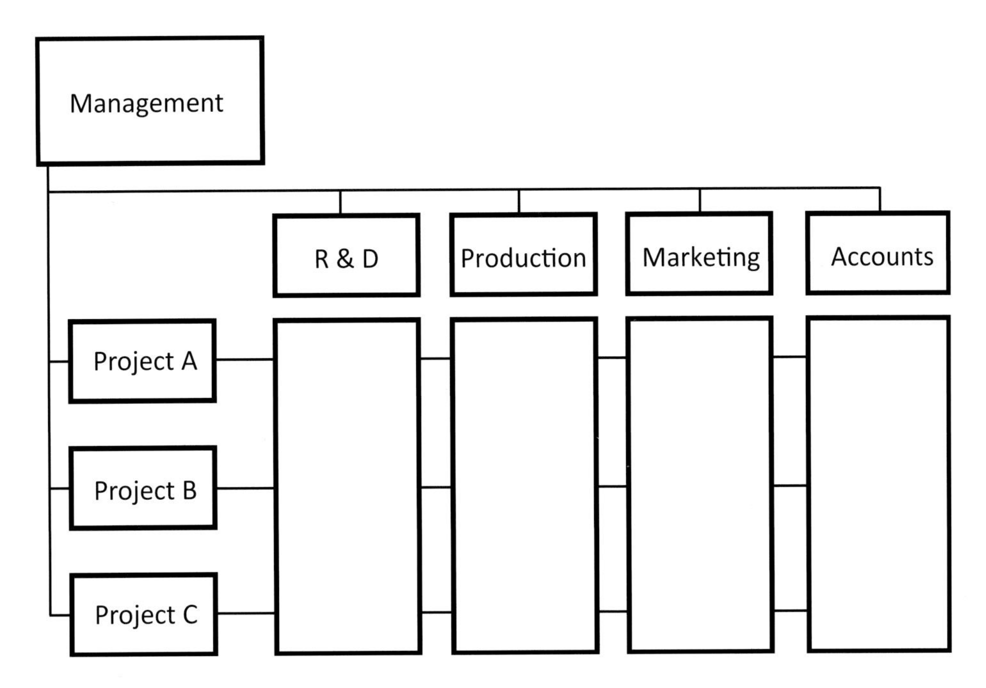

Matrix structures attempt to organise the management of different tasks in a way that cuts across traditional departmental boundaries. This structure enables people with particular specialist skills to work together in project teams. In the example above, Project A could be the formation of a new product development team. It might consist of a designer from the R&D department, an engineer from Production, a researcher from the Marketing department and a cost accountant from the Accounts department. Each individual in the team will have their own responsibility for certain aspects of the project but they will be working together to achieve a specific objective. In the diagram above three projects are ongoing: this means that more people will have the opportunity to use their abilities. However, this does mean that each member of a project team has two bosses and this can be problematic.

The matrix structure has a number of advantages:

- It allows individuals with specific skills to contribute to a number of different projects.
- It breaks down barriers to communication and ensures that projects can be better coordinated.
- It helps ideas and innovation spread throughout the business.
- There is more efficient use of human resources. The structure can improve flexibility and the motivation of employees.

Possible disadvantages:

- Defining what each employee's main responsibilities are is difficult – being answerable to two bosses may put a lot of strain on individuals. Placing too great a burden on individuals may slow down decision-making.
- Project management using a matrix structure can be expensive because extra support systems, such as ICT and office staff, may be required.
- Coordinating a team drawn from a number of different departments may be difficult as the culture and methods of operation in each department may be very different.

Each of these alternative systems has been designed with one overall objective – to improve efficiency of the organisation. It is still rare to find business organisations that have completely abandoned traditional structures; instead it is much more likely to find alternative structures operating within the hierarchy. Examples might be cell working or quality circles. These help break down barriers and overcome many of the problems that exist in traditional hierarchies.

Discussion themes
Explain what is meant by organisation by function.
Why might a wide span of control cause problems for a business?
What are the advantages and disadvantages of a matrix structure?
'Empowering workers through delayering brings more benefits than costs.' How far do you agree with this statement?
Given that traditional hierarchies can stifle innovation and communication, suggest methods of solving these problems.

Chapter 30 Motivation

Motivation theory examines the different ideas that have evolved or been proposed over the last century, each of which propose different methods and techniques of getting the best performance from the workforce. Effective motivation creates the desire and energy to complete tasks involved in a job to the highest possible standard. Motivation creates commitment to the job and the employer.

The following ideas and theories of motivation offer differing (but sometimes overlapping) philosophies for creating a motivated workforce:

- Taylor's theory of scientific management
- Mayo and the Hawthorne experiments
- Maslow's hierarchy of needs
- Herzberg's two-factor theory
- Vroom, Porter and Lawler's expectancy theories

Taylor's theory of scientific management – the science of work

Frederick Winslow Taylor, who wrote in the late nineteenth and early twentieth centuries, developed the idea of work study or time and motion study. Taylor's investigations into how jobs were performed allowed him to break tasks down into their basic components. He was then able to design jobs so that completion of the tasks was done in as simple and efficient a manner as possible.

In Taylor's view, workers can produce more output if responsibility for decision-making and planning are removed. Workers should not have to think, they should just do. His observations also indicated that a consistent approach by workers was the best way of achieving this. He argued that in each workplace the methods used by the most efficient workers should be utilised by all workers. Therefore, workers should be trained to work to the model used by those who produce most output. This idea of scientific management takes what is called a 'task-orientated' approach to managing workers. This means that the workers are just thought of as 'machines' for completing tasks.

Scientific management in practice

Taylor's ideas of scientific management based motivation on financial rewards. When applied to the workplace, there are several features that characterise scientific management. These are:

- workers are paid for carrying out specific tasks – they are not paid for thinking;
- they are paid for levels of output produced; this involves the use of piece-rate payments;
- there is a tall hierarchy within organisations, with little scope for upward communication;
- the best (most efficient) method of working is to be adopted by all workers;
- close supervision of workers and monitoring of performance exists.

To quote from Taylor:

> '...what the workmen want from employers beyond anything else is higher wages: what employers want from workmen most of all is low labour costs in manufacture.'

Taylor thought of scientific management as the best way of achieving this. The adoption of his methods led to large increases in productivity and was the foundation of the mass-production techniques applied by Henry Ford and many others. We now, of course, realise that low-cost labour manufacturing may not be the only key to success with the much greater emphasis that is now placed on quality. There is, nonetheless, still a role for scientific management. When competitiveness in labour-intensive industries depends on costs being kept to a minimum, then you will find that the ideas of Taylor are still being used today. Consider fast-food chains, with their 100-page manuals on how to prepare a burger, with little or no responsibility placed on the worker apart from maintaining a level of output. Many global fast-food chains utilise a scientific management approach by producing the same product on high streets all over the world.

Mayo and the Hawthorne experiments

Elton Mayo and his team worked in the late 1920s and early 1930s at General Electric Company's Hawthorne works. In a workplace investigative study they were trying to develop Taylor's scientific principles. However, through their work they discovered that group dynamics could be more important than any form of financial motivation in determining the pattern of work and working practices. This research also showed that the way groups of people are treated, and the way that they expect to be treated, affected the way that they worked.

The aim of the study was to establish the impact of different conditions of work on employee productivity. Initially, Mayo examined the effect of changes in the factory environment such as lighting and humidity. He then went on to study the effect of changes in employment arrangements such as breaks, hours and managerial leadership. His main conclusion was that the prevailing view of the time, that people went to work purely for money, was flawed. Work meant much more to people than simply earning money. It was first and foremost a group activity in which other people and their behaviour affected how well people worked. Morale and productivity were affected not so much by the conditions in which people worked but by the recognition they received. The rises in productivity were achieved under the interested eye of the observers; not because the conditions made the workers feel good but because the workers felt valued.

As a result of the experiments Mayo suggested that motivation at work was promoted by such factors as:

- greater communication;
- better teamwork;
- showing an interest in others;
- involving others in decision-making;
- ensuring the wellbeing of others;
- making work interesting and non-repetitive.

From Mayo's work the **Human Relations School** of motivation and management developed. The followers of this school of management regard workers and managers as interacting groups. As long as the form of interaction is tailored to the dynamics of each group, then this interactive relationship can only be of benefit to the business. Communication is now seen as important – explaining the importance of workers' roles and listening to their views.

The Human Relations School today

Group dynamics today have a very important part to play in the workplace. Managers have discovered that small groups with effective leaders are a way of transforming working practices within organisations. Working as a team allows the breaking down of traditional hierarchies and allows each worker to feel part of a small work group, motivated to achieve within their own section of the business. Managers who wish to fully gain from the benefits promised by the Human Relations School must develop an adaptive approach. This means that they must learn to treat different groups of workers in different ways. They must apply approaches, motivational methods and communication systems suited to the needs of each group within their organisation.

Maslow's hierarchy of needs

All humans have needs. The basic needs are regarded as warmth, food, clothing and shelter. These basic needs used to be what we needed to survive and for many thousands of years it was all that most humans could hope to obtain. The modern working man and woman are very different. Abraham Maslow, an American psychologist who worked in the middle part of the twentieth century, argued that we all have a hierarchy of needs. He proposed that we all wish to attain the highest level of this hierarchy. However, before we can reach this highest level the lower levels of needs must be securely in place.

Maslow's hierarchy

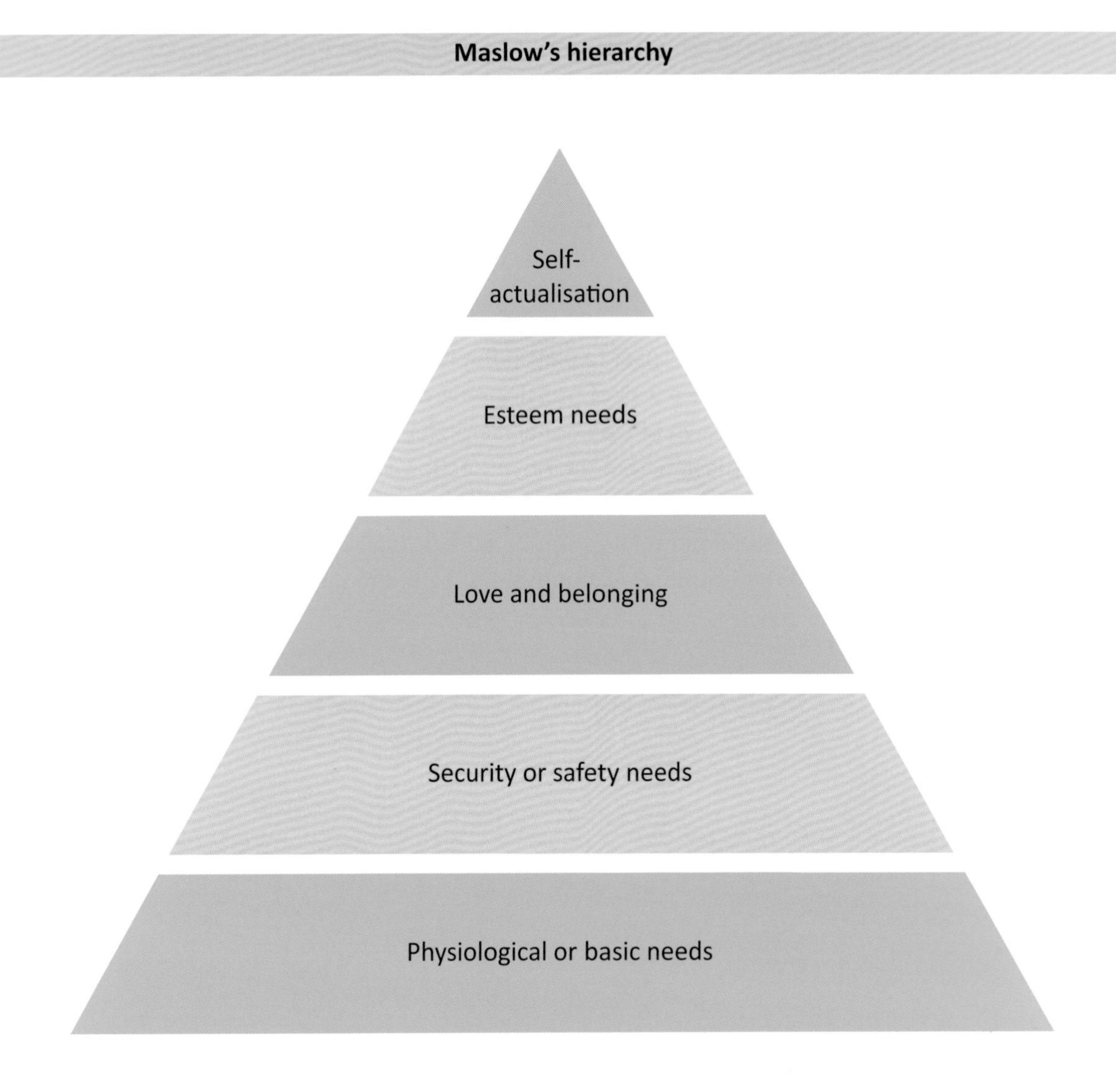

Satisfying the needs

What workers need		How employers satisfy needs
Reaching personal goals, self-expression	Self-actualisation	Promotion, control over job, empowerment, more responsibility
Feeling good about achievements	Esteem needs	Positive communication from management, bonuses, job enrichment
Interaction, trust and acceptance, leisure time	Love and belonging	Group working, leisure facilities, holidays, good communication
Confidence in the future, protection from danger	Security or safety needs	Contract of employment, pension scheme, safe working conditions
Food, warmth, clothing, shelter, rest	Physiological or basic needs	A living wage, good working conditions

When this hierarchy is applied to the workplace managers must examine how they can satisfy the needs of employees.

To satisfy the basic needs of food, warmth, clothing and shelter, workers must have an income; so a reasonable level of pay is a requirement to satisfy these needs.

The next level, security, means that workers must be able to predict their future with some degree of certainty. To allow employees to do this, managers should offer contracts of work, some form of sickness benefits and pension schemes.

The next level, love and belonging, can be satisfied by designing jobs so that they involve interactive work – this is group working again. There should be an opportunity for social interaction in the workplace, such as meeting places or provision of a social facility such as a club. Workers also need to be able to spend time with their families, so social working hours and a decent holiday entitlement are a must.

The fourth level, esteem needs, can to an extent be satisfied by communication from managers assuring the workers that they are doing good jobs. There should be the opportunity for workers to be able to train, to improve their prospects and improve the quality of their work. They must be able to give some input into the decision-making process. One way of achieving this is through participation in quality circles. Also job enrichment is an important part of satisfying this need.

At the highest level, self-actualisation, workers achieve what they are capable of doing. The key to this is promotion. Workers should be able to climb to a level within the organisation that enables them to demonstrate their talents in a job they are most suited to. They should be given as much freedom over their tasks as possible; they should be allowed to do the job in the way that they know best. The ideas of empowerment in the workplace relate to this.

Managers must consider whether all workers need to have all levels satisfied. It would be an expensive business to satisfy all the needs of all employees, up to and including self-actualisation. What managers must be aware of is the trade-off between extra quality and output that comes with satisfaction of each level of needs, and the cost of satisfying these needs. For example, it may be realistic to satisfy only basic and security needs for the mass of a business's workers, and concentrate on satisfying the higher needs of those workers who are core to the future success of the business.

Herzberg's two-factor theory

Frederick Herzberg carried out investigations into what caused satisfaction and dissatisfaction at work. Herzberg wanted to focus on the growing pool of white-collar workers and therefore used groups of accountants and engineers for his research. The method of investigation was by interview. The work was carried out in the late 1960s and he was interested in applying his findings so that improvements in job design could occur. If implemented, these improvements would lead to increased quality and levels of output.

The two factors

Analysis of Herzberg's research shows that satisfaction in work can be caused by a number of motivating factors, or 'motivators'.

Herzberg's motivators

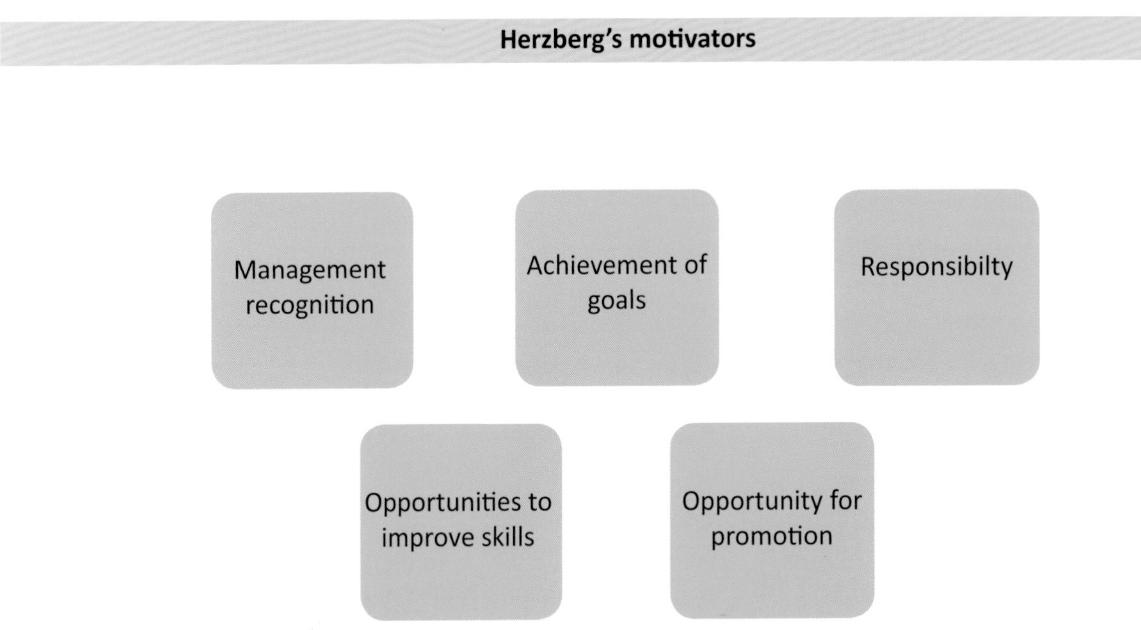

Also the research demonstrated that they were a number of factors that caused dissatisfaction. This was caused by a number of 'hygiene factors'.

Herzberg's hygiene factors

Poor working conditions

Lack of status

Unsatisfactory wages

Lack of job security

Poor workplace relationships

Application of the two factors

Herzberg said that managers must firstly provide the type of workplace and conditions of work that prevented dissatisfaction, i.e. make sure that hygiene factors are satisfied. Only when these are provided can motivation of workers happen. The basic tools to provide motivation are effective communication and training. If we look at the factors that cause motivation, we see that many of these are directly related to communication and training.

Managers should employ workers with the view that they should be trained to perform tasks they were not capable of doing at the time of employment. Jobs should be enriched progressively to allow factors that motivate to be achieved. This idea of job design is crucial to the successful use of Herzberg's ideas. Effective, flexible and challenging job design will allow workers to achieve goals in the workplace. Managers should respond to the achievement of these goals by recognising what has been achieved and communicating this recognition to the workers. Effective job design means allowing job enrichment and the opportunity for achievement in tasks. The job must allow decision-making to take place and there must be a structure in place that allows advancement/promotion.

There are two major criticisms of this theory. Firstly, the sample was taken among professional workers and skilled engineers and, therefore, the question must arise whether it will apply to semi-skilled or unskilled workers. Secondly, Herzberg ignored the effects of teamwork and the impact that it may have on motivation.

It is worth noting that there is an obvious relationship between the lower levels of Maslow's hierarchy and Herzberg's hygiene factors and between the higher levels of Maslow's hierarchy and Herzberg's motivators.

Vroom, Porter and Lawler's expectancy theories

Victor Vroom was born in Canada in 1932. Having gained a PhD at the University of Michigan, he became a business school professor at the Yale School of Management. His most well-known books are *Work and Motivation, Leadership and Decision Making* and *The New Leadership*.

Vroom assumed that people acted in their own best interests according to their beliefs about the outcomes of their own behaviour. Generally, he believed that people opted to maximise their happiness and minimise their unhappiness.

Vroom's expectancy theory actually has three components to it: valence, instrumentality and expectancy (VIE), all of which relate to an individual person's beliefs rather than to any objective reality.

1. Valence (V): according to Vroom an individual will undertake a task if they believe that they will receive a worthwhile reward as a result. Vroom called this 'valence'. The key thing is that the person expects the reward and that the reward is valued by them. The reward does not have to be monetary. People undertaking charitable work do not usually expect a financial reward. However, they do expect to receive other people's thanks and appreciation, which for them is sufficient reward. For others money is the main motivator. It depends on the individual.

Valence can be either positive or negative. If the expected outcome is favourable it is positively valent for an individual. If the outcome is not to their liking, and something they would rather avoid, it is negatively valent.

2. Instrumentality (I): by instrumentality Vroom meant that an individual needs to believe that a particular action is likely to lead to a particular result. In a work context this means that the individual will be motivated to work hard to achieve a particular target if he or she believes that it will lead to a positively valent result. For example, if the individual believes that their hard work will lead to promotion then they will be motivated to work hard. However, if they feel that, however hard they work, they will not achieve promotion, they will not be motivated to work hard. From an employer's point of view it is important that the employee understands that there is a clear link between effort and reward.

3. Expectancy (E): the third important aspect of motivation was the individual's belief in the likelihood of their being able to achieve the target that has been set for them. If the target was to run 100 metres in under ten seconds, there are very few individuals who would think it worth the effort as there would be little prospect in their achieving it. There may be other reasons why someone would want to run 100 metres but if the sole reason was to achieve a specific reward, then only Usain Bolt and a few others like him would see any point in trying. In a work context it does not make sense for an employer to set targets that employees believe are unachievable, even if the reward is something that the employee considers to be positively valent. It may be that in the future, with training and encouragement, the employee might feel more confident about their ability to achieve the required outcome.

Vroom believed that an individual's motivation was a combination of these three forces V,I and E. For an individual to be motivated they needed to believe that firstly, they could achieve a particular outcome (expectancy), and secondly, that by achieving the outcome (instrumentality) it would result in a positive valency (and not too many negative valencies).

Another example of this might be the student who thinks that getting a good job is important (positively valent) and that working hard to pass their exams will help them to get a good job (instrumentality) and that they also believe that with hard work they are capable of achieving good grades (expectancy).

Porter and Lawler also propose that an individual's motivation is affected by the reward they expect to receive for completing the task. The individual's view of the attractiveness of the possible reward will determine their level of motivation. In addition though, they categorised the reward as intrinsic and extrinsic.

Intrinsic rewards include the positive feelings that the individual experiences from completing the task – e.g. pride, satisfaction. In order to give a job more intrinsic rewards they emphasised the importance of job content. Employers needed to make sure that employees were given tasks that they found interesting and rewarding. The process involves management in job redesign and job enlargement. Job enlargement can be both horizontal, giving the worker more tasks to do, and vertical, giving the worker more control over the job. In Porter and Lawler's opinion vertical job enlargement is the more important of the two. This idea is closely related to the idea of flattening organisations and empowering workers.

Extrinsic rewards are rewards that come from outside the individual, for example material rewards such as pay increases and bonuses. Porter and Lawler realised the importance of consistency and fairness or equity when giving extrinsic rewards. The employee needs to feel that the reward is proportional to their effort, otherwise the result will be to demotivate them. The employee also needs to be aware of a direct link between the goals that they achieve and the reward that they will receive. At the same time the employer must ensure that the worker is given the training and equipment that they need in order to achieve the goals that they have been set.

Financial and non-financial motivation

When we examine methods of motivation that can actually be applied in the workplace, we normally subdivide them into financial and non-financial methods.

Financial methods directly involve monetary rewards e.g. bonuses, pay increases, improved pensions etc.

Non-financial methods, though perhaps indirectly bringing monetary rewards, are targeted at providing psychological benefits for workers.

It must be remembered that both financial and non-financial methods have costs to the employer: either through direct costs such as extra pay, or indirectly through the provision of training or management time.

Financial methods of motivation

Piece rates

The most basic method of payment is a piece rate. When a piece rate is paid workers are paid for each item they produce or for each task completed. This does have advantages in that workers will work as fast as they can to maximise their income and payment is only made when work is completed. However, there are disadvantages for both employer and employee. For the employer there must be a great deal of supervision and checking of quality as workers are motivated to achieve speed of output, not quality of output. From the employees point of view there is no guarantee of income and production may be halted by matters beyond the workers' control.

Wages

Wages are paid hourly, for example £8 an hour, and the vast majority of unskilled workers in the UK are still paid wages. There is some security in being paid a wage and those who earn wages will probably be able to work overtime to increase incomes. Lower levels of Maslow's hierarchy are quite often satisfied by a decent wage, but what does matter is the level of the wage. A minimum wage of £6.70 an hour (1 October 2015) cannot truthfully be regarded as an income likely to provide a decent standard of living. Some people argue that employers should pay a living wage of £7.85 an hour (www.livingwage.org.uk).

For many big businesses there is one large group of manual or production workers who are paid hourly and a group of administrative and marketing workers who are paid a salary. This difference in methods of payment can cause resentment and prevent the breakdown of barriers within businesses. A 'them and us' attitude can be reinforced by the artificially created separation of waged and salaried employees, when in fact the only difference may be that one group wear suits to work and the other does not.

Salaries

Salaries are paid at an annual rate, for example £25 000 per year. Salaried incomes are paid monthly, directly into a bank account. Salaries make good financial sense for businesses because they are paid monthly in arrears which means that workers will have to wait up to a month to receive income for work performed. This leads to an improved cash flow and bank balance for the business. Also it is simpler and safer to pay money by bank transfer rather than in cash. Salaried workers are not normally paid overtime but may receive other financial benefits. This non-payment of overtime does not mean that they do not work more than their contracted hours – they often do, but it does mean that employers may not be liable to pay for this extra work.

Profit-related pay

Profit-related pay links part of an employee's income to the profits of a company. Those who receive profit-related pay will have a lower salary than they might otherwise expect but will benefit overall by receiving a share of company profits.

When profit-related pay schemes were first encouraged during the 1980s it was hoped that they would catch on with all types of worker. However, in the main, they are only applied to senior management; although some businesses, such as Asda and the John Lewis Partnership, have schemes which allow all employees to share in company profits. The major problem in encouraging workers to take part in the schemes is that income is uncertain. Workers may believe that they have little influence on the profitability of the business, so they do not see why their income should fluctuate as profits fluctuate.

Bonus schemes

There are a wide variety of bonus schemes available, each designed to be suitable for different employees doing different jobs.

These schemes include the following:

- Sales bonus – this is normally paid if a sales target has been reached. For sales people this may make up a significant part of their salary.
- Performance bonus – this can be paid to an individual or on a group or factory-wide basis. It is often paid for reaching targets of output and quality. This method of payment is an important part of Human Resource management.
- Christmas bonus – often called the 13th month salary – paid for loyalty to the business. In some countries (for example, Germany) virtually all companies will pay a Christmas bonus.

Fringe benefits

Other forms of financial motivation include company cars, pension schemes, sickness benefits, subsidised meals and travel, and staff discounts. These are often grouped together under the heading of fringe benefits or perks (perquisites). Some of these fringe benefits can be regarded as essential in encouraging the right applicants for certain types of vacancies. For example, a company car is a necessity for anyone working in sales in the financial service business. Senior management in many companies would expect both an upmarket car and private health care.

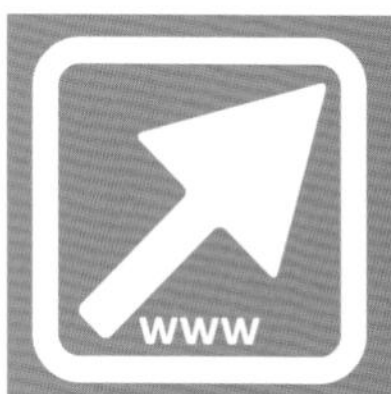

Non-monetary incentives
http://bit.ly/1S3MFSu

Non-financial methods of motivation

The use of non-financial methods of motivation demonstrates attempts by employers to apply the ideas behind the theories of the likes of Mayo, Maslow and Herzberg. Examination of these theories has shown us that motivation to achieve quality of output is best achieved through satisfaction of higher needs (Maslow), awareness of the role of groups in the workplace (Mayo) and the need to provide motivators (Herzberg). The non-financial methods of motivation outlined below can be linked to one of more of these theories.

Job enrichment – This means giving workers more control over the tasks that they complete, and allowing workers to complete tasks that have a meaning and are complete in themselves. For example, a worker who has a job fitting a circuit board to a TV may have his job enriched by testing the board and being able to make adjustments so that the required level of quality is achieved. The ability to do this range of tasks means that the worker becomes more committed to achieving quality. Effective job enrichment depends on workers having interesting tasks to complete. Job design is a key part of Herzberg's ideas.

Job enlargement – Increasing the number of tasks completed by a worker. For example, a secretary previously employed to answer calls might now have duties which include filing, letter-writing etc. This adds interest to the job and involves the employee in a more complete role within the business.

Job rotation – Changing workers' tasks which are completed at regular intervals. This can be as simple as switching places on a production line. The variety adds interest to the job and reduces the number of errors that can arise through boredom.

Job design – Jobs should include complete tasks that are of interest to the worker and challenging, which allow decision-making.

Communication – Communication is a key part of motivation and can take place in a number of ways, e.g. quality circles, works councils, cell working.

Empowerment – This means giving workers the power to control their own jobs, make decisions and implement their own ideas. It is often used in an artificial way; for example, allowing counter workers in burger bars to decide the greeting they use when they meet customers.

Quality circles – These are groups of workers that meet on a regular basis to discuss problems in the manufacturing or service-provision process and offer solutions. They may involve groups of workers from the same department or come from a variety of disciplines. For example, they may include designers, buyers and production workers. It is important that for quality circles to have value the members have the ability and the authority to implement changes suggested.

Training – The provision of a formal training scheme is important. As Herzberg stated, without training, workers will not be able to fulfil their potential. Training can be on-the-job, learning by doing; or off-the-job, such as studying for NVQs at a local college. On-the-job training has costs such as management or supervisor time spent training. Off-the-job training means lost production and disruption. Also the newly-qualified workers may seek to use their qualifications to seek better employment elsewhere.

Flexible working – Allowing workers to have elements of their schedule which are under their control. For example, the opportunity to work from home or have core hours and flexitime options around these.

The single status workplace

When all artificial barriers separating workers have been removed, then the single status workplace can be said to exist. For example, all employees wear the same basic clothes, use the same dining facilities, and have access to the same pension schemes and leisure facilities. This is strongly linked to the higher levels of Maslow.

Problems with implementing non-financial methods of motivation

Existence of Theory X managers – These managers will see no value in using expensive methods of motivation when workers have no commitment to the business or quality of the product.

Cost – All these methods are expensive in terms of management time, systems implementation and training. To effectively use these methods there is a high level of cost. Managers must balance cost against increased output and quality.

External factors – Once workers are used to having their jobs enriched, enlarged etc., it may be difficult to remotivate them when financial circumstances, caused by recession or competitors' actions, force cost-cutting on a business. Unavoidable redundancies can have a negative effect on those workers that remain as they may feel less secure in their jobs.

The structure of the workforce – If a large part of the workforce is not core to producing the added value of the business, there is probably no need to apply many of the methods given above. In the retail, hospitality and tourist industries many workers stay for only a short period of time, so motivating these workers would be very difficult.

Benefits of effective motivation

These may be summarised as follows:

- increased productivity;
- increased quality;
- lower levels of staff turnover;
- improved communication;
- higher levels of innovation;
- greater worker satisfaction;
- lower levels of industrial action;
- improved customer service;
- better reputation – easier to attract quality staff.

Discussion themes
Frederick Herzberg – Jumping for the Jellybeans lecture www.youtube.com/watch?v=o87s-2YtG4Y
Microsoft and motivation www.youtube.com/watch?v=oKyV-I8i5lg
What are the benefits of a motivated workforce?
How do the Human Relations School of motivation believe individuals are motivated?
Explain how Maslow's ideas of motivation can be applied to the workplace.
'Scientific management is not relevant to modern motivational methods.' Do you agree with this statement?
How do expectancy theories differ from the other motivational theories?
'Financial methods of motivation are more likely to motivate workers than non-financial methods.' Discuss this statement.
Evaluate the impact to a business of having a poorly-motivated workforce.

Chapter 31
Management and leadership

Management and leadership are often grouped together in business and the qualities often attributed to leadership can also apply to managers. However, there should be a distinction between the two different roles.

Leaders may perform similar functions to managers, but in addition they also inspire and motivate the workforce, they consider long-term strategy, the challenges facing the business and how to overcome them. Managers control and direct the workforce to follow the principles or values that have been established by the leaders.

Some leaders will not manage in the workplace they may rely on a deputy or a team of managers to do this on their behalf, to ensure that the right staff are recruited, products or services are produced and the business is profitable.

A successful business owner should be both a strong leader and manager to get their workforce to follow them towards their vision of success. Being a good leader involves getting people to understand and believe in your vision to work with you to achieve your goals, whereas managing is more about administering and making sure the day-to-day things are happening as they should.

The functions of management

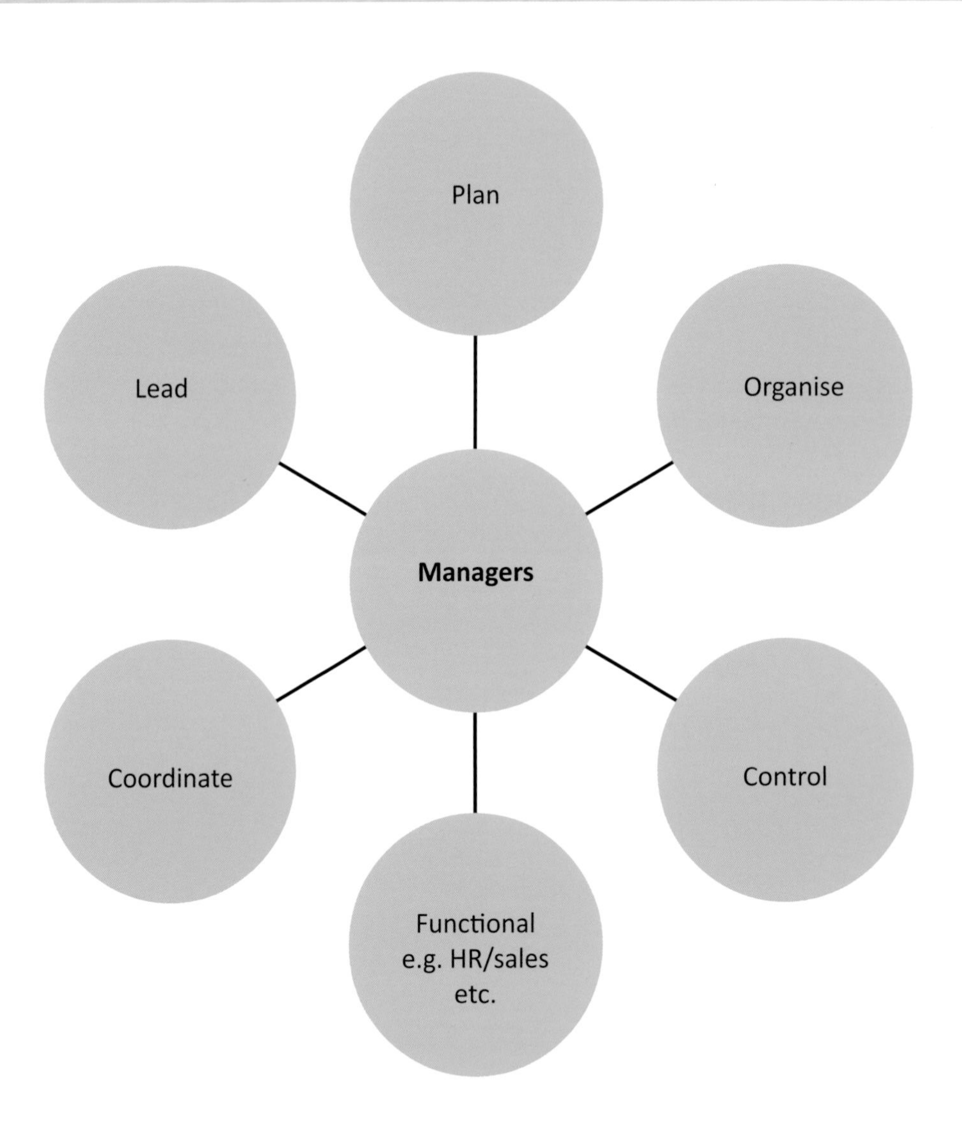

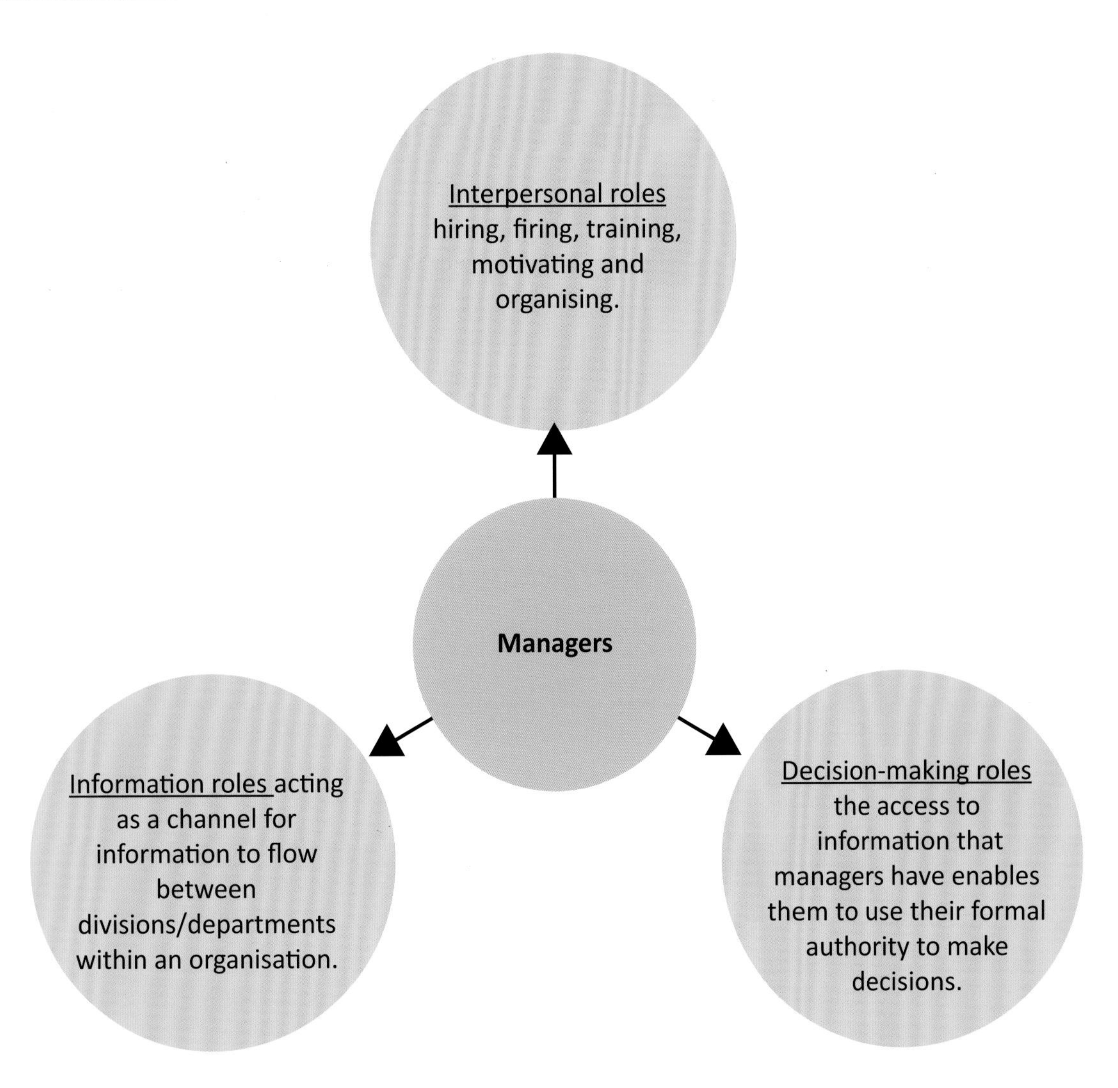

Management by objectives (MBO)

Management by objectives is a philosophy of management designed by Peter Drucker. Objectives are defined within an organisation so that the management and workers agree to the objectives and understand what they need to do in order to achieve them. It involves the breaking down and subdivision of the aims and goals of an organisation into targets and objectives for divisions, for departments, for managers and finally for workers.

The passing down and subdivision of objectives down the hierarchy should produce an end result where the targets and objectives for each individual within the organisation, when all added together, equal the same as the targets and objectives for the whole organisation.

Drucker suggested that by working together to meet the same objectives, owners, managers and workers would have a clear structure and long-term strategy that give clear goals to all stakeholders in the organisation.

An important aspect of MBO is the participative setting of objectives and planning a course of action to achieve the objectives. By including employees with the goal setting and the course of action to reach those objectives, they are more likely to be motivated and carry out their responsibilities to the best of their abilities. When the plans have been carried out it is essential that the work is monitored to measure the actual performance against the actual standards set.

The MBO process

Review objectives for the whole business (corporate objectives)

Set objectives for the management of the different functions of the business

Set objectives for individual departments and workers

Monitor progress – managers and workers check to see if the objectives are being reached

Evaluate performance and give reward if the objectives were reached

Advantages of applying management by objectives

- Improved management control of the organisation. Managers know who is doing what and what they are supposed to be achieving. Clarity of goals.
- Improved financial control. Part of the setting of the objectives process is monitoring expenditure and revenues. Any changes from (variances from) budgeted amounts need to be explained and reacted to.
- It allows managers to be aware of their responsibilities. Managers are aware of what they should be achieving and how their role fits in with organisational objectives.
- The work of departments and managers are co-ordinated. Everyone is working together towards a common goal.
- It can motivate the workforce. When managers at all levels are involved in setting and agreeing objectives they will have a commitment to ensuring that objectives and goals are achieved. Involving all employees in the whole process of goal setting will give employee empowerment. This increases employee job satisfaction and commitment.
- It can improve communication systems within the organisation. The process of setting and agreeing objectives will itself involve communication both up and down the hierarchy.

Disadvantages of applying management by objectives

The management by objectives system can have problems. The disadvantages include:

- Management time is spent on the process of setting objectives rather than managing the organisation.
- The ever-changing business environment or context in which the goals are set may change over time making the objectives unrealistic.
- Demotivation and breakdown of working relationships. If all levels of hierarchy are not involved in setting objectives, then they may not be committed to them.
- Objectives can be seen as a form of management control.
- A situation may arise where managers 'cannot see the wood for the trees'. This loss of focus means managers concentrate on short-term objectives at the cost of ignoring the long-term goals.

McGregor's Theory X and Theory Y

Douglas McGregor put forward the idea that there are two broad types of manager – Theory X managers and Theory Y managers.

Theory X managers

The first of these management styles, is founded upon the 'assumption of the mediocrity of the masses'. The Theory X type of manager makes several assumptions about employees:

- workers must be supervised or quality and quantity of output will fall;
- workers only respect the type of manager that tells them what to do and does so with complete authority;
- money is the only motivator;
- workers do not want to be involved in the decision-making process;
- workers wish to remain faceless and unknown to management;
- workers have little ambition.

Theory Y managers

Theory Y managers believe that the reverse is true. They start with several positive assumptions about employees:

- workers cannot be motivated by money alone – they seek more than financial satisfaction from their jobs;
- workers are ambitious, willing to train and contribute to improve their chances of promotion;
- workers will be more efficient if they are left to their own devices – trust breeds responsibility;
- workers want to contribute to improving efficiency – they want to be seen, be noticed, rewarded and appreciated when they work well.

Consequences of Theory X management

If managers are employed who believe that workers have little or no ambition, wish to be left alone, must not be involved in the wider business environment and must be supervised if they are to maintain quality and quantity of work, then this has major impacts on job design and control. In the case of Theory X managers, the consequences for the business will be:

- strict control of formal methods of communication;
- tasks must be designed so they are broken down into their simplest units;
- responsibilities must be clear and unambiguous;
- supervisors must maintain quality;
- high level of dependence on the decision-making of senior management.

Consequences of Theory Y management

Theory Y managers are likely to create an open structure, with both formal and informal paths of communication and delegated powers. Workers will be given responsibilities and a wider range of tasks. Theory Y managers are facilitators. It is likely that managers will adopt a democratic style – this is based on encouraging participation in decision-making. In the case of Theory Y managers, the consequences for the business will be:

- requirement for training;
- use of cell working – restructuring of production and service methods;
- setting up of formal communication channels, with both vertical and lateral communication;
- promotion structures;
- flexible working practices.

An important part of this theory of management is that the managers will, over a period of time, influence how workers behave. So if we have a Theory Y manager placed in a business where workers have previously behaved within the Theory X pattern, it is quite possible for change to take place. The existing workers may be transformed from being uncooperative, demotivated and unconcerned with the success of the business into contributors who are motivated to improve quality and ambitious for personal and company success. It also follows from this that lack of motivation amongst workers and poor quality of output is a management-created problem. It is the role of management to create methods of production and management of human resources that will allow these resources to realise their full potential.

Character traits of effective managers

A number of character traits of effective managers have been identified and are shown in the diagram below.

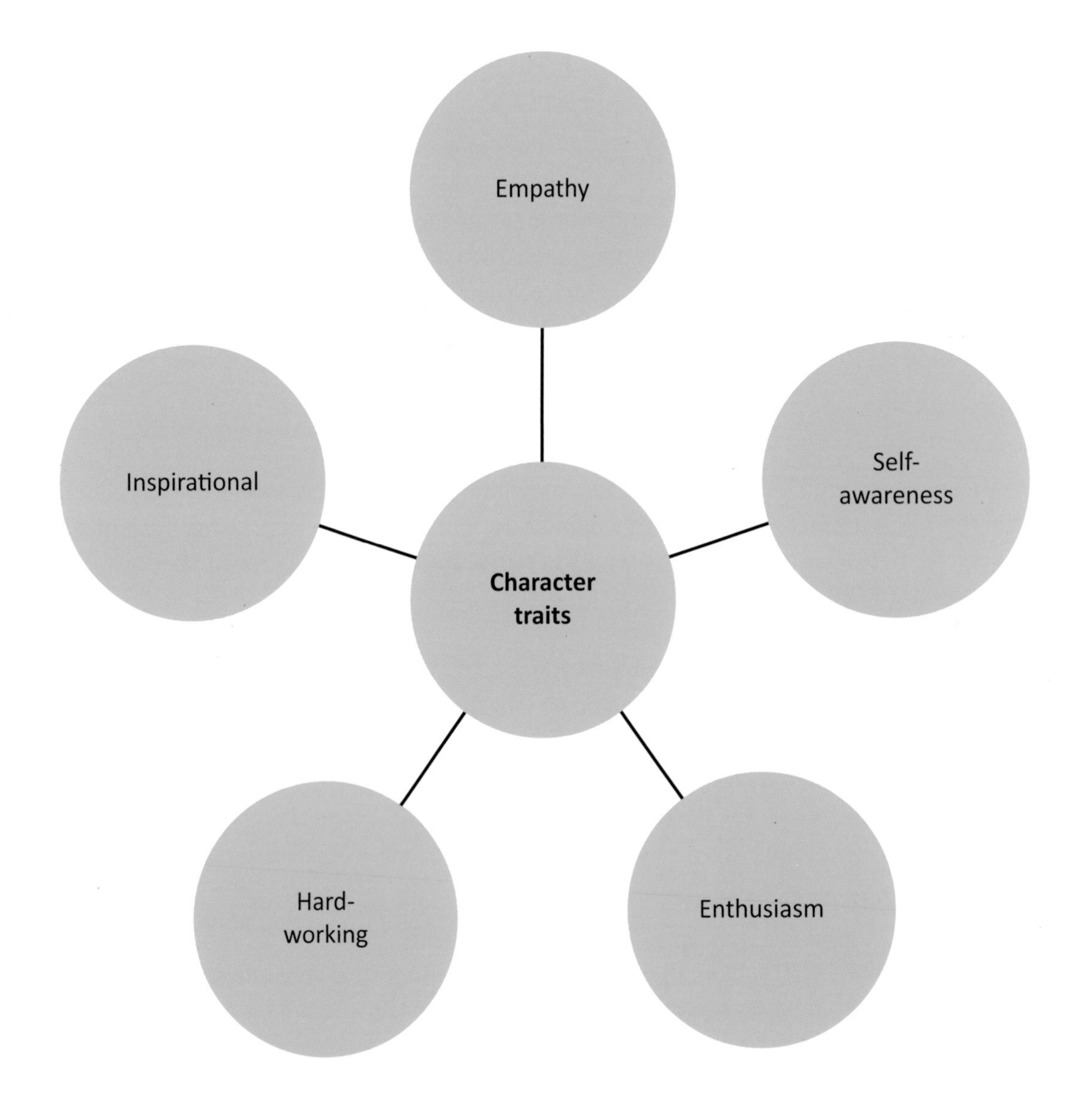

Leadership

As explained earlier, leaders may perform similar functions to managers, but in addition they also inspire and motivate the workforce, they consider long-term strategy, the challenges facing the business and how to overcome them. Managers control and direct the workforce to follow the principles or values that have been established by the leaders.

Being a good leader involves getting people to understand and believe in your vision to work with you to achieve your goals.

Role of leaders

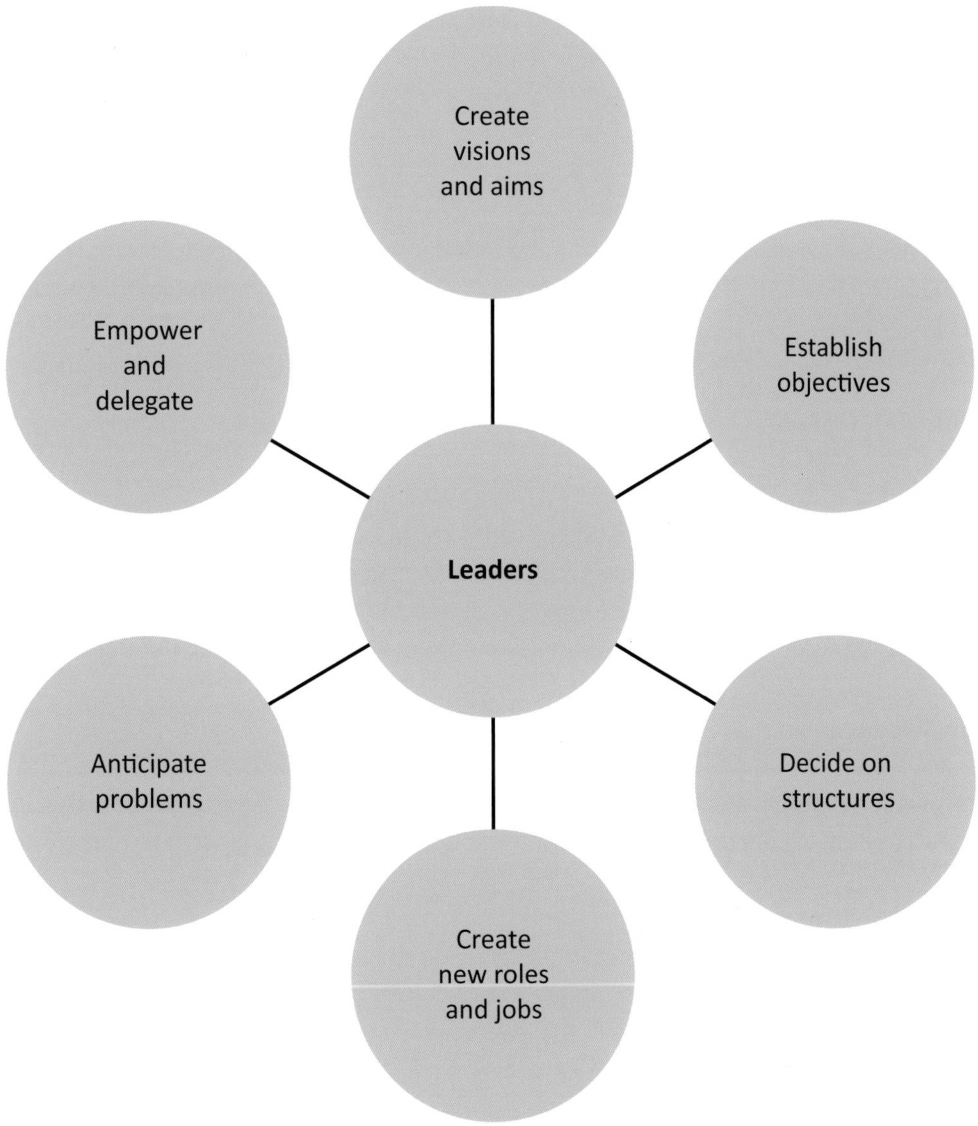

Leaders

Create visions and aims

Establish objectives

Decide on structures

Create new roles and jobs

Anticipate problems

Empower and delegate

Because leaders need to lead and fulfil a number of challenging roles, a leader needs to have a number of characteristics that will help them lead their business. These might include the following:

- intellectual skills;
- interpersonal skills;
- realistic aspirations;
- vision;
- communicative skills;

- creativity;
- innovation;
- commitment;
- identify and respond to changes.

It is unlikely that any leader will have all of these characteristics – indeed no single one of these characteristics is essential for a leader to be successful. A good leader is the one that adapts to the needs of the employees through identifying problems and creating solutions.

Leadership styles

In the long run, there is no one leadership style that suits any particular organisation. Market circumstances change, internal circumstances change, external pressures change, or alternatively there may be a period of stability. These factors mean that as the business adapts to these different circumstances, then the type of leader that is best suited to the business will also alter. The type of leadership required to force through restructuring or rebranding of an organisation will be very different from the leader who most effectively oversees a period of stability.

The leadership styles we examine below may then be broadly suited to a particular business form or structure but there will be times when the style is easily transferable to organisations that have previously been run in different ways.

Different leadership styles

Autocratic leadership
This style of leader gives orders which are to be obeyed without question. Probably a Theory X manager, who has no time for consideration of Maslow's higher needs or Herzberg's motivating factors. This type of manager can be effective when rapid restructuring is required but to be effective he/she will rely upon a strictly hierarchical organisational structure. There is no employee involvement in the decision-making.

Paternalistic leadership
These leaders are similar to autocratic leaders in that they make all the decisions and there is no employee involvement. However, paternalistic leaders may attempt to persuade the employees that the decisions made are in the best interest of all concerned. Paternalistic leaders will consider the welfare of the employees.

Democratic or participative leadership
This type of leader consults with subordinates in the decision-making process. Subordinates are involved with managers in designing their jobs and the tasks involved. This philosophy is ideally suited to the implementation of 'soft' HRM policies. Democratic leaders will need to communicate effectively with employees in order to consult, persuade and receive feedback. A democratic style of leadership can result in a workforce that is motivated and committed to the organisation and can also promote creativity and better quality decisions.

Laissez-faire leadership
This occurs when the leader has minimal input and subordinates are largely left to get on with their jobs. Minimum guidance is offered and workers are given a great deal of scope to demonstrate their capabilities. The danger with this style of leadership is that if workers are not motivated or committed to their work, their productivity can be low.

Bureaucratic leadership

Bureaucratic leaders focus on developing the specialisation of jobs and departments. They have a reliance on formal procedures and clearly-marked status definitions. Bureaucratic leadership operates within hierarchical structures. Employees are allowed to use discretion only within delegated limits. Job roles are defined formally by the use of clear job descriptions, and an obligation to stick to these job descriptions severely limits the employees' ability to act in situations that are unusual or unexpected.

It is argued that in a bureaucracy each employee within the organisation knows precisely what their duties are and therefore many tasks will be performed a lot quicker and more efficiently. Another advantage is that workers who are secure in their roles are, therefore, more likely to cooperate with other workers. The main disadvantage of this type of leadership is the discouragement of innovation and the ability to adapt to change.

What makes successful leadership is open to question. Different styles suit different circumstances and the same leader can use different styles with different groups of workers. A good leader is one who can adapt their style or approach to different situations; this is known as a contingency approach to leadership. Leaders can be task or people-orientated and this orientation will dictate their approach to control, job design and motivation.

Leaders must plan, motivate and control, but how they best do this is a question of circumstance. Using an autocratic style with a group of computer games developers may be a mistake but using the same style within the armed forces makes a great deal of sense.

Theories of leadership

Fiedler's contingency model

Fiedler believed that the quality of leadership was the most important factor affecting the success or failure of an organisation. He realised that most people are effective in some situations but not in others. For example, a successful military leader would probably not be good directing a research laboratory or a film director would not make a very good manager of an accounts department. Fiedler devised a way of helping people decide what type of leader they are in order to help them become more effective.

Fiedler's contingency model states "that the effectiveness of a group or an organisation depends on two interacting or 'contingent' factors. The first factor is the personality of the leaders which determine their leadership style. The second factor is the amount of control and influence which the situation provides leaders over their group's behaviour, the task and the outcome. This factor is called 'situational control'. For more details, see the following publication: F. E. Fiedler, M. M. Chemers and L. Mahar, *Improving Leadership Effectiveness: The Leader Match Concept* (John Wiley and Sons, New York, 1976).

In order to identify a manager's leadership style Fiedler got them to fill in a questionnaire about the person they would **least** like to work with (see below). This was known as 'The Least Preferred Co-worker (LPC) Scale'. This scale was used to identify two types of leadership style.

Least preferred co-worker (LPC) scale

			Scoring
Pleasant	8 7 6 5 4 3 2 1	Unpleasant	
Friendly	8 7 6 5 4 3 2 1	Unfriendly	
Rejecting	1 2 3 4 5 6 7 8	Accepting	
Tense	1 2 3 4 5 6 7 8	Relaxed	
Distant	1 2 3 4 5 6 7 8	Close	
Cold	1 2 3 4 5 6 7 8	Warm	
Supportive	8 7 6 5 4 3 2 1	Hostile	
Boring	1 2 3 4 5 6 7 8	Interesting	
Quarrelsome	1 2 3 4 5 6 7 8	Harmonious	
Gloomy	1 2 3 4 5 6 7 8	Cheerful	
Open	8 7 6 5 4 3 2 1	Guarded	
Backbiting	1 2 3 4 5 6 7 8	Loyal	
Untrustworthy	1 2 3 4 5 6 7 8	Trustworthy	
Considerate	8 7 6 5 4 3 2 1	Inconsiderate	
Nasty	1 2 3 4 5 6 7 8	Nice	
Agreeable	8 7 6 5 4 3 2 1	Disagreeable	
Insincere	1 2 3 4 5 6 7 8	Sincere	
Kind	8 7 6 5 4 3 2 1	Unkind	
		Total	

A high score of 64 or more indicated a **high** LPC person; such a person is called relationship-motivated. A score of 57 or below indicated a **low** LPC person. This type of individual is called **task-motivated**. An in-between score makes it difficult to identify which group the individual belongs to.

The high LPC leader sees other people as relatively pleasant, industrious or sincere even if they find it difficult to work with them. The low LPC person, who sees their co-worker in negative terms, is determined to get the job done and believes that a poor co-worker is bad in almost every possible respect.

Relationship-orientated leaders (high LPC) are most effective in less extreme circumstances. That is, in situations that are neither favourable nor unfavourable or situations that are only moderately favourable or moderately unfavourable.

Task-orientated leaders are most effective when facing a situation that is either extremely favourable or extremely unfavourable. In the case of an extremely favourable situation, they are effective:

- when there is enormous trust, respect and confidence;
- when the task is very clear;
- when followers accept the leader's power without question.

In an extremely unfavourable situation, they are effective:

- when trust and respect do not exist;
- when the challenge people face is vague and undefined;
- when the atmosphere is anarchic or even rebellious (for example, an emergency or crisis).

Fielder did not believe that leaders were very good at changing or even adapting their style, making it difficult for leaders to alter their approach to suit changing circumstances.

Fiedler's model gives organisations a way to identify the best potential leaders for a particular situation, group of workers or task. This approach also gives individual leaders an idea as to which types of situation they are best suited for. He called his approach the 'leadership match concept'.

Not everything was black and white for Fiedler as he appreciated that there is a great deal of middle ground in 'The Least Preferred Co-worker' scale, which makes it difficult to be clear if a particular leader is task-focused or relationship-focused.

Fiedler has been criticised because he does not give enough credibility to the flexibility of leaders, since there is evidence that many leaders are quite good at adapting to changing circumstances.

Wright and Taylor

P. Wright and D. Taylor believed that a lot of leadership theory was theoretically correct but did not actually show leaders how they could improve the way that they worked. They believed that it is possible to improve a leader's performance and that this could be done through education.

Wright and Taylor identified two specific gaps in existing approaches to the study of leadership. Firstly, there is not enough emphasis on what leaders actually do when they interact with their subordinates. Secondly, the element of skill is largely ignored. In answer to these deficiencies Wright and Taylor were concerned with improving leadership skills. The way that they did this was by providing a checklist for improving work performance.

The skills that leaders needed to learn are both verbal and non-verbal. At the same time leaders need to improve their ability to diagnose what needs to be done in any particular work situation and also to develop an accurate perception and evaluation of people and events. In other words they did not believe that it is possible to have a 'one size fits all' type of solution. Every situation requires a different and appropriate response by leaders in order to improve the performance of their followers.

Whilst Wright and Taylor refer to autocratic and democratic leaders they believed that most people would rather work for interpersonally skilful leaders, irrespective of his or her leadership style.

As far as improving an individual's performance goes, Wright and Taylor believed that ability and motivation are the key factors. An individual will not perform a task well unless they want to do it and have the necessary ability to do it. If an individual is not performing well the leader will need to talk to them to find out why, then he or she will need to find skilful ways of influencing their behaviour. They recognised that this process should nearly always involve encouragement rather than punishment.

Wright and Taylor devised the following checklist in order to help leaders analyse performance problems.

They did not expect that the checklist would, in itself, find the solution to the problem since it is likely that more information would be required. Its main purpose is to provide a means of thinking over a problem systematically. They also stressed that any potential solution should be considered on a cost-benefit basis since there would be no point in spending more on it than the likely savings that would be generated by it.

Figure 1: Checklist for improving work performance

1. What is the problem in behavioural terms? What precisely is the individual doing or not doing which is adversely influencing his or her performance?
2. Is the problem really serious enough to spend time and effort on?
3. What reasons might there be for the performance problem? (See column 1)
4. What actions might be taken to improve the situation? (See column 2)

Possible reasons for the performance problem	Possible solutions
Goal clarity Is the person fully aware of the job requirements?	Give guidance concerning expected goals and standards. Set targets. MBO.
Ability Does the person have the capacity to do the job well?	Provide formal training, on the job coaching, practice, secondment, etc.
Task difficulty Does the person find the task too demanding?	Simplify task, reduce work load, reduce time pressures etc.
Intrinsic motivation Does the person find the task rewarding in itself?	Redesign job to match job-holders needs.
Extrinsic motivation Is good performance rewarded by others?	Arrange positive consequences for good performance and zero or negative consequences for poor performance.
Feedback Does the person receive adequate feedback about his/her performance?	Provide or arrange feedback.
Resources Does the person have adequate resources for satisfactory task performance?	Provide staff equipment, raw materials as appropriate.
Working conditions Do working conditions, physical or social, interfere with performance?	Improve light, heat, layout, remove distractions, etc. as appropriate.

5. Do you have sufficient information to select the most appropriate solutions? If not, collect the information required e.g. consult records, observe work behaviour, talk to person concerned.
6. Select most appropriate solution(s).

7. Is the solution worthwhile in cost benefit terms?
a. If so, implement it.
b. If not, work through the checklist again, or relocate the individual, or reorganise the department/organisation, or live with the problem.
8. Could you have handled the problem better? If so, review own performance. If not, and the problem is solved, reward yourself and tackle next problem.

Discussion themes
Explain the differences between management and leadership.
'There is no one best style of leadership. It depends on the type of business and the objectives of the business.' To what extent do you agree with this statement.
Explain what is meant by MBO.
'Theory Y managers will always be more effective in the management of the workforce than Theory X managers.' Do you agree with this statement?
Explain the difference between democratic and bureaucratic styles of leadership.
Complete Fiedler's Least Preferred Co-worker (LPC) Scale, total up your score. What does this tell you about the type of leader you would be.

Chapter 32
Employer/employee relationships

In the UK, employer/employee relationships are founded on the contract of employment which lays out the roles and responsibilities of both employer and employee. Employment law also makes specific rules that each side are expected to abide by. The relationship is also affected by trade unions who act in the interests of employees. In the past, in many employment sectors, the relationship has been seen as somewhat adversarial (one side against the other) but in recent times much more of a partnership type of relationship has been established, with employers and employees each recognising the others' role in long-term business success. Nonetheless, industrial disputes still occur, but not as frequently as has been the case in the past.

The duties and rights of employers and employees

Under health and safety legislation, employers have a duty to take all reasonable care to ensure the well-being and safety of their employees. Employers have a legal responsibility to ensure that working environments are safe and that employees are trained to deal with the risks involved in their jobs. Employees also have responsibilities, such as taking reasonable care and ensuring that they abide by health and safety rules: e.g. wearing hard hats on building sites.

Workers also have rights with regards to their terms and conditions of employment. Employees must be provided with a written contract of employment within 12 weeks of starting employment. The contract must state levels of pay, holiday entitlement, pension rights, disciplinary procedures and length of notice period. This act also protects employees against unfair dismissal; however, this protection only comes into effect after two years of service (or even longer for some part-time workers).

European legislation also helps protect workers. The UK signing up for the Social Chapter of the Maastricht Treaty has established within UK law further rights for workers, such as a legal limit on the hours in a working week (maximum of 48 hours), and paid maternity and paternity leave. It is also illegal to discriminate on the grounds of sex, race, age or disability. It used to be the normal situation for men and women doing identical jobs or jobs of similar value to have very different pay. Since the mid 1970s this has been illegal. Anti-discrimination laws protect workers from being treated differently because of their race, colour or culture and employers with workforces of over 20 must make efforts to ensure that workplaces, where possible, are suitable for disabled employees.

The minimum wage

The National Minimum Wage, when first introduced in April 1999, was set cautiously low at just £3.60 an hour, so as not to undermine a business's competitiveness by pushing up costs. The change to the minimum wage was expected to benefit about two million people – more than half of them in the service sector. Some wage packets were boosted by up to a third.

Minimum wages for each group of employees in October 2015:

- Main (adult) rate for workers aged 21 and over – £6.70 per hour.
- Development rate for workers aged 18–20 inclusive – £5.30 per hour.
- Rate for under 18 year olds – £3.87 per hour.

Impact of the minimum wage on employment

The introduction of the minimum wage has added only around 0.5% to the national wage bill. In contrast to the views of many pessimists, there was no measurable impact on overall employment following introduction of the minimum wage. In fact, in the areas of the economy where the minimum wage was expected to have the greatest impact on employment levels, we saw the greatest growth in employment. However, it could of course be argued that there would have been even greater growth in jobs without the minimum wage. The first large-scale research into the impact of the minimum wage on employment levels by Income Data Services said that the introduction of the minimum wage had not caused job losses or upset industry pay structures.

Effects of the minimum wage on employees

Firstly, it is worth noting that most employees have not been affected by the introduction of the minimum wage. Only around 7–8% of the workforce were in occupations that paid below the minimum wage, so the mass of employees were not directly affected by its introduction. However, there has been some pressure to maintain differentials, meaning that wage rates of those above the minimum wage have moved up in line with those receiving the minimum wage. The workers who have benefited the most have been younger workers in low-paid industries – these include care services, office services and areas such as cleaning, catering and fast food. For the lowest paid, the minimum wage has allowed a move away from poverty and removed some aspects of the poverty trap.

Employment has continued to grow in low-paying sectors following the introduction of the minimum wage and there have been no signs of a significant minimum wage effect in the unemployment figures between 2000 and 2008. In fact, in the lowest paying sectors of the economy such as the hotel industry, catering and care services, employment levels had grown strongly over the first eight years of the minimum wage. The impact of the recession seems to be have felt across most employment sectors, with those on the minimum wage not seeing any greater increase in unemployment levels. Job creation over the last two years (2013–2015) has also been strong in minimum wage sectors.

Effects of the minimum wage on employers

- It is argued that the minimum wage has made the UK much less attractive to inward investment – discouraging investment in the UK by foreign companies. Also some businesses have moved production and investment to low labour-cost countries in the east of Europe and Asia.
- Small businesses have been most affected, especially those that are labour intensive. The focus for the owners and managers of these businesses, as encouraged by the government and bodies such as the Low Pay Commission, has been to make workers more productive through training and education. When viewed from this perspective, the minimum wage could be argued to increase efficiency.
- Overall wage costs could have increased because of the pressure to keep existing wage differentials in place – as the wage of the lowest paid workers increases, so must the wages of those on the next level up and so on.
- Employers who have felt the worst of the impact are found in the industries mentioned earlier – sectors such as the care home industry, where rising costs have outpaced increases in income. This has led to the closure of many care homes, resulting in shortages of beds for the elderly in some areas of the country.

Equal opportunities

The Equality Act 2010 legally protects people from discrimination in the workplace and in wider society. It is against the law to discriminate against anyone because of:

- age;
- being or becoming a transsexual person;
- being married or in a civil partnership;
- being pregnant or having a child;
- disability;
- race including colour, nationality, ethnic or national origin;
- religion, belief or lack of religion/belief;
- sex;
- sexual orientation.

The above are known as 'protected characteristics'.

Any of the following is regarded as discrimination:

- direct discrimination – treating someone with a protected characteristic less favourably than others;
- indirect discrimination – putting rules or arrangements in place that apply to everyone, but that put someone with a protected characteristic at an unfair disadvantage;
- harassment – unwanted behaviour linked to a protected characteristic that violates someone's dignity or creates an offensive environment for them;
- victimisation – treating someone unfairly because they have complained about discrimination or harassment.

In the workplace the law protects people against discrimination in relation to:

- dismissal;
- imposition of unfair employment terms and conditions;
- pay and benefits;
- promotion and transfer opportunities;
- opportunities for training;
- recruitment;
- redundancy.

The first equal opportunities legislation was passed in the 1970s but there are still issues regarding discrimination in the workplace. Circumstantial evidence is sometimes put forward to indicate discrimination: examples include comparisons between the numbers of black footballers and the numbers of black managers, lack of women running large companies and age discrimination on TV where we see ageing male presenters but few older females.

What are trade unions?

Trade unions were traditionally organisations that represented workers in a particular trade, industry or occupation. More recently we have seen the growth of general trade unions (e.g. Unite), representing a wide range of workers. All sorts of occupations are represented by trade unions, including manual and professional workers. Their purpose is to protect and improve their members' terms and conditions of employment.
An individual worker alone has very little power to influence decisions, but by joining together, workers

have more chance of having a voice and influence. This is known as collective bargaining. Trade unions also campaign for laws and policies which will benefit working people.

Trade unions are financed and run by their members. Many were formed over 100 years ago. Almost every working person has the legal right to join or not to join a trade union. The Trades Union Congress (TUC) is made up of representatives of most of the major unions and has a role in national negotiations with employers and the government.

Why do people join unions?

- **Representation**. This means that unions represent members faced with redundancy, a grievance, disciplinary procedures and legal action.
- **Negotiation of pay and conditions with employers**. This is 'collective bargaining', and benefits workers. About half of the UK workforce is covered by collective bargaining arrangements. Negotiation does not have to be done on an individual basis but through a representative of a large section, or even the whole, of the workforce.
- **Help ensure high standards of health and safety**. The provision of a network of health and safety representatives in Britain's workplaces.
- **Union members can benefit from a wide range of services** which are not directly related to the workplace. These include financial, legal and welfare services.
- **Unions support the development of equal opportunities policies**. Most large companies, and many smaller ones, now operate policies which attempt to eliminate discrimination at work. Trade unions have not only supported their members who have been discriminated against but also helped the workforce to understand the policies.

Most employers are happy to have trade unions representing workers because:

- **Collective bargaining assists employers** because it simplifies the process of negotiating with workers. Negotiation does not have to be done on an individual basis, which would be very time consuming and disruptive.
- **Trade unions can also help ensure that agreements are complied with by workers** and can assist with communication between management and workers.
- **Trade unions are able to take a longer term view than individuals** and are therefore able to see why difficult decisions have to be made. Individual workers may be blinded by short-term desires such as improving their pay, when raising costs may make the business uncompetitive.

What is the role of trade unions in industrial disputes?

When disagreements between employers and employees occur they need to be resolved fairly and swiftly. Good industrial relations contribute to the smooth running of business – so disputes between managers and employees should be avoided whenever possible.

Even so, disagreements between employers and employees can occur for a wide range of reasons. These include disputes over wages, hours and conditions of work, the introduction of new machinery, new work rotas, overtime, job losses, redundancies, health and safety issues and equal rights.

If there is a disagreement on any of these issues, it is often the unions' local representative, the shop steward, who will negotiate with the management. When an agreement between management and the local union representatives cannot be reached straight away, the national trade union officials may be consulted and involved in negotiations. On the whole, differences are sorted out without any industrial action being taken. There may even be a national agreement in place which the employer and employees are bound by – this agreement can then be used to resolve issues.

However, there are occasions when the two sides cannot agree. In these cases, a trade union will use a number of strategies before calling a strike. Strikes are often in the news but they are rare in most workplaces. Many more working days are lost through work-related sickness than through strikes.

Types of industrial action

- **An overtime ban** – workers just work basic hours and refuse to do any extra work. This is a useful tactic if the employer has a lot of work on and is trying to meet high levels of demand.
- **A work-to-rule** – workers stick very closely to every rule in the workplace, especially health and safety rules. This slows down production and reduces output.
- **Strikes** – a withdrawal of labour. An all-out strike is called as a very last resort. Both sides have much to lose – the workers' income and the employers' profits. Letting down customers can have a lasting impact on a business as they may seek alternative suppliers and never return.

There is no doubt that the British record on industrial action has improved dramatically over the last 30 years: this new realism by trade unions is probably more the result of trade union legislation, limiting the powers of trade unions, than any other factor.

ACAS

Sometimes an outside body is called in to arbitrate (try to bring the two sides together) during employer/employee negotiations. The Advisory, Conciliation and Arbitration Service (ACAS) is often used to help find a solution which is acceptable to both sides. ACAS plays an important role in settling disputes but only has a role to play when it is invited by both sides to conciliate (offer and suggest solutions) or arbitrate (when ACAS's solution will be accepted by both sides).

The advisory role of ACAS

Employment law is complex. The advisory role is to give employers and employees a point of contact so that issues regarding employment law and procedures can be made clear. Any employer or employee can contact ACAS to gain advice, or to discuss appropriate steps to take to help resolve employment issues.

The conciliation role of ACAS

The conciliation process involves an invited independent ACAS conciliator discussing disputed workplace issues with both parties in order to help them reach a better understanding of each other's position and underlying interest. The impartial conciliator tries to encourage the parties in dispute to come to an agreement between themselves and so avoid the disruption and expense of progressing the dispute through industrial action. With conciliation, the recommendations and advice given is in no way binding on either side.

The arbitration role of ACAS

Arbitration involves an impartial ACAS advisor being asked to make a decision on a dispute. The arbitrator makes a firm decision on a case, based on the evidence presented by the parties. Arbitration is voluntary, so both sides must agree to go to arbitration; they should also agree in advance that they will abide by the arbitrator's decision. Arbitration is often used in collective employment-related disputes. For example, a trade union might be in dispute with an employer over the annual pay rise. The union could agree with the employer to ask ACAS to appoint an independent arbitrator from their panel to hear the two sides' cases and then make an independent and impartial decision. Arbitration can also be used to settle individual disputes. For example, an individual and an employer might decide to go to arbitration to avoid the stress and expense of an employment tribunal.

Discussion themes
Why are good employer/employee relationships important?
'The introduction of the National Minimum Wage has had more benefits than drawbacks.' Discuss this statement.
'The National Minimum Wage should increase every year.' Discuss this statement.
Why do workers join a trade union?
What is meant by collective bargaining? What workplace issues might be covered in the collective bargaining process?
Explain the roles of ACAS in helping prevent industrial disputes.
Do you think that the action taken in these cases is justified? Christina McAnea, Head of Health for UNISON, explains why UNISON's members working in the NHS are taking industrial action https://www.youtube.com/watch?v=bz_nCcKsQeQ Midwifery strike action https://www.youtube.com/watch?v=NIKQyNbOufI

Chapter 33
Added value

During the production process a business adds value to the raw materials which it uses when making a product.

Calculation of added value – the difference between the cost of purchasing raw materials and the price for which the finished good is sold for.

Raw materials (inputs)	Processes	Finished product (output)
Wood – £20 Brackets – £2 Screws – £0.50 Paint – £1 Varnish – £0.50	Cutting Sanding Joining Painting Varnishing	
£24	**Added value = £80**	£104

In the example above a carpenter uses inputs such as wood, screws and other raw materials to make a table. The total cost of all the materials adds up to £24. In order to make the table the carpenter has carried out a variety of processes. The final output – the table – is sold for £104. The added value in this case is £80 (£104 – £24 = £80).

Added value **is not to be confused with profit**. Out of the £80 added value in this example the wages of the carpenter plus any overheads his business may have, such as transport and insurance, must be deducted.

Added value does not only apply to the production of goods – **it also applies to the provision of services**. For example, when a wholesale business buys a thousand tins of baked beans from a manufacturer it will sell the beans on for more than it paid for them. This difference in price is regarded as added value. The wholesaler has provided a service and has therefore added value by making it convenient for local retailers to come to the warehouse and pick up the amount of baked beans they need to sell to their own customers in their shops.

How might added value be increased?

There are a variety of ways in which added value may be increased for both goods and services:

- Purchasing cheaper raw materials – however, care must be taken that quality is not compromised when doing this. As a business grows it may be able to take advantage of purchasing economies of scale and achieve greater added value as a result.

- Improving the efficiency of the production process – for example, this may be achieved by purchasing up-to-date machinery or by training the workforce.
- Raising the price of the product – price elasticity of demand is a key issue here. If the business raises the price of a product, the demand for which is price sensitive, it will result in a fall in overall revenue – which is clearly something it would not want to do.
- Achieving brand status for a product can create added value. Chanel perfume sells for a great deal more than the majority of its competitors, but the processes involved in production will be virtually identical.
- Offering additional services with a product can result in added value. A telephone helpline to help with technical questions, or the willingness to install new equipment and ethically dispose of old equipment are examples of this.
- Improving customer access or convenience is a well-proven method of adding value. Drive-through fast-food outlets and home-delivery pizza are typical examples.

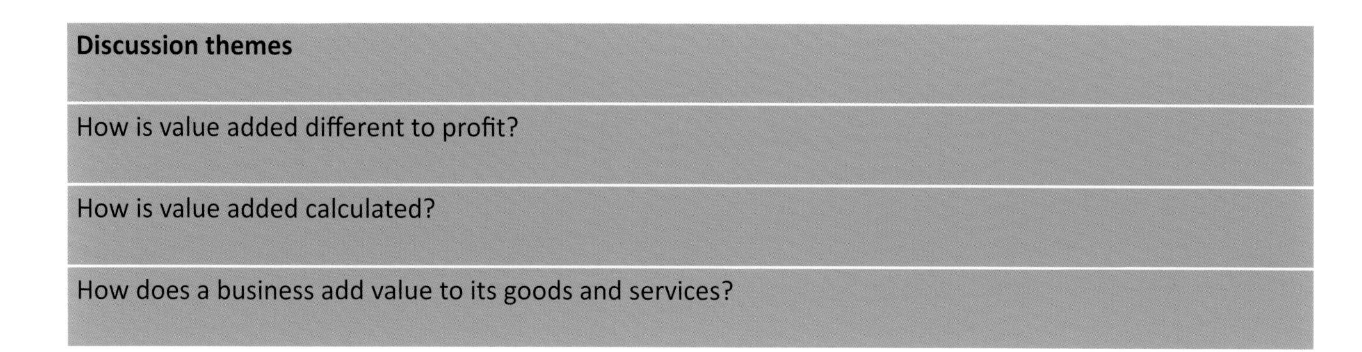

Discussion themes
How is value added different to profit?
How is value added calculated?
How does a business add value to its goods and services?

Chapter 34
Production

There are a number of different ways that a business can organise how it produces its products. The method which the business operates will depend on many factors including cost, volume, quality and the skills of its workforce.

There are three types of production – ways of producing goods. These are:

Job production

Single items, usually to the buyer's specification, are made using job production. This method produces unique products and they are made one at a time. Job production is labour-intensive and produced by skilled workers. Examples of goods made by job production are wedding dresses and tailor-made suits. Other, large-scale examples may include buildings, bridges and ships.

Job production results in high-quality products that are matched to customer needs. Employees producing goods using job production can be highly skilled and have interesting and challenging jobs. Design is flexible and can be adapted to customer needs. However, goods made using job production methods can take a long time to make compared to goods made using mass production. Prices of any goods produced are also likely to be a great deal higher, as skilled workers will command higher payments for their time and expertise.

Batch production

This is the method which involves manufacturing a limited number of identical products. At each stage of the production process work will be completed for the whole batch before the next stage is begun. A typical industry using batch production is baking. For example, stage one would involve mixing sufficient dough for 500 granary loaves. Stage two might require leaving the dough to rise for a period of time. Stage three would be to divide the dough into loaves, stage four to bake the loaves, stage five to slice the loaves and stage six would be the packaging. Batch production is also often used by potters and furniture manufacturers.

Batch production will have lower unit costs and higher output than job production. Employees are likely to be semi-skilled and there can be a reliance on capital investment. Batch production allows businesses to aim at niche markets, using the same assets or capital equipment to produce a range of goods. Time is lost when machines have to be reset for new production and the business may not be equipped to deal with large scale orders. However, some economies of scale will be gained when compared with job production.

Flow or mass production

Flow production involves the production of products on production lines. There is a continuous process – the product flows from one stage of production to the next. This method allows identical products to be made in large volumes. The production process is broken down into a number of small, simple tasks enabling machines or robots to be utilised. The production of the products is much faster than job or batch production so a business can meet the demand of large quantities.

Workers, when used, can be unskilled or have skills limited to particular simple tasks. This can lower labour costs, although motivation can become difficult. There are often large amounts of capital investment involved through high set-up costs – production line machines/robotics can be very expensive. Also breakdowns and hold-ups can be very expensive. However, unit costs are low and businesses will benefit from economies of scale, thereby reducing costs. The products produced through flow production are identical and this method does not allow for a wide product range.

The type of production used will depend on a number of factors:

- the product being produced;
- the cost of labour;
- the cost of capital;
- the availability of money for investment;
- technology;
- the skills of labour;
- the size of the market;
- customer requirements.

Discussion themes
Explain the factors which determine which type of production is used in each clip. Methods of production Job production: https://www.youtube.com/watch?v=u2rujM6QKJ8 Batch production: https://www.youtube.com/watch?v=XKGak-4yh-8 Mass production: https://www.youtube.com/watch?v=VreG1iC65Lc
Summarise the main points for each method of production.
'Flow production is always the best option for a business producing a high volume of products.' Discuss this statement.

Chapter 35
Productivity

Productivity is a measurement of the efficiency with which a business turns production inputs into output. Labour productivity (output per worker) is the most common measure of productivity.

$$\textbf{Labour productivity} = \frac{\textbf{Output (per period)}}{\textbf{Number of employees (per period)}}$$

$$\textbf{Capital productivity} = \frac{\textbf{Output}}{\textbf{Capital employed}}$$

If a factory produces 1000 bicycles a day and employs 100 workers, then productivity is 1000 bicycles/100 workers = 10 bicycles per worker per day. The fixed measure of input does not have to be labour – it could be a value of capital (output per £1000 of capital invested), or of machines used (200 pairs of shoes per machine per day). Productivity in retailing can be measured through sales per square foot. If a department store has sales of £3 000 000 in a week, and the square footage of the shop is 20 000, then sales per square foot are £150. The higher the productivity, the more efficient production or sales generation is.

How to improve productivity in manufacturing

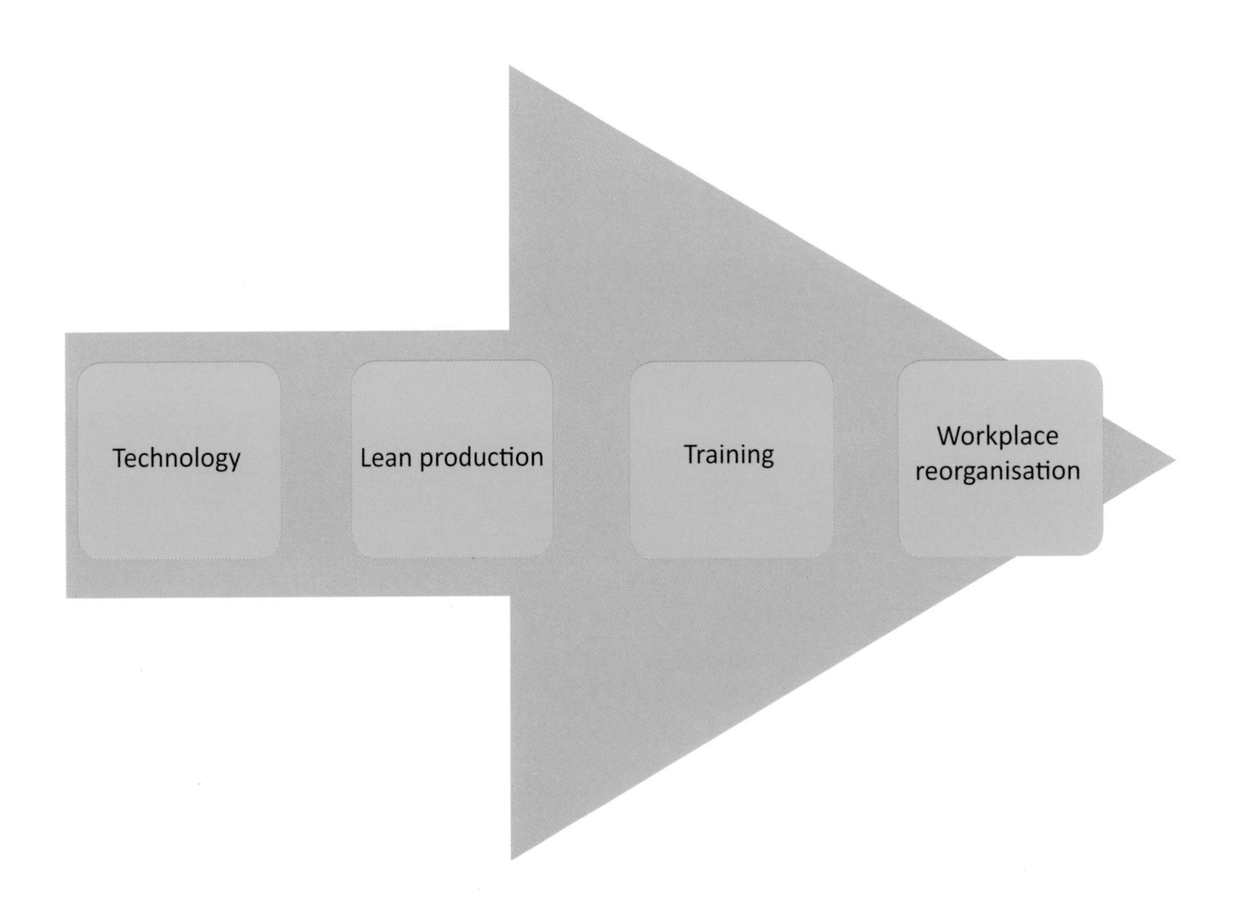

Advantages of high productivity

- Increased economies of sale
- Increased competitiveness
- Spreading of fixed costs over higher output
- Lower unit costs
- Performance bonuses to workers - motivation

Capacity utilisation

It is normally only when the economy is booming and demand is buoyant that businesses are able to operate at full or near full capacity. Full capacity means that all employed factors of production are being used to their optimum level of efficiency – producing the maximum level of output, given the business's current investment levels. At most other times in the economic or business cycle businesses will be operating below full capacity. This means that they have the capability to produce greater levels of output than they are actually producing – therefore spare capacity exists.

To measure spare capacity we look at output as a % of total capacity. If a factory is capable of producing 2000 car exhausts per day and is only producing 1700, then spare capacity is 300. This represents 15% of maximum capacity and the business is therefore operating at 85% of full capacity. In this case resources are underused, or underutilised.

Problems of spare capacity

If the level of spare capacity is significant (i.e. large enough to be of concern), then this underutilisation of factors of production can have major effects on businesses.
These effects include:

- **Demotivation of staff.** Overtime is probably not available, bonuses will be limited and there may be a threat of redundancy.
- **Increased costs to the business.** Businesses may be forced to make workers redundant and redundancy payments will have to be made. Also management time will need to be spent on reorganisation.

- **Reduced profits.** This will limit capital for investment and research and development, causing a reduction in long-term competitiveness.
- **Lack of return on investment capital.** Producer goods will continue to depreciate, even though they are not being used to full capacity. Technology will move on, putting pressure on businesses to replace fixed assets that otherwise have plenty of productive potential.

Resolving the problems of capacity underutilisation – spare capacity

Businesses have several options open to them. These include:

Subcontracting of production

If there is low utilisation then it might make sense to subcontract to another business. This means getting someone else to produce the goods for you. By using subcontractors there is a reduction in risk to the business. This risk reduction is achieved through a reduction in capital investment required. If the business is not making the goods it does not have to buy the machines to make the goods, lease the factory space or employ and train the workers.

However, subcontacting can bring problems of its own. Firstly, there is a lack of control – especially with regard to quality. Secondly, if there are a limited number of potential subcontractors then prices of the goods can become prohibitively high – reducing profitability. In addition, there can be delays in delivery, leading to customer dissatisfaction.

Rationalisation

This means concentrating on core products or services and disposing of those products or services that are not seen as profitable or necessary to the business's long-term success. There can be costs to rationalisation, such as writing down (reducing) the book value of assets, but it does allow management to concentrate and focus upon the business strengths. There is a risk, however, that customers will be lost. Some customers, especially business customers, who bought into the business's whole package of products, may be less loyal when 'one-stop shopping' is not now available. Rationalisation also implies redundancy costs.

Increasing the use of assets

This is potentially the most attractive option as it removes many of the costs associated with the other methods of rationalisation. Retailers can sublet some of their shop floor space – for example, supermarkets could include hairdressers or chemists. Manufacturing businesses can expand their ranges by looking for new markets or market niches (although development and marketing investment costs must be considered). They could possibly act as subcontractors for other producers. This increased use of investment goods is often referred to as 'making your assets sweat'.

Because of the short-term expense of solving problems of spare capacity, businesses often try to ride out this type of situation in the expectation that the market in which they operate will recover and demand will increase.

Problems with working at full capacity

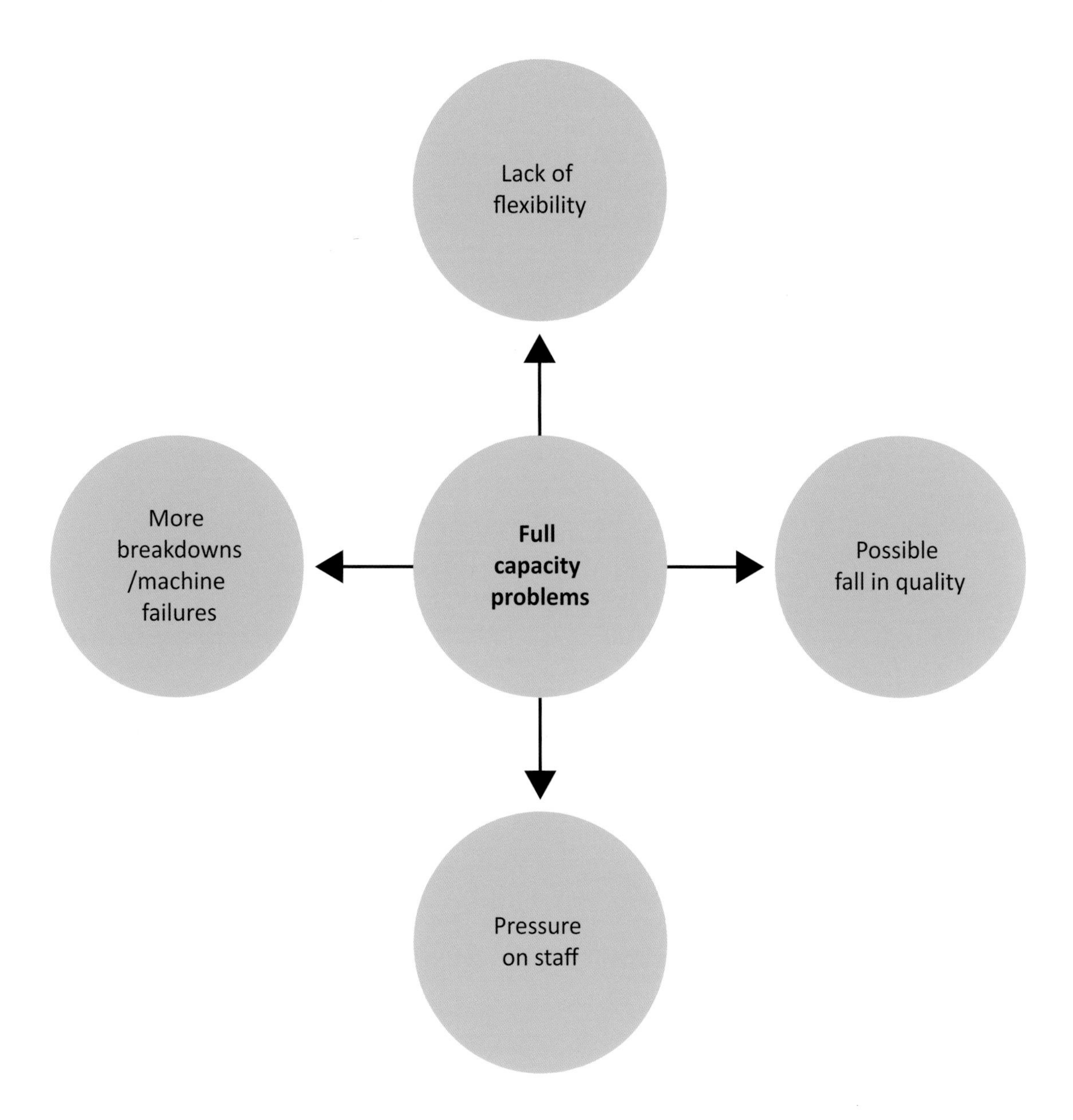

Discussion themes
What is meant by productivity?
How is productivity measured?
Explain the concept of capacity utilisation.
Operating a full capacity for an extended period can bring problems. Describe the problems that can arise.
Describe how subcontracting production can resolve spare capacity.
Make the best use of spare capacity: http://research.nus.biz/Documents/Insights%20and%20Commentaries/BT_Factiva7.htm Explain how spare capacity can be reduced by creating new demand.

Chapter 36
Technology

Technology has been used in making things ever since the first caveman or cavewoman sharpened a piece of flint to make an arrowhead with a second piece of flint. Of course things have moved on a little since the Stone Age and when we talk about modern technology today we think of computerisation, robots and digital communication.

The effective use of new technology by businesses has changed the way we live our lives. The development of mass production methods reduced the price of goods like cars in the 1920s, making them affordable to the middle classes. By the 1950s consumer durables like cars, washing machines and fridges were available at affordable prices to the mass of the population. Technology in production improves efficiency and forces down prices.

What are the most important technologies used in production today?

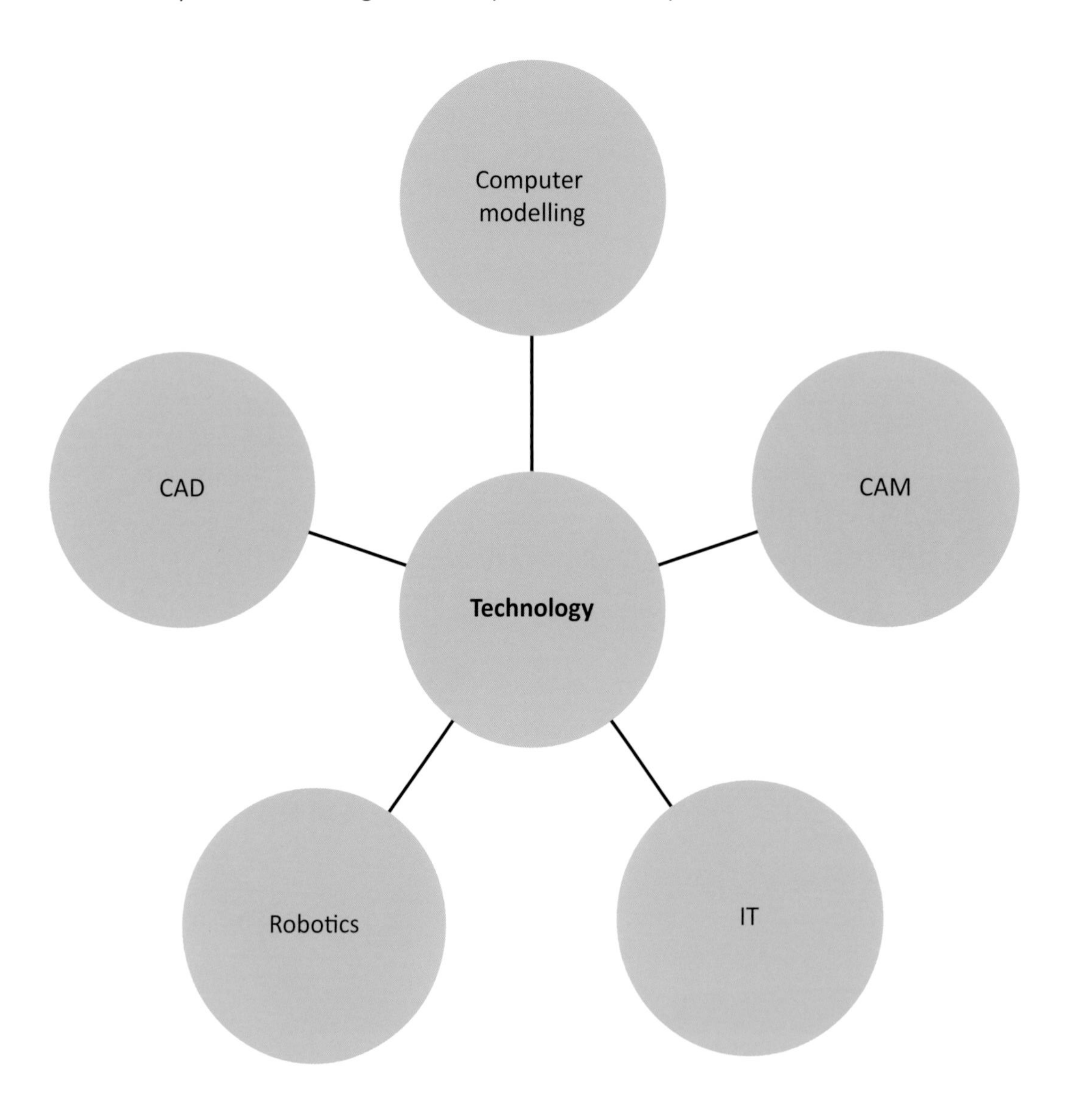

Computer-aided design (CAD)

Computer-aided design is an interactive computer system which is capable of generating, storing and using computer graphics. It assists design engineers in solving design problems. CAD has reduced the length of time between the initial design concept and actual production. The shorter the time between an original idea and getting a product on the shelves or into the showroom, the more competitive the business can be.

In the 1970s it could take five years from the initial car concept to actual production. Businesses like Kia and Honda can now do the same thing in 14 months. Computer-aided design also allows an infinite variation on design themes, allowing all possibilities to be tested. Modifications or changes can be easily made, without having to go back to the 'drawing board'. Also CAD can identify design problems at an early stage, preventing the need for expensive reworking of ideas and reducing the chance of faulty products reaching the market.

Computer-aided manufacture (CAM)

The use of computers in production occurs in all sorts of industries. There is the obvious example of robotic welders in vehicle production. Another, more unusual example is the use of CAM in packaging vegetables for supermarkets, where machines digitally photograph every vegetable and then automatically sort them into bags based on size and shape. These sorting machines always produce output of the same quality, day in day out, guaranteeing customer satisfaction.

The use of CAM can also aid flexibility in production. For example, reprogramming a welding machine is quite simple, but training a welder may be a great deal more complex and expensive. CAM can even cut costs in small businesses. Tailors and dressmakers use CAM machines to cut material in the most economical way, ensuring that waste is minimised.

Computer modelling

Computers with the right information input can be used to model anything from wear and tear of a pair of shoes to the electricity generated from a wind turbine in different wind conditions. Use of modelling allows developers to try a huge range of 'what if' scenarios, such as 'what happens to the life of the shoe when we change the stitching?', or 'what will happen to the efficiency of the wind turbine if we alter the angle of the blades by a few fractions of a degree?'. Using computer models allows businesses to perfect their products and continually improve efficiency of production.

Robotics

It is difficult to define exactly what a robot in manufacturing is – when does a machine become a robot? The basic rule is that a robot is defined not by its appearance but by how it is controlled. The more automated it is and the more it can determine its own behaviour, the more likely it is to count as a robot. For businesses robots have huge potential. For example, robots with machine vision can check to see that bottles and jars are filled to the right level so that the tops and caps fit and that the right labels are correctly stuck on. Robots put chocolates into boxes, sort apples and make salads without having to take a rest or visit the toilet. Robots even work in bakeries slicing cakes because they are more accurate than people – if you make thousands of cakes a day all those wasted crumbs add up.

Information Technology (IT)

IT is used throughout businesses increasing their productivity in a number of ways. Secretaries have preformatted letters, databases are held on customers improving customer relations, cash flow is modelled so improving financial efficiency, bar codes and EPOS systems are used to manage stock – and these are just the tip of the iceberg.

Marketing is a key aspect of the effective use of information technology. Most businesses have a web presence. In its simplest form it may be 'how to find or contact us'; in its most complex form the web is used to gather detailed customer profiles to build a database and an attempt is made to match these profiles. The internet allows a much wider geographical market to be targeted, cheaper advertising and improved customer convenience. Information gathered from browsing and purchasing habits allows sophisticated targeted marketing to take place, generating potential sales automatically. The digital revolution has had a huge effect on the business world – social networking is now a well-established marketing tool, tablets and portable devices are used in offices, and mobile phones are used to buy products online.

Communications technology allows flexibility in the location of services and customer relations centres. Calls to the directory enquiries number 118118 are answered in Cardiff during the day and in the Philippines during the night. Costs are therefore reduced and service standards improved.

Why use technology?

The advantages to businesses of using technology include:

- improved quality – thanks to their high precision and the ability to do the same thing in the same way day after day, robots and CAM processes have the ability to consistently produce top-quality products and accurately perform repetitive tasks;
- faster innovation – it is much easier, and less expensive, to model and test new products using CAD and computer modelling;
- more effective marketing and sales – marketing new products encourages consumers to dump old products and buy new ones on a regular basis;
- less dependency on labour – this is important to the business in reducing costs, especially if workers had used their bargaining power to push for higher wages and improved conditions;
- increased productivity;
- reduced waste and costs;
- improved communications.

Potential costs of using new technology

All technology costs money and to build a state-of-the-art car plant costs hundreds of millions of pounds. There is always pressure to buy the latest machine, the fastest computer or the newest robotics. Also technology does not always work, or there are huge cost overruns. In addition, there are a number of different labour costs related to the implementation of technology. Some workers are likely to lose their jobs, especially those who are not adaptable, cannot be retrained or do not have specialised skills. Workers who remain after redundancies have occurred may feel less secure and less motivated in their work and may need retraining, which will cost the business. There will, of course, be new opportunities for workers with the skills now needed to run the latest technology.

Discussion themes
What is the difference between CAD and CAM?
Explain how technology is used in the production, finance and marketing functions of a business.
'Improved technology will always benefit businesses and their stakeholders.' Discuss this statement.
Should workers be worried about the widespread use of robotics? The Guardian: When robots take our jobs, humans will be the new 1% http://www.theguardian.com/commentisfree/2014/mar/22/robot-jobs-humans-used-to-do-fight-back
Describe how Amazon have incorporated a range of technology into their business. BBC documentary on Amazon http://www.youtube.com/watch?v=RXLAlziEzAE

Chapter 37
Lean production

The idea of lean production encompasses theories of modern Japanese industrial management that are all designed to achieve the reduction and removal of waste within a business.

Lean production is a term that has come into widespread use within UK industry over the last 25 years. Lean production methods teach us that waste is any process that does not give 'added value' to a product.

- Raw materials lying around unused can be seen as waste.
- Work in progress which is sitting in parts bins waiting to be used in production can be seen as waste.
- The finished product sitting in a warehouse waiting to be delivered to customers is an example of waste.
- Skills and knowledge of workers not being used by management is an example of waste.

Lean production aims to remove all these elements of waste from the production process and as a result increase productivity and reduce costs.

Lean production in practice

For lean production to work there must be a complete change of business approach, away from the traditional hierarchical, function-centred business (so typical of many UK businesses) to a more modern, flexible, people-based structure. Also a number of complex systems must be adopted before effective lean production can take place.

The most important component parts of an effective lean production system are:

- Just-in-time;
- Kaizen;
- Cell production;
- Time-based management methods.

Just-in-time

Perhaps the best known of the lean production processes is just-in-time. Just-in-time (JIT) tries to ensure that parts, raw materials and components are received and products are made only when there is demand for the parts and demand for the products. In other words;

'If it isn't wanted don't order it; if it isn't sold don't make it'.

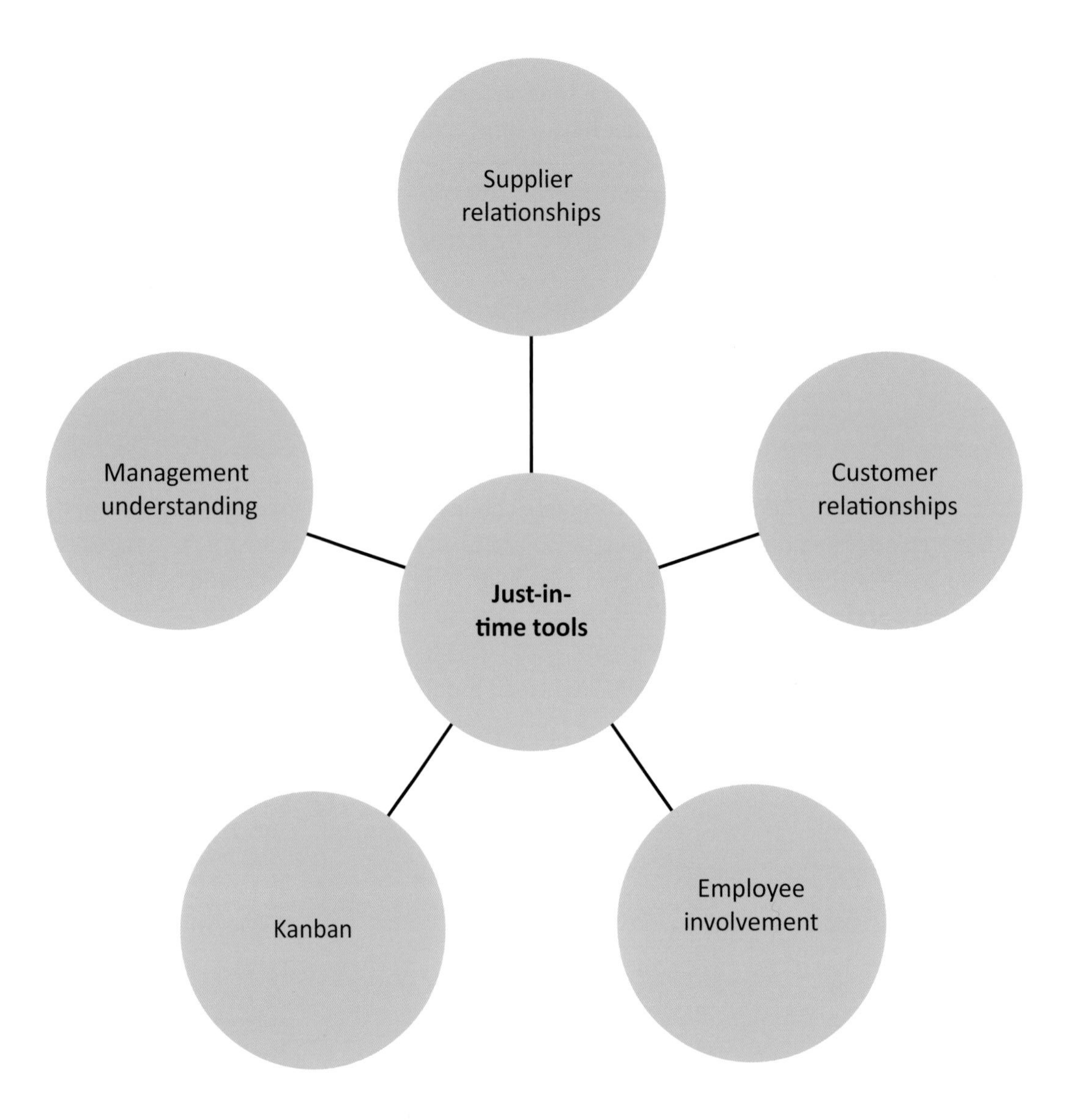

Management understanding

The first stage in incorporating an effective just-in-time programme is a full understanding of the production process. Managers must 'walk the line' (follow the whole production process from start to end) to understand the processes used to complete the finished product. Only when managers fully understand the production process can just-in-time be incorporated. It may seem surprising that managers do not fully understand the production process, but it is not unusual.

Supplier relationships and stockholding

Effective incorporation of just-in-time systems requires that relationships with suppliers are strong and communications systems are effective. There is no point in reducing stockholdings if stock cannot be topped up at the appropriate time.

Suppliers must be told when stock is needed and how much stock is required. Many businesses have bar codes on work in progress, which are read as the product moves along the production line. These bar codes, when read, automatically order stock from suppliers at the appropriate time. Some car manufacturers use such sophisticated just-in-time systems that suppliers can be automatically notified when a car starts on the production line, so that components can be delivered to the production line at exactly the right time. The effectiveness of such a process would of course depend on proximity and flexibility of suppliers and the use of electronic ordering systems.

Kanban

Another example of a just-in-time system is the idea of Kanban. This involves the use of order cards to ensure a regular and timely supply of components. It is not unusual when using a Kanban system to find an employee of the supplier continually working on a shop floor, ensuring that the parts arrive in the right place and at the right time.

Employee involvement

Another key element of just-in-time is a strong relationship with employees. There must be a people-centred approach from managers. Employees must be trained to use the systems of lean production effectively and understand their role in ensuring that the system continues to work. Cells of production are an important part of this process. Cell working will encourage the use of job enrichment. There will be more employee control over tasks. This helps ensure employee commitment to the JIT system. It is always worth involving employees when designing a just-in-time system, as employees often understand their part of the process of manufacturing better than management. There is a strong relationship between the use of just-in-time and the use of the latest motivation theories and human resource management principles. Flexible working practices must exist within the organisation and the view must be held that quality and production problems are best solved by workers and management together.

Customer relationships

The final part of incorporating a just-in-time system is strengthening relationships with customers. Often customers are able to use electronic point of sales systems (EPOS), and these can be tied in with the manufacturing process. Orders can be placed electronically so that finished product can go straight from the production line to delivery, rather than being stored in a warehouse where storage can lead to loss of value.

Kaizen

Kaizen is a Japanese word meaning **continuous improvement**.

Continuous improvement is an important aspect of lean production and is a theme of all world-class businesses. These world-class businesses take the view that one of the main objectives of their existence is to be continually making small incremental steps in the improvement of quality, design and waste reduction.

Before Kaizen

Before the use of Kaizen became widespread amongst leading British businesses, improvements in quality of output were made in large one-off steps. These stepped improvements were often forced upon businesses because of the actions of competitors. Therefore, a business would be under competitive pressure to invest in retooling the workplace or to purchase new technology: thereby creating a one-off improvement in productivity. Things would then remain pretty much the same until external pressures forced a new process to be implemented or staff to be retrained etc.

The problem with this approach was that businesses were often playing 'catch-up' in terms of quality and productive efficiency. As soon as businesses had finished implementing new processes that were supposed to make them competitive, the competition had already moved on. This was because the competition, often foreign, was using the idea of continuous improvement. Also British businesses had other problems which resulted from using the stepped approach. Large-scale changes in production processes often meant lower demand for workers, which led to redundancies. This, in turn, led to a breakdown in relationships with trade unions and caused large-scale disruptions in the workplace. Also because of the high cost of the large one-off improvements, implementing these depended on raising finance and this was often expensive or unobtainable.

Using and applying Kaizen

The main working element of Kaizen is the use of Kaizen groups. These are groups of workers who have a common stake in part of the production process. For example, a Kaizen group may involve the designer of a component, the installation workers from the production line and the production managers. These groups will meet regularly to discuss problems and to suggest improvements. Often improvements can be made at nil or minimal cost. This means that over time the whole cost base of the business can be reduced whilst indicators of quality and levels of production increase. All this is achieved with minimal capital investment.

Key elements of Kaizen

- All employees, from the managing director down to the shop floor workers, should be asking, 'How can I do what I do better'? – 'How can we do what we do better'?
- Kaizen does not ignore the need for new technology or large-scale capital investment: however, it does recognise that these are not the only methods of achieving increased competitiveness.
- A motivated workforce – the workers must be committed to the business.
- A management with belief in the capabilities of the workforce.
- A trained workforce – the workers must have the ability to understand their roles and complete their tasks efficiently.
- Effective communication systems – workers must be able to communicate suggestions to superiors and other relevant employees. This can be done through Kaizen groups, but other methods of communication must also be available.
- Security of jobs. Workers will not suggest process improvements if their jobs are threatened by these improvements. Kaizen does suggest that demand for labour will fall, although this should be achieved through natural wastage.
- Management must have a clear understanding of the production processes in order that they can organise, control and plan to enable workers to meet the needs and quality requirements of the 'customers' within the organisation.

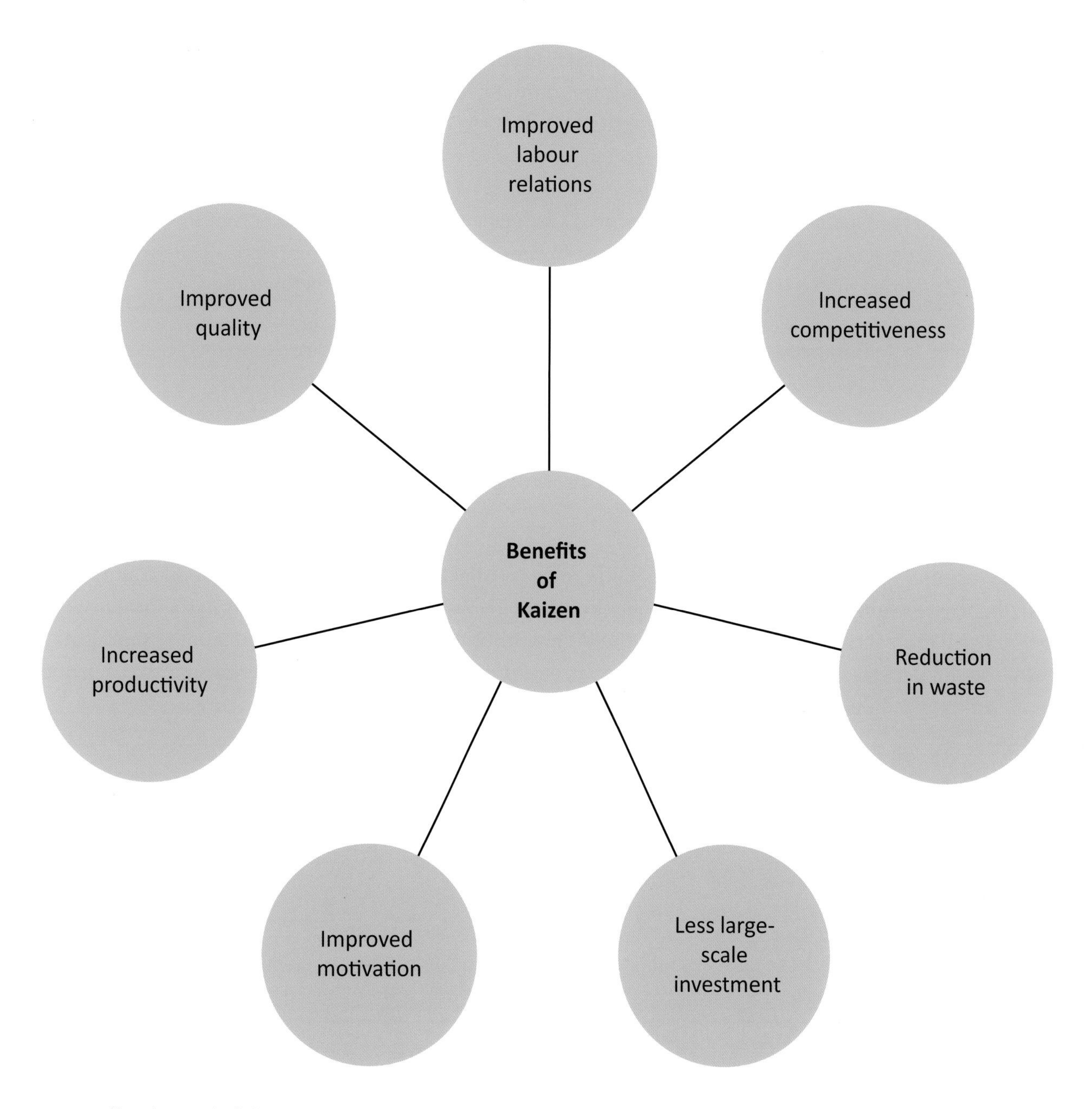

Kaizen will only work if there is a committed management and workforce. Each group must believe in the integrity and ability of the other group, so that all continually work towards the same goals. Kaizen is an ongoing system of beliefs, not something that can be used as and when management pleases and ignored when trading becomes difficult.

Cell production

With cell production the production line is subdivided into a number of cells. These cells are groups of workers involved in related tasks. The workers are trained so that they can fulfil a number of tasks within the cell, and this allows job rotation. The skills of the workers mean that they can each play a role in improving quality, and also creating flexibility in the production process. Also communication is improved, and the job enrichment and enlargement elements of cell design improve motivation. It is possible for cells to be self-managing with regards to many human resource management issues such as shift arrangements, breaks and holidays.

Time-based management methods

With this approach **time is regarded as a key business resource**. Speed of development, speed of response and speed of delivery are becoming increasingly important. Speed adds value, as we can witness in the battle between internet retailers when seeking to get their products to their customers' doorsteps as quickly as possible.

With time-based management, emphasis is placed on reducing time taken in all aspects of the whole production process. It involves concepts such as **just-in-time**, the use of **CAD** (computer-aided design) and **CAM** (computer-aided manufacture), **critical path analysis** and **simultaneous engineering**.

When engaging in **simultaneous engineering**, emphasis is placed on carrying out, as near as possible at the same time, the functions involved in designing, producing and marketing a product. Obviously it is impossible to manufacture a product before it has been designed, but it may be possible to get the production lines ready or to work out at least the basics of a marketing plan. This strategy can be effective in reducing the time a product takes to reach the market and is of increasing importance as product life cycles continue to shorten.

For simultaneous engineering to be effective, there must be effective communication between the functional departments involved, as well as regular product meetings involving all those taking part in the product development. Project teams are created from the different business and engineering functions. Specialists drawn from R&D, design, transport, market research, accounting etc., work together to ensure that activities are carried out in conjunction with one another.

Discussion themes
What is lean production?
What lean production practices have been adopted by Dell? Lean production at Dell http://www.youtube.com/watch?v=uufjHILLnE4
Explain what is meant by 'waste' in lean production.
Explain circumstances when JIT may not be the best stock management method.
Given that Kaizen brings so many advantages to businesses, why is the system not used more widely?
What are the benefits of adopting lean production?

Chapter 38
Quality

What is quality?

Quality is a difficult concept to define. W. Edwards Deming, the American quality guru, stated that 'quality is defined by the customer'. Customers may require certain specifications or demand exceptional levels of comfort. It is true to say that consumers are increasingly conscious of quality and this is reflected in the mission statement of the successful computer manufacturer Dell. It states: 'Customers must have a quality experience and be pleased, not just satisfied'.

Quality is often defined simply as 'fitness for purpose'. After all, if the product does the job it was designed to do, it must therefore have some level of quality. Another way to define quality could be the features of a product or service that allows it to satisfy customers' wants.

Whichever way we choose to define 'quality' the importance of the concept continues to grow. Businesses are placing greater and greater emphasis on trying to provide quality goods and services in an increasingly competitive global marketplace.

Benefits of quality

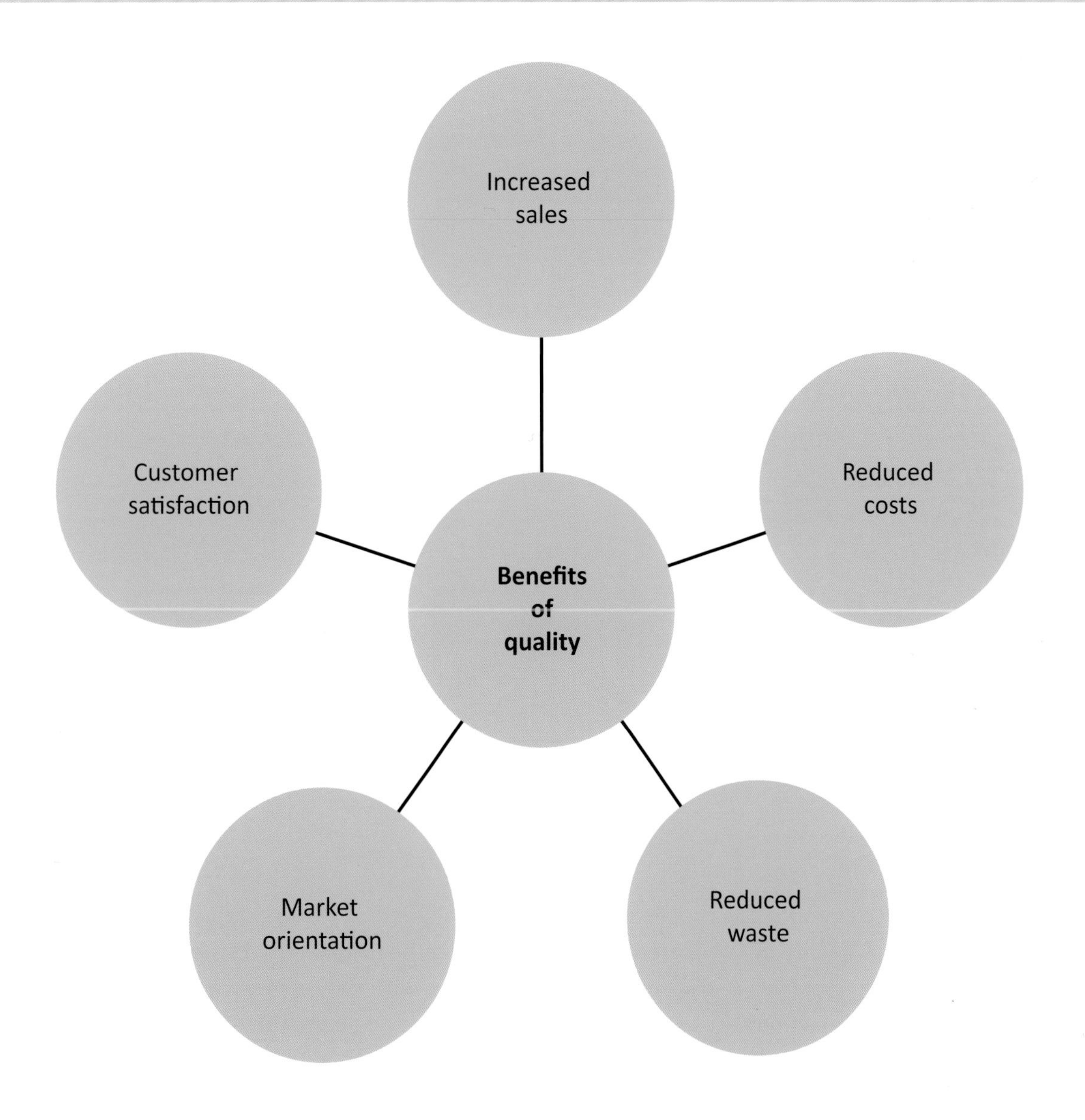

Achieving quality

For large manufacturing and service companies, achieving quality is a complex task which combines the work of several separate functional departments within an organisation. These departments typically include:

- Purchasing – ensuring that the right quantity and quality of raw materials or components are available for the production process.
- Operations – structuring and managing the manufacturing process.
- Finance – ensuring that capital is available for appropriate investment.
- Human Resources – ensuring that the factor of production labour is available in the right quantities with the right skills.
- Marketing – providing market research information in order that customer wants can be satisfied.

Quality assurance

It is the view of world-class manufacturers that quality must be 'built in'. This means that when the finished goods roll off the production line, management is confident that there is no need to check quality. Inspection is carried out during the production process. The emphasis is placed on preventing the production of poor quality products, as opposed to checking quality at the end of the production line.

Quality assurance methods

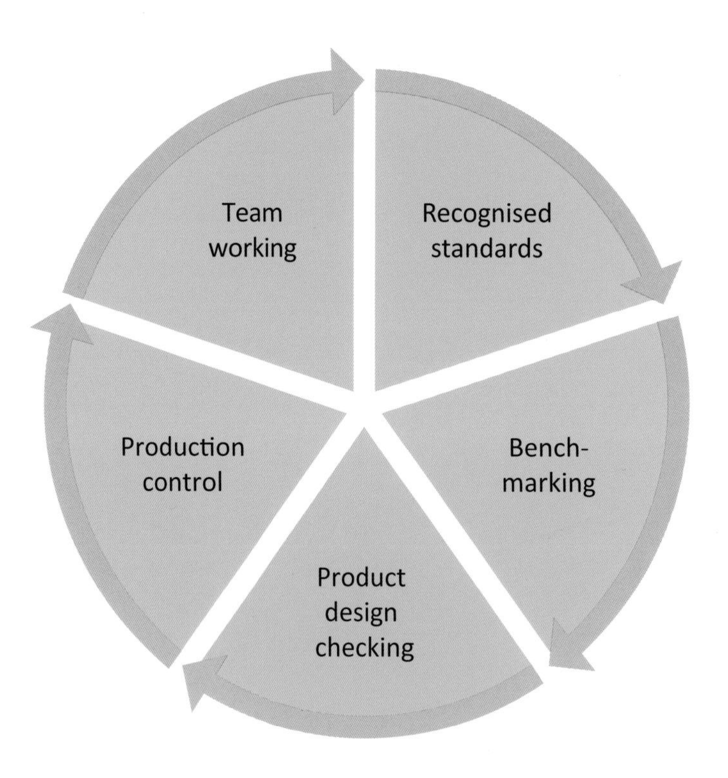

Team working

A team is responsible for a production process, such as the installation of a conservatory. The team is empowered to check the quality of raw materials, interact during the installation process and check the quality of the finished product. This implies that responsibility lies with the team – we know exactly where the 'buck stops'. Team work can build trust and morale, whilst improving communication between members. It is regarded as a key element in achieving quality.

Product design checking

In addition to monitoring raw materials and components, the total design of the product must also be checked for quality. The failure of the Mercedes A Class to reach independent test standards is an example of poor design. The problem has since been rectified, but only at great cost, both financially and with regard to corporate image. Another example was Persil Power washing powder, which was so powerful that it seemed to shred and dissolve clothes – a serious design problem! Time, effort and money must be put into product design.

Benchmarking

If the highest standards are to be achieved, what standards are to be targeted? There is no point in saying that we intend to improve our standard from one fault in 50 to one fault in 100, if our competitors are achieving one fault in 1000. This is where benchmarking comes in. Benchmarking is the process of setting standards of quality and output which are based on the best that competitors can offer.

The first stage in the benchmarking process is discovering the appropriate figures for competitors. This information may be hard to come by, but research organisations may be able to produce figures on competitors' levels of sales, quality and consumer satisfaction.

The second stage in the benchmarking process is setting new targets to be achieved in the manufacturing process which match those of the best competitor. Methods of production need to be designed which ensure that the benchmark levels of productivity and quality are achieved.

The key stage in benchmarking is gaining a commitment from the whole work force. All levels of hierarchy must be committed to the achievement of these standards.

The great advantage of benchmarking is that targets set are based on the activities of competitors. This increases the focus on the market and so increases market orientation.

Application of recognised standards

The use of recognised standards such as ISO 9000 is widespread amongst businesses. Achievement of these standards by businesses is often an indication of achievement and maintenance of quality.

ISO 9000 is supposed to guarantee quality of management of the whole organisation. Achievement of this standard depends on proving that quality targets for all parts of the organisation have been met. However, critics often state that if low target levels are set then there is no real guarantee of quality. Another failing of using recognised standards to achieve quality is that unless targets are related to external benchmarks then the quality process only results in increased product orientation – when often what is required is increased market orientation.

Production control

This is the method of ensuring that standards set, and processes designed to meet these targets, are actually being used in the workplace.

Production control involves:

- monitoring of costs through use of budgeting and variance analysis;

- control of operations through use of critical path analysis and monitoring of individual processes;
- supervision of output (now largely replaced by cell and teamwork);
- feedback methods, involving the monitoring of customer satisfaction, and the feedback of problems to the relevant department.

These methods of control have now spread from the manufacturing industry to service industries and have found a new home in call centres. Call centres are centralised departments that deal with customer enquiries. Each worker will have a requirement to answer calls in a specific period of time, spend a certain amount of time on each call and achieve a targeted level of sales. Information Technology (IT) allows the performance of each worker to be monitored and any variation from required standards and targets will be responded to by management. Workers will be retrained to ensure that standards can be met.

Quality control

Quality control is a system of maintaining standards in manufacturing by testing a sample of the output against expected standards. The data collected from the sample is then used to make judgements on action to be taken. The sample may indicate that quality is of the required standard, or the reverse may be found. If standards have not been achieved then appropriate steps to achieve standards must be made – for example, defective units must be repaired or rejected. If too many failures to achieve standards occur, a plan must be devised to improve the production process.

Total quality management – TQM

Total quality management is an operations management system that creates structures within an organisation that satisfy internal and external customers and suppliers. It creates quality through continuous improvement, development of systems and products and by creating an organisational **culture of quality**.

T stands for Total – it is the integration of the staff, suppliers, customers and other stakeholders. These are all seen as part of a single system, an unbroken chain of production – a chain of quality.

Q stands for Quality – quality can be the speed in which a service is delivered. It can be consistency. It can be innovation. It can be reflected in low maintenance or favourable repair history. According to W. Edwards Deming (one of the founders of the TQM system), 'a product or service possesses quality if it helps somebody and enjoys a good and sustainable market.'

M stands for Management – The need is for management to improve processes and to monitor them continually in order to identify improvement opportunities. The responsibility for ensuring the improvement of the processes in an organisation lies with top management. As part of the management of quality the system includes 'process owners' who coordinate the various functions and work activities at all levels of a process. Process owners have the authority to make changes in the process as required – they manage the process end to end so as to ensure optimal overall performance.

How does TQM work in practice?

For TQM to be effective a number of production management and control methods need to be used:

- **Quality chains** are based on cross-functional teams where processes involve internal customers. The next person in the production process is treated as a customer and customer satisfaction is the objective.
- **Empowerment** – giving workers control over tasks completed.

- **Monitoring** – checking that standards at each link in the chain are being achieved and the use of statistical tools to measure levels of failure to achieve quality.
- **Teamwork** – cells of production and a team approach to product or service improvement.
- **Quality circles** – Employee involvement in the decision-making and product-improvement process. Employees meet to identify and solve problems.
- **Zero defects** – attempting to achieve perfect product quality, time after time.
- **Benchmarking** – standards based on the best of the competition.

Total quality management
http://bit.ly/1S3V9cj

Stakeholders and quality

The view that the quality control department takes care of all problems of quality has largely changed – now all employees are responsible and this puts pressure on employees to adapt. When quality is the responsibility of the process operators, jobs may become more stressful. Often a TQM-based product is cheaper to produce because there is no need to repair or scrap the end product. The quality of the final output produces a more marketable product, meaning that consumers of the product will benefit. Management now have to communicate the aims of the organisation to all members of the organisation and this may be difficult for 'Theory X' managers to adapt to. The traditional structure of many manufacturing businesses has changed, resulting in less management control and the loss of power of traditional groups such as unions.

Achieving quality is a complex task. We have seen that effective quality control involves the monitoring of the whole production process, feedback of requirements from marketing, management of resources and the use of external standards. The overall objective is greater efficiency, achieving product quality and improving productivity – all of which help the business achieve customer satisfaction.

Discussion themes
Explain how quality can be achieved in business.
What is the difference between quality control and quality assurance?
How can benchmarking help a business improve the quality of its products?
What are the core parts of successful TQM?
Lean production and quality in business: https://www.youtube.com/watch?v=CCyziyskYuE

Chapter 39
Purchasing

Effective stock management, whether it is of raw materials, work in progress or of finished goods, is an important part of an efficient operations management plan. Purchasing of stock at the required quality and quantities is a key factor in the production process. Ensuring a smooth flow of goods from the production line to the final consumer is a complex process, which may involve numerous different suppliers.

Key aspects of effective stock management

Businesses must ensure that stock is available for use within the manufacturing process as and when it is needed.

Part-finished goods (work in progress) do not sit around the factory floor unused and losing value: instead they are brought to the next stage as soon as possible.

Finished goods are available for timely delivery to customers and are not made before customers are found for them.

Traditionally the main method of ensuring a ready supply of raw materials has been the maintenance of large buffer stocks. These are relatively large stock holdings held 'just in case' they might be needed. This method of stock management was to an extent understandable. Businesses in the 1970s and 1980s were operating during times of considerable industrial strife, with interruptions to supplies an everyday occurrence. However, the industrial landscape has changed and this has allowed the operations management emphasis now to be on the reduction of stock holdings and the freeing-up of working capital. The old idea of buffer stocks has been largely abandoned in favour of the effective use of just-in-time systems.

A traditional stock management chart

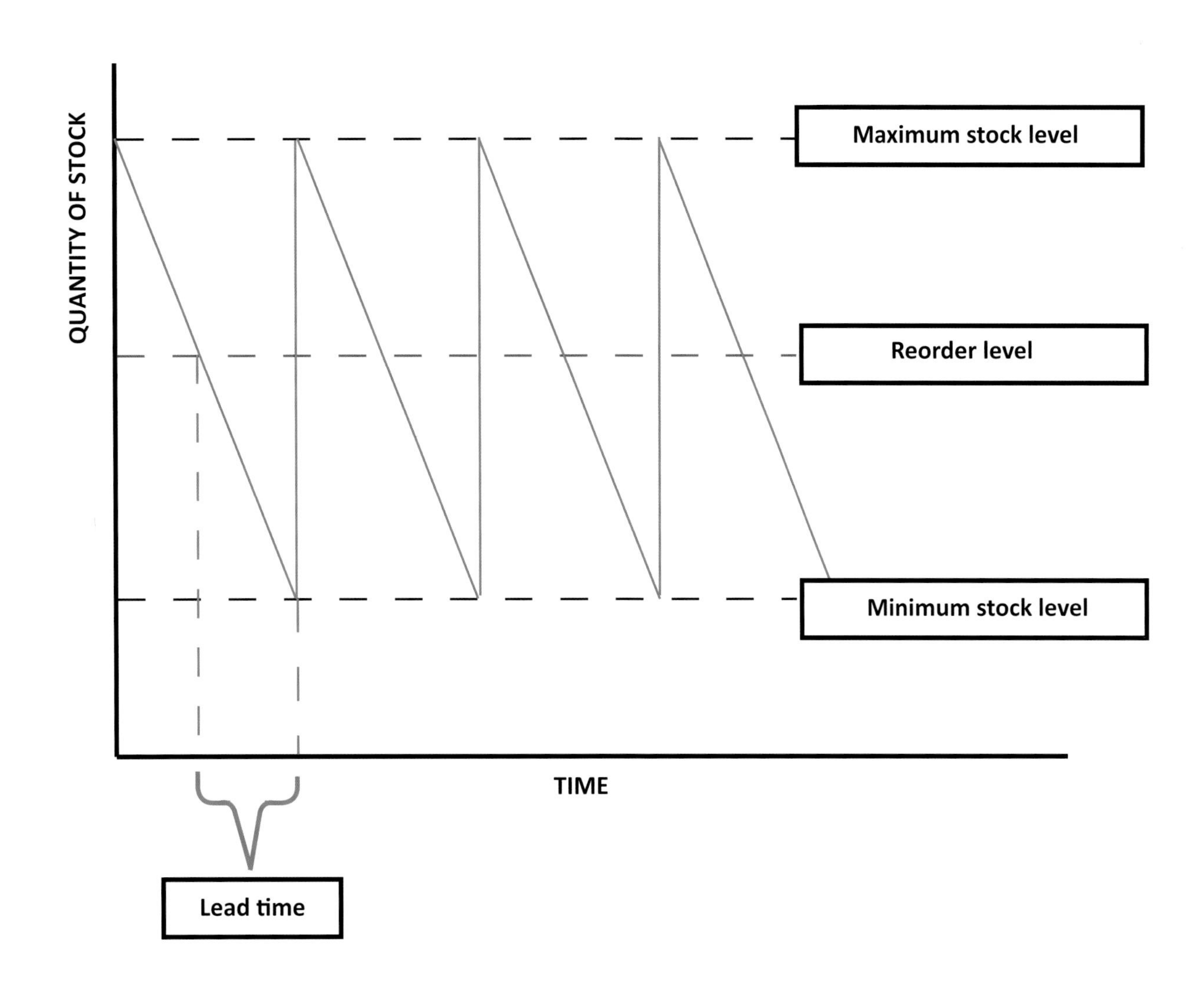

reorder level — This is the level of stock at which a new order is placed.

reorder quantity — This is measured by the difference between the maximum and minimum stock holding levels.

lead time — This is the amount of time taken for delivery to take place following the placement of an order.

buffer stock — This is the stock level that will always be held in case of problems with delivery – i.e. the amount of stock below the minimum stock holding level and zero stock.

Computerised stock control

Businesses today hold their stock details on computer databases. This improves efficiency and accuracy. When the quantity of stock decreases or increases, the database is updated instantly which allows for accurate stock checks and the automatic reordering of stock if the level falls below the reorder level. The best example of this is the stock control systems used by the main supermarkets. The system is connected via computers to the checkout tills, and when products are scanned in the stock control database is automatically updated.

Just-in-time (JIT)

Many businesses today operate a JIT manufacturing system which is designed to minimise the costs of holding stocks of raw materials, components, work in progress and finished goods. This is achieved by carefully planned scheduling in order that resources can flow through the production process smoothly. There are a number of key requirements for JIT to operate effectively:

- a very efficient ordering system;
- suppliers that reliably deliver raw materials and components just when they are required;
- a well-trained workforce which can be trusted and who are willing to work in teams;
- a cooperative (non-confrontational) culture, whereby management encourage workers to achieve their goals and work flexibly.

Under a JIT system materials are delivered shortly before they are required by the manufacturers and go straight onto the production line – virtually no stock is stored on site. Products are not made unless an order has already been placed, and when the goods are complete they leave the factory to be delivered to the customer.

The operation of a JIT system is not without its problems. Ordering and administration costs are likely to rise and the advantages of bulk buying may be lost. Suppliers who do not deliver on time can bring the whole production line to a halt, leading to a manufacturer's reputation being damaged if customers do not receive their goods on time.

Systems for effective stock management

For effective stock management to work there must be systems and relationships put in place. These systems and relationships include:

- **Effective relationships with suppliers and customers.** Suppliers must be able to switch to the new, very efficient ordering system. There is no point in expecting to have regular and timely deliveries just when they are required if suppliers are unable to comply with this requirement. Often this type of ordering and delivery system will involve some integration between the two companies. This type of integration of systems can be achieved by the use of EPOS and bar coding systems.

- **Effective internal relationships**. There must be a customer chain within the manufacturing process. This means that internal supply operates on the same basis as external supply - in other words, each team within the production process treats the next as its customer. Goods and parts are only supplied precisely when they are needed in the next stage of production.

Advantages of effective stock management

- **Reduction in working capital**. This frees money for investment and improves liquidity. There is an opportunity cost of holding stock. This means that if money is tied up in stock it is not free for use elsewhere in the business.
- **Improved relationships with customers**. Helping to guarantee ongoing orders.
- **Freeing of storage space**. This can release retail or manufacturing space.
- **Less stock wastage and discounting**. Smaller buffer stocks and supplies of finished goods will mean that stock is less likely to be damaged before it is used and finished goods are less likely to become out of date or out of fashion.
- **Easier stock rotation**. Stock rotation means ensuring that older stock is used before newer stock. When buffer stocks are small and deliveries are regular this becomes easier – this is because stock is used shortly after delivery.

Discussion themes
Why is it important to a business to have an efficient purchasing function?
Explain how a business can control its stock.
Why does it cost to hold stock?
What is meant by lead time and buffer stock?
Explain the possible advantages to a business of adapting a JIT stock control system.
Explain how technology has improved stock control.
'It is better to have too much stock than too little'. Do you agree with this statement?

Chapter 40
Research and development

Research and development (R&D) is essential today for businesses to compete in a dynamic marketplace. It involves the identification of new ideas and turning them into products, services and processes. Businesses who invest in R&D are considered to be innovative and always looking to bring new ideas and products to the market.

Innovation

The commercial exploitation of an invention.

Bringing a new idea to the marketplace is known as 'product innovation'. Doing so in the workplace is known as 'process innovation'. Innovation is not cheap and resources have to be committed by the businesses to bring new products to the marketplace. Governments try to encourage innovation within the business community because an innovative culture will help grow the whole economy, creating both employment and wealth.

Research

Research is the inquiry into, and discovery of, new ideas.

Methods used to generate new ideas include:

- Pure research – research just to find out how or why, with no product objective. This type of research is often carried out by universities or research institutes.
- Laboratory research – for example, the testing of new pharmaceutical compounds on animals.
- Evaluation of existing products – are there problems with this product? How can such problems be resolved?
- Brainstorming using discussion groups – thinking outside of the box, novel ideas for solving existing problems.

Development

Development is the process which changes ideas that result from the research process into commercially viable products or processes.

Development is a costly and complicated process, which for some products may take many years. Concorde was originally conceived in 1962, but it did not enter regular service until 1975. Development of pharmaceuticals can take years as they progress through different stages of testing until approval is achieved.

It is important that businesses reduce the development time of new products. Shorter product life cycles are now the norm. Prior to the turn of the century, with a few cosmetic adjustments, a car model could last a decade. Now, for motor manufacturers to stay competitive, a new model launch or major revamp of an existing model three times a decade is the norm. Development can be phenomenally expensive, costing hundreds of millions of pounds for car manufacturers, and even then success is not guaranteed.

The product design and development process

The development of new products have a number of distinct stages which takes the idea through to the launch:

1 **Identification of problem**
2. **Research**
3. **Development of ideas and solutions to solve the problem**
4. **Development of prototypes**
5. **Final design**
6. **Testing**
7. **Manufacturing and launch.**

Why invest in research and development?

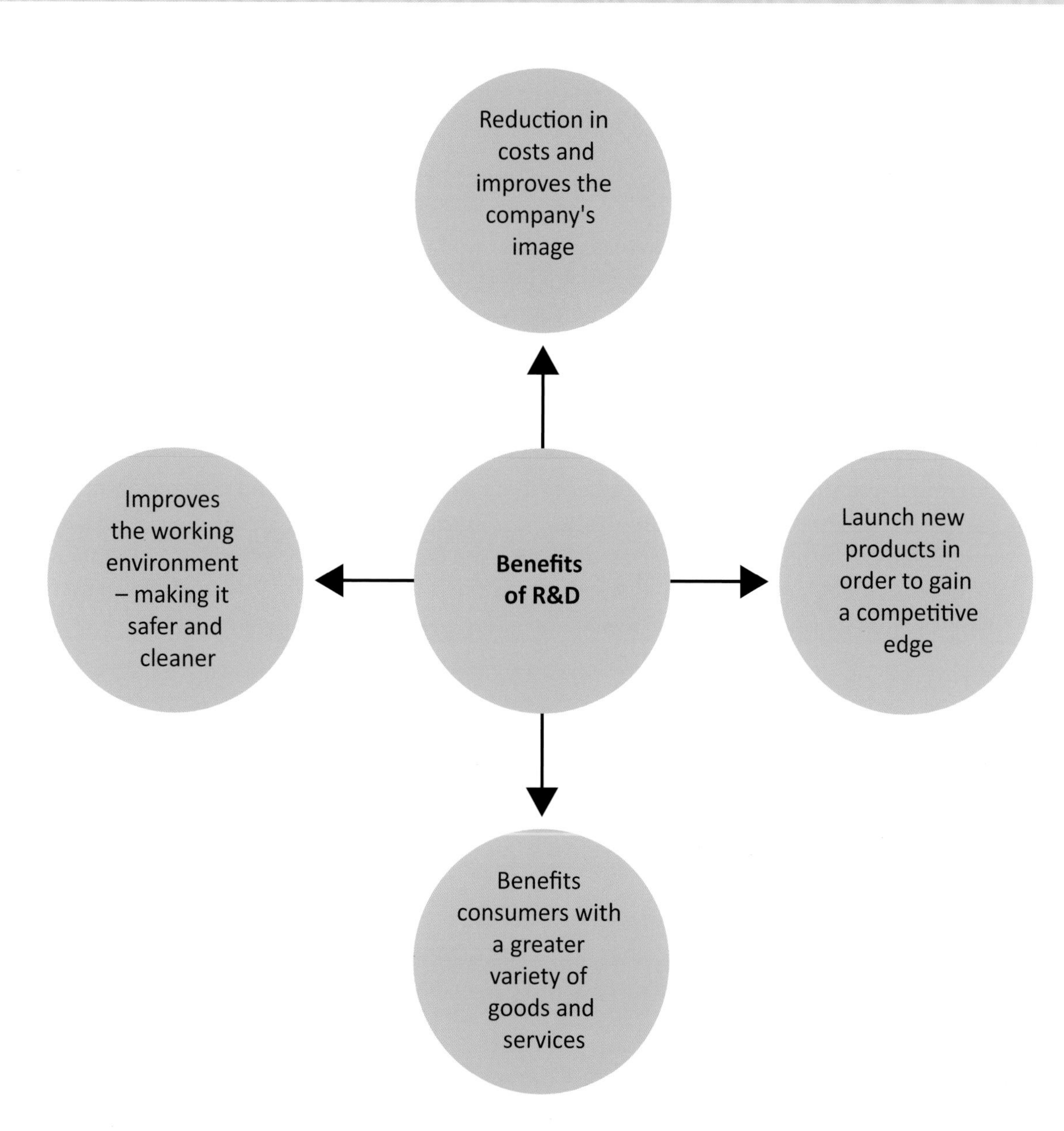

Research and development is needed by businesses because in most markets there is a constant requirement for invention and innovation to keep up with competition and attract customers. New products are required not only for a business to grow, but also to survive. It is often the case, however, that other businesses can wait for others to take the risk of launching new products or technologies and then move into the market once an idea has been proven. The expression, 'it is the second mouse that gets the cheese', is one that is worth remembering and copycat behaviour is often well rewarded.

Which type of companies rely on research and development?

For pharmaceutical, aircraft and electronics companies R&D is their lifeblood – without new products they will die. This is because their existing products are guaranteed to be redundant within a relatively small number of years as customers demand new and improved versions.

For a second group, which include car manufacturers and the construction industry, R&D has an important role to play: but in these industries there can be an element of waiting to see what the competition are up to. For example, it was only with the launch of the first successful SUV (Sports Utility Vehicle) that design departments in major motor companies throughout the world suddenly became covered in drawings of the Qashqai, Duster, Evoque and the like.

For a third group R&D can take a back seat – instead marketing comes to the fore. This group of industries includes retailers, who often just borrow ideas from each other.

UK businesses and R&D

In the past Britain had been a world leader in research. One study showed that of all the inventions and resulting products of the last 60 years that had a major effect on people's lifestyles, over 50% were originally conceived by British businesses, British inventors or British research scientists.

However, research and development has to be budgeted for as it is a **highly expensive business activity**. Companies must reinvest profits into R&D to grow. For many years Britain has had a poor investment record in this area, with many companies looking for short-term gains and profits. Such companies turned away from organic growth (growing from within) to easier external growth (takeovers and mergers). More recently there has been some reversal of this trend. Businesses have started to link with universities, providing funding and research fellowships, so that the latest science and technology can be used in R&D. Money is now more often used for pure research and many universities now have science parks attached to their campus, where small companies develop ideas that are based on university research work.

Product life cycles and R&D

Effective research and streamlined development shortens life cycles and is also used in a response to shorter life cycles. The example of cars used above demonstrates how R&D allows businesses to stay competitive, but also forces continually higher spending on R&D.

One effect of this shortening of product life cycles is that small businesses find it hard to survive because of the resulting R&D costs. In the UK, Lotus, Rolls Royce and Aston Martin have all become parts of larger motor groups as a direct result of being unable to afford the increased costs of R&D spending, which were necessary if they were to stay competitive.

Market research and R&D

Market research can be the foundation of targeted R&D. If latent (unfulfilled) demand is discovered, then products need to be developed to meet this demand. This product development to satisfy market demand is part of being market-orientated.

Also, market research is used to help develop existing products. Market research is continuously being carried out, with the objective of discovering consumer attitudes to products. Product revamps and redesigns often occur as a direct response to market research findings.

NB – A common error learners make is to confuse research and development with market research. They are very different things, even though market research may lead on to R&D taking place. Learn the definitions thoroughly and you will not make this mistake.

Discussion themes
'Businesses that do not invest in R&D are doomed to failure.' To what extent do you agree with this statement?
Why is R&D considered risky by some stakeholders?
Evaluate the costs and benefits of innovation for a business and its stakeholders.
Why did the Canadian business buy this UK-based business? Cardiff University spin-out technology firm Mesuro acquired by Canadian firm http://www.walesonline.co.uk/business/business-news/cardiff-university-spin-out-technology-firm-8530959

Chapter 41
Economies of scale

As businesses grow and their output increases, they commonly benefit from a reduction in average costs of production. Total costs will increase as output increases. However, the cost of producing each unit falls as output increases. This fall in average costs as output increases indicates that a business is benefitting from **economies of scale**. This reduction in average costs is what gives larger businesses a competitive advantage over smaller businesses.

Economies of scale are an important aspect of efficiency in production. Economies of scale can be defined as: '**the reduction in average costs of production that occur as a business increases its scale of production**'.

Costs in the short and long run

When examining economies of scale it is worth looking at both the short run and long run average costs of the business. In the short run costs can be both variable and fixed, but in the long run all costs become variable. For example, rent negotiated over a 12 month contract is a fixed cost in the short run – i.e. it does not alter in relation to changes in demand or output. However, if rent rises after 12 months, then it too is regarded as a variable cost. It is this switch to all costs becoming variable that separates the short run from the long run.

Each business's long run average cost curve is made up of a series of short run average cost curves. As a business grows it moves from one short run average cost curve to another short run average cost curve, each one being progressively lower and so reducing average costs of output. This is represented in the graph below.

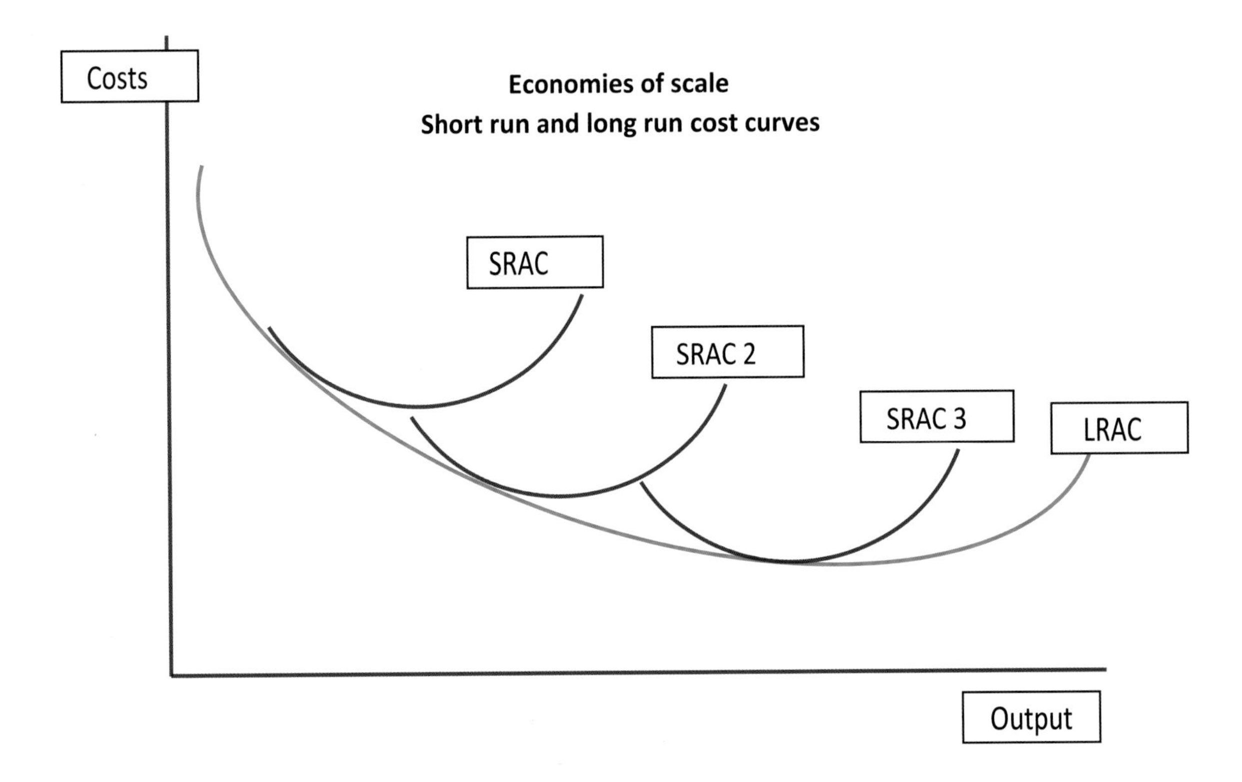

Imagine a building site with one foreman and one worker. The worker's role is digging trenches; the foreman's role is to oversee the digging of trenches. The foreman earns £10 an hour, the worker's wage is £5 an hour. The worker is capable of digging five metres of trench in an hour. With one worker, each metre of trench would therefore cost £3: i.e. the £5 wages of the worker and the £10 wages of the supervisor divided by 5 metres dug – equalling £3 per metre.

If another worker was taken on then we would now have 10m of trench per hour at a total cost of £20 (£10 + £5 + £5). Therefore the cost per metre of the trench is now £2. With three workers, we now have 15 metres of trench at a total cost of £25; which gives a cost of £1.66 per metre. This represents decreasing average costs in the short run.

In the long run the building site could, instead of using workers and spades, use a digger. This would allow a move on to another short run average cost curve – lowering potential average costs even further. This is an example of how economies of scale reduce average costs of production.

Internal and external economies of scale

We can break down economies of scale into two broad groups – these are internal and external.

Internal economies of scale

Reductions in average cost per unit of output as a result of increasing internal efficiencies of the business.

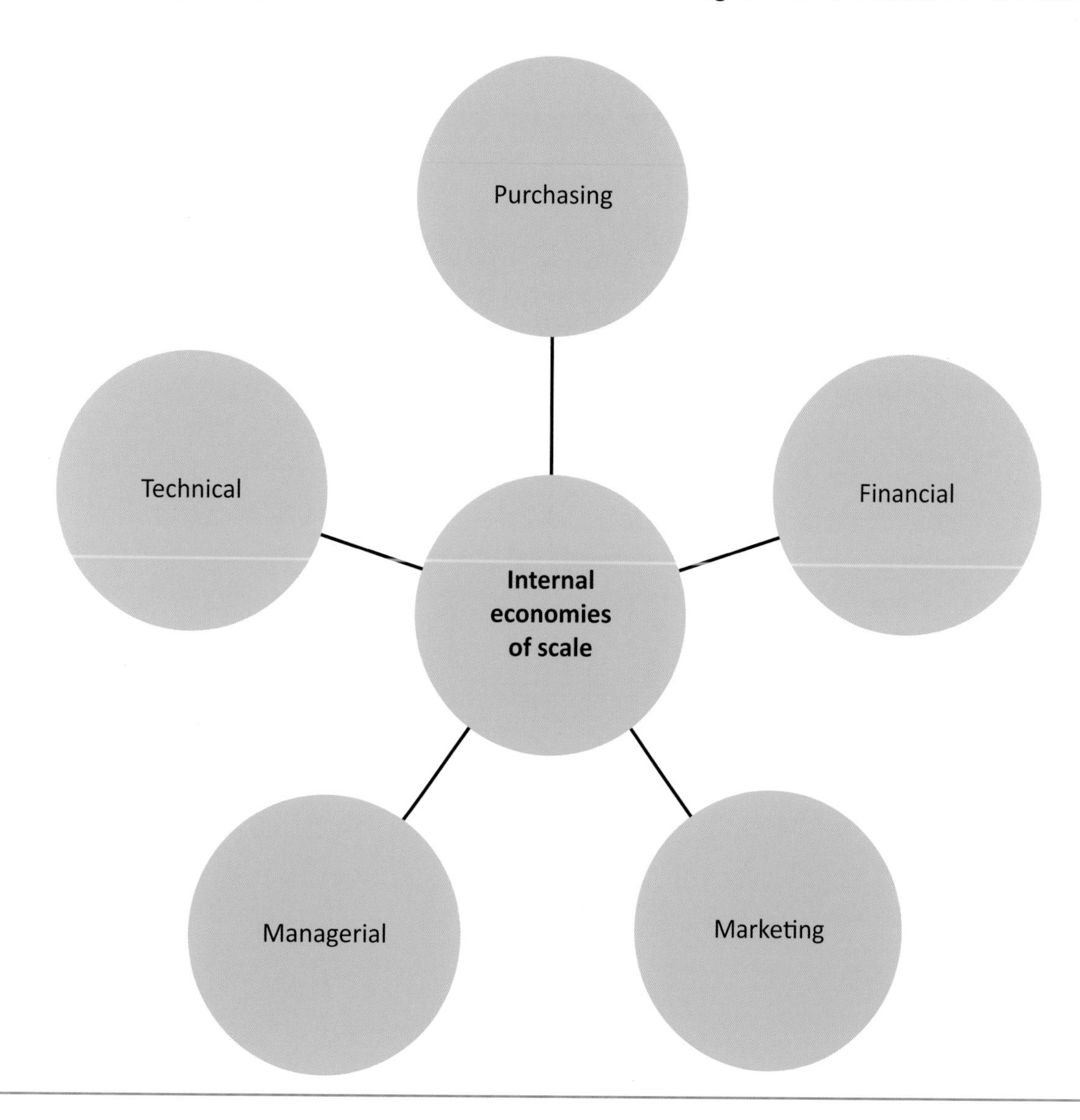

Purchasing economies – as businesses grow they increase the size of orders for raw materials or components. This may then result in discounts being given and the cost of each individual component purchased will fall. This will therefore reduce the average cost of production.

Technical economies – as businesses grow they are able to purchase the latest equipment and incorporate new methods of production. This increases efficiency and productivity, reducing average costs of output.

Financial economies – as businesses grow they will have access to a wider range of finance. As the assets of businesses grow, they are able to offer more security when seeking to borrow money – reducing the risk to the lender. As a result, larger businesses can often negotiate more favourable rates of interest on any money they do borrow.

Managerial economies – as businesses grow they are able to employ specialist managers. These managers will know how to get the best value for each pound (£) spent in the business, whether it is in production, marketing or purchasing. This will increase efficiency and thereby reduce the average costs of producing goods and selling the goods or services on offer.

Marketing economies – as businesses grow each pound (£) spent on advertising will have greater benefit for the business. Imagine a chain of local supermarkets: a TV advertisement is placed to cover the region. If there were 10 stores in the chain the cost of the advert must be borne by each of the 10 stores. However, if they have 20 stores, then the cost of the advert would be spread across each of the 20 stores and the benefit of the advert applies to each of the 20 stores.

External economies of scale

The advantages of scale that benefit a whole industry and not just an individual business.

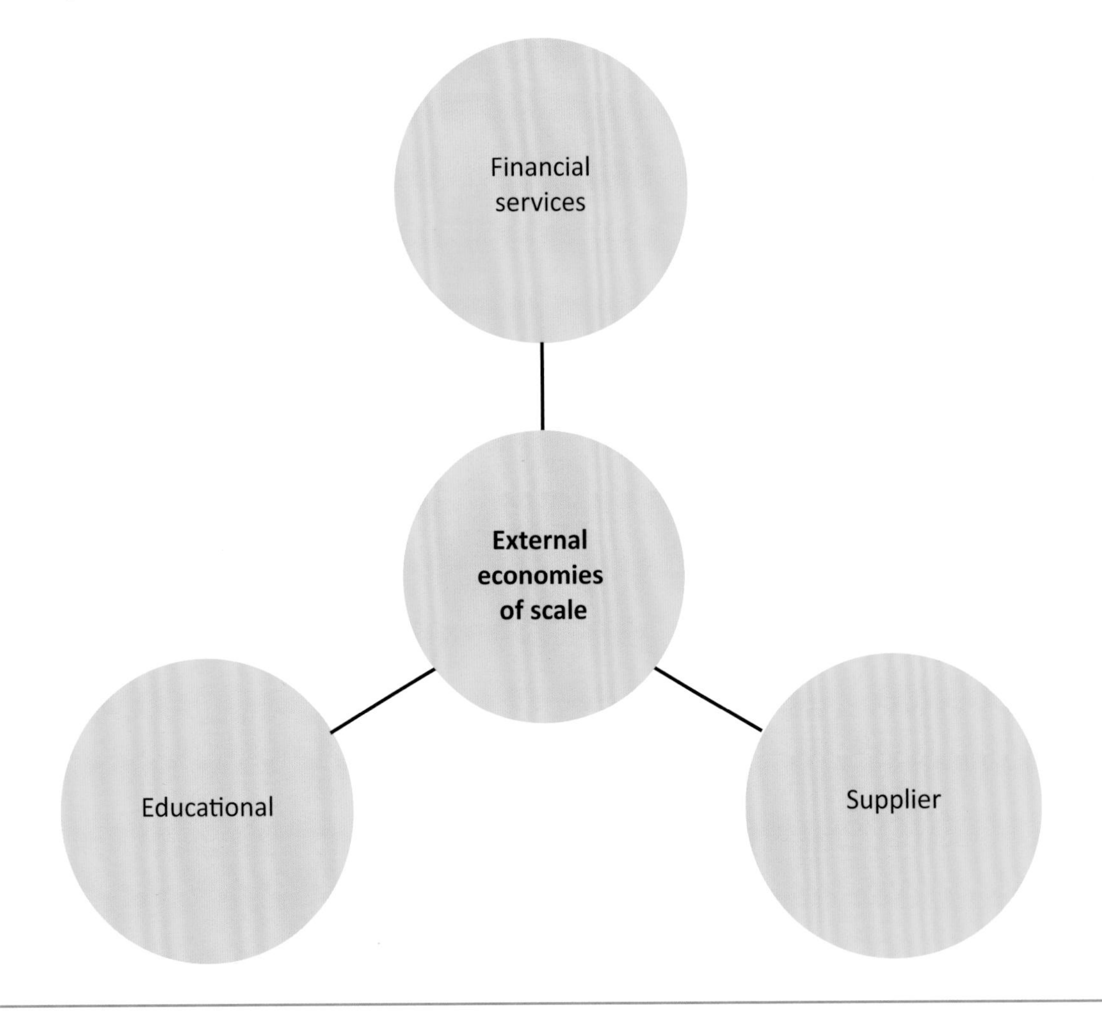

The largest businesses often benefit from external economies of scale, especially if the industry is concentrated in one geographical area.

Supplier economies – a network of suppliers may be attracted to an area where a particular industry is growing. The setting up locally of supplier businesses, often in competition with one another, reduces buying costs and allows the use of systems such as Just-in-Time.

Educational economies – local colleges will set up training schemes suited to the largest employers' needs, giving an available pool of skilled labour. This reduces recruitment and training costs for those businesses who make up the industry concerned.

Financial economies – financial services can improve, with banks and other financial institutions providing services that may be particularly geared towards a particular industry. For example, for an industry where cash flow may be a particular problem, debt factoring services may be made available at competitive rates.

These economies of scale can be regarded as quantitative in nature, i.e. they can be measured using financial methods. We know exactly how much is saved on purchasing raw materials, we know exactly how much is saved when a loan is renegotiated at a lower interest rate.

Diseconomies of scale

The factors that cause higher costs per unit of output when the scale of an organisation continues to increase – the causes of inefficiency in large organisations.

When diseconomies occur, the average costs of production rise with output. Let's go back to the example of the building site.

Maybe the foreman is capable of looking after 10 workers effectively and ensuring that each digs five metres per hour; but if there were 15 workers average output may start to fall. This happens because the supervisor is not able to supervise all the workers and ensure that each is working to their maximum capacity and some may take advantage of this and work more slowly. Now there are increasing average costs of output. We have diseconomies of scale.

Like economies of scale, diseconomies can be both internal and external.

Internal diseconomies of scale

Coordination issues – The larger an organisation becomes, the more difficult it is to coordinate. Inevitably there is a good deal of delegation and this empowerment of more and more managers to make their own decisions can result in different departments heading in different directions. To counter this, numerous management meetings have to be held. The time that managers spend in meetings, in an attempt to ensure better coordination within large organisations, can be viewed as a significant overhead cost.

Communication issues – As an organisation grows and levels of hierarchy increase, the efficiency and effectiveness of communication breaks down. This leads to increasing misunderstanding and inefficiency as each level of hierarchy grows further and further apart and messages become distorted, resulting in increasing average costs.

Motivation issues – With larger businesses it is harder to satisfy and motivate workers as many may feel that their views are ignored, as they distanced from the organisation's decision makers. This means that they may not give of their best as they are not focused on the organisation's aims and objectives.

These diseconomies of scale are often **qualitative** in nature and are difficult to measure financially – nonetheless, they still reduce the efficiency of the organisation.

External diseconomies of scale

Overcrowding in industrial areas – Traffic congestion may occur – resulting in late deliveries and staff arriving late for work. Local residents may resent this and public relations may suffer.

Increased price of resources – More businesses in an area means increased demand for labour to work in that industry and the best employees may be harder to recruit and keep. Land, services and materials may all become more expensive as the industry grows and demand for such resources increases.

Economies of scale and stakeholders

- Economies of scale have led to significant price drops in some market segments which have been advantageous to consumers. Electronics, clothes and phone services are just three of the sectors that have seen real price falls over the last 20 years. Therefore, consumers do benefit from the fall in a business's costs if they are reflected in lower prices.
- **Shareholders** may well benefit if economies of scale have helped businesses prosper as they have increased in size, resulting in increased share values.
- Some businesses have increased their scale to such an extent that they have become monopoly suppliers and eliminated their **competitors**. These were no longer able to compete as their larger competitors took more and more advantage of the economies of scale available to them.
- **Suppliers** are increasingly finding themselves under pressure to provide cheaper goods and services to businesses who operate on a large scale. This has proven to be the case with large supermarkets, resulting in many farmers going out of business as the profit margins that they were operating proved to be unsustainable.

Survival of small businesses

Small businesses are unlikely to benefit in any major way from economies of scale, so they will be less efficient and have higher costs than their bigger competitors. How do they survive? Well of course many don't. We have all seen local businesses and independent stores close as a result of larger competition moving into the area. However, many still do well, and there are a number of possible reasons for their success.

They provide a service that is difficult to scale up. Most plumbers, electricians and roofers are local small businesses. They seem better able to deal with fluctuations in demand, adapting their target market to changing market conditions. In this case it seems that flexibility is the key. Other factors leading to the survival of small businesses are:

- **Target market size** – sometimes the potential sales are suited to small businesses, for example dog grooming services or kennels.
- **Population density** – large businesses need large target markets: if these don't exist then the market is left to small businesses.
- **Quality of service and product** – often it is this added value aspect of the business that justifies the

higher prices charged.

- **Customer loyalty** – even in the modern retailing environment there are customers that remain loyal to local shops and service providers.
- **Niche markets** – sometimes the segment the small business is targeting is just too small to be worthwhile to big business or the product is legally protected for a period of time.

Discussion themes
Watch the economies of scale video to identify the main types. https://www.youtube.com/watch?v=6ihehRMtRWc
Explain how Apple benefits from economies of scale. Does Apple suffer from any disadvantages from being so big? Apple – Economies and diseconomies of scale https://fayblack.wordpress.com/2012/09/11/economies-of-scale-apple/
What are diseconomies of scale?
Some small businesses survive and thrive even though they are unable to benefit from economies of scale. Explain why this happens.